M000238070

Who Do I Say That You Are?

Who Do I Say That You Are?

Anthropology and the Theology of Theosis
in the Finnish School of Tuomo Mannermaa

WILLIAM W. SCHUMACHER

WIPF & STOCK · Eugene, Oregon

WHO DO I SAY THAT YOU ARE?
Anthropology and the Theology of *Theosis* in the Finnish School
of Tuomo Mannermaa

Copyright © 2010 William W. Schumacher. All rights reserved. Except for brief
quotations in critical publications or reviews, no part of this book may be
reproduced in any manner without prior written permission from the publisher.
Write: Permissions, Wipf and Stock Publishers, 199 W. 8th Ave., Suite 3, Eugene, OR
97401.

Wipf & Stock
An Imprint of Wipf and Stock Publishers
199 W. 8th Ave., Suite 3
Eugene, OR 97401

www.wipfandstock.com

ISBN 13: 978-1-60608-320-8

Manufactured in the U.S.A.

To Tamara:
sine qua nihil

Contents

Abbreviations

AE *Luther's Works.* Jaroslav Pelikan and Helmut T. Lehmann, general editors. 55 volumes. St. Louis: Concordia Publishing House, 1957–1986.

WA *D. Martin Luthers Werke: kritische Gesamtausgabe.* Weimar: Böhlau, 1883–1993.

WA Br *D. Martin Luthers Briefwechsel, D. Martin Luthers Werke: kritische Gesamtausgabe.* Konrad Burdach et al., editors. 11 volumes. Weimar: Böhlau, 1930 ff.

WA TR *Tischreden, D. Martin Luthers Werke: kritische Gesamtausgabe.* Karl Drescher, editor. 6 volumes. Weimar: Böhlau, 1912 ff.

AWA *Archiv zur Weimarer Ausgabe der Werke Martin Luthers. Texte und Untersuchungen.* Cologne & Vienna: Böhlau Verlag, 1981.

CA Augsburg Confession

Ap Apology of the Augsburg Confession

SA Smalcald Articles

SC Small Catechism

LC Large Catechism

FC Formula of Concord

Ep Epitome of the Formula of Concord

SD Solid Declaration of the Formula of Concord

AOG *Andreas Osiander d. Ä. Gesamtausgabe.* Herhard Müller and Gottfried Seebaß, editors. 10 volumes. Gütersloh: Gütersloher Verlagshaus, 1975–1997.

Introduction

The Confusion of Contemporary Anthropology

"WHO DO YOU SAY THAT YOU ARE?"

"WE LIVE IN AN age of anthropology."[1] Over the last century and a half, our understanding of ourselves has undergone enormous changes, and these changes have resulted in a fragmented view of human nature. Such a fragmented anthropology, in turn, is both a cause and a symptom of a wider fragmentation of society. The title presents an intentional inversion of the well-known Christological question; it is intended to connote three related facets of human beings' knowledge of themselves. First, just as the Christological question reveals the prevailing confusion about Christ, so the anthropological question uncovers the prevailing state of perplexity or confusion as humans seek to understand themselves. Secondly, at the same time, it is meant to suggest that there is a close relationship between anthropology and Christology, an inherent link between what one says about Christ and how one understands humanity. And thirdly, the question points us in the direction of an answer, namely that the essential being of human creatures is determined and defined by a word said about them—indeed, by a word said to them. What does it mean, at root, to be human? We will attempt first to set this question in the broader context of the fragmented intellectual culture of our day, and then turn to specifically theological approaches to anthropology. As we shall see, changes in the way human beings define their identity challenge traditional dogmatic formulations and call for new theological reflection about what it means to be human creatures, both *coram Deo* and *coram hominibus.*

Numerous possibilities present themselves as ways of answering the anthropological question. "Western" philosophical responses since

1. Pannenberg, *What Is Man?*, 1.

1

the enlightenment seem to revolve around a self-existing ego of rational subjectivity: the *ego* implicit in Descartes' *cogito* and thus also in the *sum*. An entire civilization has been built around this idea of humans as autonomous individuals, most notably in the United States in the last two centuries or so. The philosophical revolution begun by Descartes made possible a parallel revolution in political thought, through which the autonomous and self-existing individual was placed at the center of modern democratic nation-states. Of course, the idea can be pursued *ad absurdum*, with results that constitute the various alarming pathologies of American society at the beginning of the twenty-first century. The symptoms range from a shallow, seemingly innocuous hedonism to a murderous and diabolical will to power. The destructive—and self-destructive—permutations on the theme of individualism are evident on every scale, from chaotic personal lives to the unprecedented brutality that characterized the twentieth-century history of nations.

In competition with this view of the autonomous self and its subjective ego is a materialistic alternative, namely the conception of human beings in unambiguous continuity with the natural world. At its extreme this view is reductionistic and deterministic, as in the thought of B. F. Skinner. But the rigorous exploration of the continuity of the natural world, and of human beings within nature, began with the descriptive efforts of Newton, Galileo, Linnaeus, and others. The scientific revolution made possible a new perspective on the meaning of humanity. Humans comprise one species of animals (*Homo sapiens*, in the order *mammalia*) among many others, inhabiting one planet among many others, orbiting one rather ordinary star among countless others. Human nature is ultimately a matter of biology, or of biochemistry, and in this sense he stands in the whole continuum of observable and describable phenomena in the universe, from quarks to aardvarks to globular clusters. This is not, of course, to equate human beings with other organisms, much less with inorganic matter, any more than scientists would think of "equating" parrots with amoebas or quartz crystals. But modern scientific thought is constructed around a worldview that considers the universe to be a self-contained continuum of the same kinds of "stuff," with human beings fitting neatly and without remainder in that continuum of matter and energy. This worldview has gained remarkable acceptance in the twentieth century, and is reinforced in popular thinking by the perceived triumph of science and technology. The advance of medicine and the increase in our knowledge of how human organisms function may serve as two instances. We now know with some certainty that the structure of human DNA is not qualitatively different from that of other organisms. We share the same amino acids with other forms of life. The fruits of such a scientific approach to the world, and to humans as part of the world, are undeniable and extremely useful. Thus a materialistic view of humanity is in some ways a pragmatic working assumption that can simplify a host of technical problems and yield practical solutions. If one understands "myth" in the sense of an axiomatic assertion that serves as both a filter for perceptions and an interpretive framework for understanding reality, then this materialistic view of human beings in unambiguous continuity with nature has become the dominant myth in the technological culture at the close of this century. It is the presupposition for various forms of "myth" about the origins of the human species (evolution). At the same time, the materialist myth is also manifest in neo-romantic reactions against technological manipulation of the natural world, such as extreme forms of ideological environmentalism that border on pantheism.[2] A fundamental shift has taken place in how we think about ourselves as human beings: "Today the sciences concerned with man are following the best route toward taking the place in the general consciousness held in earlier centuries by metaphysics."[3]

The materialistic myth also underlies the anthropology of Marxism in its various forms.[4] The definition of human nature in strictly material terms, coupled with a dubious pseudo-scientific understanding of history, led to deliberate and sustained efforts to cultivate a new kind of human, a so-called "*Homo sovieticus*," in which the immaterial and individual self was supposed to be submerged in, and contingent upon, the collective embodiment of the state. At the same time, as Thielicke points out, "the idea of radical evil is totally eliminated from Marxist eschatology."[5] In other words, a Marxist view of human existence posited the ultimate perfectibility of humanity, but at the expense of the freedom and responsibility of the individual human self. The dramatic failure of such a view in the former Soviet Union and its entire sphere of influence should not lead

---

2. E.g., Rosemary Radford Ruether, *Gaia & God*.

3. Pannenberg, *What Is Man?*, 1.

4. Thielicke, *Being Human. Becoming Human*, 246–50.

5. Ibid., 248.

one to dismiss Marxist anthropology as merely a relic of the past, since at least a quarter of the human beings on the planet are still undergoing a similar experiment in anthropological engineering.

There are, of course, other alternative ways to approach the whole question of human identity, approaches that arise from other cultures. In many Bantu languages in sub-Saharan Africa, proverbs express the culture's fundamental understanding of who people are and how the universe is put together. The Motswana says, "*Motho ke motho ka motho yo mongwe*"—"A human being is human through (by means of) another human being." To be human is at root to be in relationship with others. Those relationships are not the result of voluntary choices by an autonomous self, but are rather imposed and defined from outside by one's social environment. One's existence and identity consist in one's interconnections with others. I know who I am because I know how I am related to other people: where I fit in my extended family (spanning generations both long dead and unborn and thus including the spirits of the ancestors as well). Those relationships create and describe my responsibilities toward others and theirs toward me. In this view, understanding human "nature"—and the term "nature" itself is difficult to express in many African languages—starts with, and largely consists in, understanding the intricate and dynamic web of human relationships. However, this anthropology is proving to be inadequate to meet the demands of new realities, such as rapid urbanization. People increasingly find themselves isolated as strangers in crowds of strangers, alone in groups that do not cohere as communities, cut off from the traditional relationships by which a person is defined and shaped. What they are left with is an anthropological oxymoron, the self-contradiction of a person without relationships. The ultimate inadequacy of understanding humanity as consisting purely in relationships is not avoided by post-modern efforts in the West to define human identity in terms of autonomously chosen (but essentially arbitrary) relationships.[6]

---

6. This is one weakness in the whole shape of the debate about "personhood" as a decisive category for establishing the acceptable limits of human responsibility. For a "person" is generally thought to be someone capable of meaningful human relationships. Redrawing the "anthropological boundaries" in this way happens to leave out the weakest members of the species at both the beginning and the end of life. The extent to which that exclusion is not perceived as a problem is cause for profound concern.

4

Somewhat surprisingly, recent developments in technology seem to offer us new ways to define ourselves as individuals and to relate with others. Esther Dyson has written of two seemingly contradictory "advantages" of so-called digital life: "community" and "anonymity."[7] These two values reflect the inner contradictions in contemporary ideas of human life: the need to be in meaningful, healthy relationships as "person-in-community," and the image of the anonymous, self-contained, autonomous individual with an absolute need to control others' access to him.[8] In some way an emerging new culture based on digital information technology allows a person to have it both ways: to be both enmeshed in a network of significant (but self-chosen) human relationships and yet to remain an autonomous, anonymous individual. The contemporary notion of what it means to be human is not only fragmented throughout the culture as various ideas make competing claims, but even a single individual can reflect the fragmentation and self-contradiction of antithetical views of human nature. Human beings at the beginning of the twenty-first century know vastly more about the universe than ever before in history—and less about themselves. How else, as novelist Walker Percy asks, is it possible for an average human to glance at a picture of Saturn or Jupiter and recognize it instantly, yet be baffled and deceived by his own reflection in a store window?[9]

In fact, neither the ontology of the autonomous self (*cogito ergo sum*), nor the materialistic scientism of human-being-as-animal (the "naked ape"),[10] nor the quest for identity through human relationships offers an ultimately satisfactory answer to the anthropological question, even though each describes part of what we know about what it means to be human. The history of our understanding of what it means to be human is characterized not by progress toward clearer knowledge, but

7. Dyson, *Release 2.0*.

8. The "digital community" consists in individuals who are free *absolutely* to define their own existence and identity. The "virtual" identity fostered on the internet produces a new kind of radically individual self whose rights and freedoms are no longer understood either as endowments of a Creator or as limited by real others to whom one is concretely responsible—a self who is therefore accountable to no one and even *ontologically* self-defined. As the old internet joke has it, the great thing about cyberspace is that no one knows that you're a dog!

9. Percy, *Lost in the Cosmos*.

10. E.g., Morris, *The Naked Ape*. It is instructive to compare Luther's "Disputation Concerning Man," Theses 1–2 and 6 (LW 34:137).

by fragmentation and loss of coherence, a pattern reflected through the many approaches to anthropology. The same loss of a unified or cohesive view of the essence of being human emerges as the insights and assertions from psychology, sociology, linguistics, ecology, and other disciplines are compared.[11] Each discipline formulates its own working definition of the human person for use within the framework of the discipline, and each of these can be shown to fail when pressed to give an ultimate or comprehensive account of humanity. While all such efforts to construct an anthropology account for certain kinds of data, and each is useful in a pragmatic sense, they all are nevertheless bounded and incomplete. Each fails precisely when its inherent limitations are forgotten or ignored, that is, when the "working model" it presents is absolutized and it pretends to tell us who we really are. The result is that people at the beginning of the twenty-first century have a much more confused idea of what it means to be human than their great-grandparents had at the beginning of the twentieth century. There was a shared sense of human uniqueness that people of the sixteenth century had in common with people of the fourth. But that shared understanding of humanity has largely been lost, and anthropology has become a "problem."

THE NEED FOR A RENEWAL
OF CHRISTIAN ANTHROPOLOGY

It should be obvious, in the light of this current confusion about anthropology, that Christian theology is called upon for fresh reflection and response to what it means to be human. The doctrine of human nature and existence has renewed relevance. That is to say, there is a new opportunity to communicate those elements of the biblical message that can help us answer the new (and not-so-new) anthropological questions. An important mode of deliberately Christian response to modern anthropologies is a flourishing discipline which may be termed "missionary anthropology." This is an adaptation of the social sciences of cultural anthropology, psychology, linguistics, and sociology, in the service of evangelism and mission. This discipline is championed in evangelical circles by scholars

11. Numerous works can be cited as evidence and documentation of this fragmentation. Teilhard de Chardin, *Man's Place in Nature*; Friedman, *The Hidden Human Image* (and others); Heschel, *Who Is Man?*; van Leeuwen, *The Person in Psychology*; Stevenson and Haberman, *Ten Theories of Human Nature*; Marin, "The Disappearance of Man."

and missionaries such as Charles Kraft, whose recent *Anthropology for Christian Witness* provides an excellent orientation to the perspectives and insights of cultural anthropology as a discipline, as well as its utility (indeed, necessity) for effective communication of the gospel.[12] The practical utility of such an approach is undeniable, but it still does not reflect on the theological meaning of humanity. In fact, the object of study in this kind of "missionary anthropology" is actually not "humans" *per se*, but rather human artifacts, the things which humans make for themselves. Missionary anthropology studies that conglomerate of physical, social, and intellectual artifacts we call "culture." And this study of human creations is not quite the same as the study of human creatures themselves.[13]

What does it mean, then, to understand human creatures theologically? In this climate of often useful but incomplete attempts of humans to understand themselves, there is a need to do more than find ways to apply the results of disparate disciplines to the practical problems of extending and managing the church. The anthropology of Christian theology urgently begs renewed attention. The doctrinal *locus de homine* sets out to answer the anthropological question by asserting that human identity can only be adequately understood by taking into account the contingent and dependent[14] nature of the human being as a creature of God.[15] As creatures, we cannot know ourselves rightly without a right knowledge of the source of our life, our Creator.[16] This is what lies beneath the paradox and inadequacy of the various non-theological anthropologies. The fragmentation of human knowledge of humanity results from and mirrors our fractured relationship with God. Our actual identity (ontology)

---

12. Kraft, *Anthropology for Christian Witness*.

13. For example, Kraft includes chapters on technology (Ibid., 164–79) and economic systems (180–95), both of which are important as "artifacts" of human communities, but neither of which can be properly identified as inherent to human nature itself. The area of language (236–53) is somewhat more ambiguous, since the phenomenon of linguistic communication seems to be a common feature of human life, while almost none of the details of any particular language can claim to be universal.

14. Cf. Arand, "Autonomy."

15. Pannenberg regards precisely this characteristic "infinite dependence" of human beings as the ground and cause of their "openness to the world."

16. This fundamental insight about human origin in God is a decisive point in Luther's "Disputation Concerning Man": "Nor is there any hope that man in this principal part can himself know what he is until he sees himself in his origin which is God." (LW 34:138; WA 39I.17536f.).

and our knowledge of ourselves (epistemology) are bound inextricably to our relationship with our Creator. That relationship turns out to be more complex than one might suppose at first, and we are drawn into the mystery of the Trinity. The gospel asserts that our relationship has been definitively and uniquely restored by the action of God in the person of Christ, in whom the divine and the human natures are uniquely united. Anthropology and Christology are thus intimately and necessarily connected. Christ not only reveals to us God's true being and nature, but also embodies perfectly what it means to be fully human, and recreates humanity by his death and resurrection, continuing his saving, re-creating work in human life through the Holy Spirit. Theological anthropology explores this inner connection between the creating and saving work of God, which also finds expression at times in the church's worship, as for example in one of the Christmas collects which addresses God as "our Maker and Redeemer, who wonderfully created us and in the incarnation of your Son yet more wondrously restored our human nature."

But in Lutheran theology this connection is often not made so explicit, and its implications have remained largely unexplored. Various contemporary Christologies generally affirm the full humanity of Christ, without careful examination about what that humanity entails.[17] Dogmatic treatments in the Lutheran tradition often ignore the connection between anthropology and Christology. The *locus de homine* is relegated to a sort of transition between the doctrine of God (and its corollary or sub-locus, the doctrine of creation), and a more detailed discussion of sin. Pieper's *Christliche Dogmatik* offers an excellent example of this approach to anthropology. He devotes 13 pages to the doctrine of humanity as created by God, which is less space than he uses to discuss angels.[18] Pieper's "anthropology" is actually limited to a description of the *imago Dei*. The section on human beings *per se* actually functions, for Pieper, as the introduction to a much more extensive section on sin (more than 60 pages). Surely this prompts the serious question: Is sin the only thing worth saying about the meaning of being human?

That kind of cursory or superficial treatment of anthropology does not do justice to the theological heritage of Luther and the Reformation. Indeed, Luther could sum up the whole *proprium* of theology as including

17. In the "myth of God incarnate" debate, for instance, the issue is the deity of Jesus. His humanity remains largely unexplored. See Hick, *The Myth of God Incarnate*

18. Pieper, *Christliche Dogmatik*, 617–29; see also 600–616.

a right understanding of humanity: "The knowledge of God and of man is the divine, and properly theological, wisdom."[19] As Gerhard Ebeling points out, Luther's insight into the place of anthropology in theology, the *cognitio hominis*, was profound. Luther's approach differed instructively in this respect from that of Zwingli and Calvin, who began with God and then considered human nature. This sequence has an obvious and intuitive attraction, and it has, in fact, become the dogmatic sequence most generally accepted also in Lutheran theology. Luther, on the other hand, was less interested in consistent logical systems than in the *ordo rei*, the reality of human existence *coram Deo*. For Luther, true theological knowledge apprehends the inescapable but often obscured fact of the human condition as *homo peccator*, and only that fact makes intelligible the revelation of God as *deus iustificans*. And both realities, *homo peccator* and *deus iustificans*, are grounded in the prior fact of God as Creator.

Creation is the matrix for salvation history: the paper on which the drama of sin and redemption is written. Luther's insight into and expression of the Christian view of life is counter-intuitive and somewhat paradoxical. Viewed theologically, the movement of human existence is not "life and death," as might naturally be supposed on the basis of direct empirical observation. Theology begins in the midst of the creaturely— yet fallen—human existence. Precisely against that background the gospel transforms the observable "life and death" sequence into "death and life": a radical re-ordering of the experience of being human. When Lutheran dogmatics give short shrift to the *locus de homine*, these insights about human creaturely existence are easily overlooked as resources for theological engagement with the contemporary world.

The dogmatic neglect of anthropology has had several consequences. For one thing, in the absence of theological anthropology, the whole question of what it means to be human is left, for all practical purposes, to be answered from other sources. The result is the fragmentation and confusion in the wider culture that we have briefly described, which are reflected also in the church. This explains why the "missionary anthropology" mentioned above has flourished as a version of the social science, largely unencumbered by genuine theological reflection. Christians have generally seen anthropology as a secular discipline, one that may be carefully used by Christians for their own purposes, but nevertheless remains

19. "*Cognitio Dei et hominis est sapientia divina et proprie theologica.*" In "Interpretation of Psalm 51," WA 402: 327. Cf. Ebeling, "Cognitio Dei."

distinct from the study of Christian doctrine. Yet the proper theological *cognitio hominis* itself is woven into the whole fabric of the *doctrina evangelii*. That branch of social science called anthropology, while helpful for missiology, is not enough for the church's theological task. Genuine theological anthropology is necessary for the church's confession and evangelization, since it is integrally connected with the chief article of the faith. The fragmented, disintegrated anthropologies devised by humans who are finally unable to understand themselves can obscure the message of the gospel. The message of forgiveness, reconciliation, and new life has little meaning for people who do not understand themselves in the first place as creatures *coram Deo*.

There is a fundamental and necessary connection between what it means to be human and the credal confession of the humanity of Christ, and this connection has also received inadequate study. Put another way, this means we have not explored in enough detail how theological anthropology is related to Christology. The creeds imply that there is an underlying connection between what we confess in the First Article (creation) and the Second (salvation). Yet that connection is no longer apparent in Lutheran theology; indeed, there sometimes appears to be a wide gulf between the two.[20] Gustaf Wingren's work is extremely helpful in this respect. He identifies what has become a prevalent neglect of the doctrine of creation through Protestant theology's almost exclusive preoccupation with epistemology since the nineteenth century.[21] In the wake of Wingren's convincing argument for a recovery of creation's place in Christian theology, it seems clear that any progress toward developing theological anthropology in our day will need to be matrixed with a renewed appreciation for the theology of creation.[22]

20. Cf. Albrecht Peters's commentary on Luther's Catechisms, in which he discusses the apparent discontinuity between Luther's explanations of these two articles. Peters, *Der Glaube*, 50. It should be noted that the discontinuity Peters identifies between the First and Second Articles does not reflect a discontinuity in the giving nature of God, which is in the foreground in Luther's explanations, but rather to a fault line within the person of the confessing "I" who speaks. The human believer, who speaks in the Catechism, experiences a fracture between her unproblematic existence as creature and her status as a "verlornen und verdammpten Menschen." More will be said about the continuity between the creation and redemption in chapter 4.

21. Wingren, *Creation and Law*.

22. In recent decades there has been a resurgence of interest in theological anthropology. Notable has been the work of Wolfhart Pannenberg, who has engaged the wider

Genuine theological anthropology will help us to integrate all that we know about what it means to be human, rather than ignoring (much less simply negating) the real insights from other approaches to anthropology. In rejecting or reacting against the reductionist or materialist distortions of anthropology that dominate twentieth-century culture, Christian theology can be tempted to give an answer to the anthropological questions that is too theological—in the sense of neglecting the importance of the common, everyday, "natural" dimensions of human life. In other words, theological anthropology can sometimes operate as if the real nature of human creatures had nothing to do with the rest of the universe and existed purely and exclusively in relation to God. The result is that the secular confusion and distortion concerning human beings is replaced by a different distortion of the understanding of humanity, but in this case a distortion that may hold special appeal within theological circles. Despite the limited special appeal of this sort of "purely theological" anthropology, such an account of humanity is doomed to remain unintelligible or irrelevant to the wider culture.

It is a presupposition of this study that theology and theological discourse ought not to become an exclusive or "in-house" exercise by which specialists speak and write only for each other, but at its best will also interact with other disciplines in the wider intellectual culture. In so doing it may even serve as an invitation to human beings to integrate their knowledge of themselves as creatures of God, fallen yet redeemed and restored in Christ.

THEOLOGICAL ANTHROPOLOGY
AND THE FINNISH SCHOOL

This study interacts with several recent theological studies that distort theological anthropology precisely by being too theological, in a way that is perhaps new to us in the West but not new to Christianity. The theologians of the so-called "Finnish school," led by Tuomo Mannermaa, have re-opened the discussion of soteriology and anthropology in provocative

---

culture's understanding of human nature and human history and related it to the incarnation of Christ. Pannenberg's theological anthropology deserves an extended study by itself. Only occasional references will be made to his thought in this dissertation. Some of his important works are available in English: *What Is Man?*; "The Christological Foundation of Christian Anthropology"; *Anthropology in Theological Perspective*; *Toward a Theology of Nature*; and his *Systematic Theology*.

ways, largely through their contacts with the theology of the Orthodox Church. Their approach, while challenging the "mainstream" of Luther research, has found favorable response within a number of theological circles. Martin Brecht, for example, responded with cautious optimism to what he called the "*neue Ansätze*" offered by the Finnish Luther research, while at the same time noting that some of their ideas are still in need of clarification ("*klärungsbedürftig*") and only "new" in a limited sense ("*nur begrenzt neu*").[23] He calls for further engagement with the impulses coming from Mannermaa and the Finnish school, and welcomes the fact that the Finns are conducting "engaged Lutheran theology," which, he adds dryly, "*heute nicht selbstverständlich ist.*" Gert Haendler, in an early review of the Finnish school's work, took note of the rather one-sided systematic approach and the lack of historical contributions to the project, but he also was positively inclined to serious consideration of their proposals: "The quiet worry about the one-sided primacy of systematics in Luther research should not diminish the thanks due to this volume, which imparts such multifaceted stimuli."[24]

Since most of the results of their scholarship have been published in German, the Finnish school and their works have been better known in Europe than in North America up to now.[25] But there are also signs that the program of the Finnish school is beginning to gain wider acceptance on this side of the Atlantic. Carl Braaten has hailed their approach as a "breakthrough," and Robert Jenson has also written favorably on the same theme.[26] The editors of *Luther Digest* have introduced English readers to this current of thought by giving prominent notice to the Finnish *theosis* studies.[27] One of Tuomo Mannermaa's seminal essays has also appeared in English translation.[28] The most complete and important English publication from the Finnish school to date is *Union with Christ: the New*

23. Brecht, "Neue Ansätze."

24. Haendler, review of *Thesaurus Lutheri.*

25. See also Plathow, review of Mannermaa, and the helpful and insightful piece Wenz, "*Mannermaa, Tuomo.*"

26. Braaten, "Finnish Breakthrough." Jenson, "Theosis."

27. See a number of articles abridged in *Luther Digest*, 3 (1995): 134–75; and 5 (1997): 162–81.

28. Mannermaa, "Justification and Christology." (This is the first and most important chapter of Mannermaa's *Der im Glauben gegenwärtige Christus.*) While the present study was in preparation, a complete translation of Mannermaa's key book was published as *Christ Present in Faith: Luther's View of Justification.*

Finnish Interpretation of Luther,[29] in which the earlier impression of enthusiastic response from editors Braaten and Jenson is emphatically confirmed (as in Jenson's unreserved endorsement of the whole project: "Since my attention was first called to the contemporary Finnish school, I have thought that Professor Mannermaa and his associates were simply and wholly right in their chief contentions"[30]).

Working from a starting point of ecumenical engagement especially with the Orthodox Church in Finland and Russia, Mannermaa and his school have explored the theme of *theosis*, or deification, as a possible key for understanding Luther's theology. This is certainly a departure from earlier approaches to Luther, in which the attention was concentrated on identifying the distinctively evangelical insight in Luther's development, and tracing ways such a "breakthrough" (however it may be precisely defined) worked itself out over Luther's career.[31] Mannermaa and those of his school are generally uninterested in such questions. Instead, in various studies of the Finnish school, the *theosis* of the believer through his "real-ontic" union with Christ has been used as a new way to map the structure of Luther's thought.

One positive influence of this initiative of the Finnish theologians has undoubtedly been their effort to re-connect theological anthropology and Christology, and to explore the connection between what it means to be human and what God gives us as he saves us in Christ. The *theosis* studies of the Finnish school have helped put anthropology back on the theological table, so to speak, and they have done so in a time when our theological understanding of what it means to be human urgently needs to be recovered and revitalized. This is important for Lutheran theology. If we are to renew theological anthropology as a meaningful and functional dimension of our theology (as I believe we must do), then our theological answers to the questions about humanity must be explicitly related to Jesus Christ. The quest to understand the manner and meaning of that relation between anthropology and Christology will underlie much of this study.

29. Braaten and Jenson, eds., *Union with Christ*.

30. Ibid., 21.

31. Some important figures and themes of this "mainstream" of Luther research are collected in two volumes edited by Bernhard Lohse: *Durchbruch* and *Neuere Untersuchungen*.

A sense of the necessity of that relation may account for the attraction of the central thesis of the Finnish school. The anthropology of *theosis* is explicitly Christo-centric. Under the general theme of *theosis* Mannermaa and his colleagues offer a number of interrelated perspectives, which urge a critical rethinking of Lutheran theology. They challenge us to consider what are for most Lutheran Christians new ways of approaching theology. *Theosis* is in this sense not so much a single doctrine as an entire frame of reference for thinking about salvation: namely, as an ontological reality in which our own humanity is really connected with God's nature through faith in Christ. This ontological claim about salvation also indicates a way to understand the person and work of Christ. Rather than focus attention especially on Christ's vicarious obedience and atoning sacrifice, the theology of *theosis* tends to regard the union of deity and humanity in the incarnation of the Logos as the decisive salvific event. This then leads to *theosis* as a new way to understand anthropology. Because the Finnish theologians concentrate on the theme of *theosis*, and focus their interest exclusively on soteriology, they fail to appreciate Luther's own recovery of creation as a positive good. Theology centered on deification makes the incarnation of Christ paradigmatic for restored humanity, and conceives human destiny in terms that move human beings "beyond" creation. To be truly human is to become divine: the genuine human being is "more than human" ("*mehr als ein Mensch*").

As we study the anthropology of *theosis* in the Mannermaa school, it will be necessary to sharpen our theological understanding of humanity, but in ways that guard against two wrong approaches to what it means to be human creatures *coram Deo*. The first has characterized a good deal of Luther research since Ritschl; it understands "being" (including our being as humans) as exclusively "being in relation." This seems to imply a kind of independent self-existence for human beings who are thus able to exist "in relation to" God. Risto Saarinen has made a major contribution to Luther studies by examining the philosophical roots of this conception.[32] But at the same time, it is mistaken to think of human nature and being in purely "substantial" terms, as if the primary point of reference for our existence were "in us." Our theological anthropology cannot content itself with a definition and description of the nature of human creatures in and of themselves ("*homo in se ipso*"). What is decisive in a theological

---

32. Saarinen, *Gottes Wirken auf uns.*

understanding of human existence is the Word of God, a word that is not merely descriptive but creative and performative. That is to say, the word is not only the source of accurate theological information from which we piece together our anthropology, but also the source and cause of human existence itself. Our being as human creatures hangs continually on the word by which we are addressed by God, or as Gerhard Ebeling puts it, "the word decides about man's being as man."[33] To the basic human question "Who are you?" such an anthropology begins by answering: "I am the one to whom it is said: 'I am the Lord your God.' I am the one who is created by this word."[34]

In creation, God's word brings about what it says: he speaks, and it happens. Since the first rebellion of human creatures against their Creator, God's descriptive word ("alien" word) to us is a word of law, which exposes our self-distortion and is experienced by us as condemnation and judgment; thus it is an accusing—indeed, a killing—word. But the word of the gospel, God's "proper" word, works creatively: it performs and does and gives what it says. This is the "strong word," which, in the words of Martin Franzmann's hymn, "bespeaks us righteous." From beginning to end, the word not only describes and defines, but actually brings about and establishes the "being" of human creatures. This fact allows us to speak of human existence in terms of an "ontology of the word," in contrast to the kind of ontology which occupies the interest of the Finnish school.

Tuomo Mannermaa and his colleagues develop an ontology of justified human nature, a way of understanding what it means to be human, which differs significantly from that just described. For them, genuine humanity can only be defined by a "real-ontic" union with Christ's divine nature, into which the human being is drawn. The word of God is not decisive in such a system, because it is understood more as a vehicle for information than as the effective cause of new realities. In this way the Finnish theology of *theosis* shares certain fundamental features with the theology of Andreas Osiander (1498–1552). Osiander regarded the word of justification, by which the sinner was declared righteous, to be a descriptive word which presupposed a prior "real" change in the sinner by the indwelling of God's own essential righteousness. The connection between the *theosis* theme in the Mannermaa school and the "essential

---

33. Ebeling, *"Problem des Natürlichen,"* 284.
34. Bayer, "Geistgabe und Bildungsarbeit," 2.

righteousness" taught by Osiander demands closer attention, and it will be my argument that the Finnish scholars have revived a number of major ideas found in Osiander's theology, ideas which separate them both from Luther and from the tradition of Lutheran theology since the Formula of Concord. For now it is worth noting that their studies have contributed to a new openness to reconsider Osiander's doctrine of justification. The connection is made by Carl Braaten, who disclaims—yet at the same time hints at—a "rehabilitation" of Osiander.

> The Finnish theologians are careful to point out that they are not merely rehabilitating Andreas Osiander, whose teaching on justification was condemned in the 16th century Lutheran *Formula of Concord*. However, recent research based on the latest critical edition of Osiander's writings raises questions about what precisely was found wanting in his teaching. Osiander emphasized that justification by faith brings about an ontological participation in the divine nature, that through faith sinners receive the essential righteousness of God, at the deepest level of personal being— ideas Osiander shared with Luther. In rejecting Osiander did the Lutheran tradition overreact by throwing the baby out with the bath? All these matters are now being re-investigated by the Mannermaa circle of scholars.[35]

This present study seeks to be another contribution to that reinvestigation and reconsideration of the theme of anthropology as it grows out of the Lutheran understanding of the justification of the sinner before God. Its conclusions are less sanguine about the theological program of the Mannermaa school (and Osiander's, by the way) than those of Braaten and some others.

PROCEDURE AND METHOD

The first chapter of this study outlines the main features of the *theosis* theme as a way of interpreting the theology of Martin Luther; this part of the study concentrates on the influential work of Tuomo Mannermaa. Following that, the second chapter focuses specifically on the ramifications of *theosis* for questions of theological anthropology, notably as this theme is developed in the work of Simo Peura. The third and fourth chapters present a response to the theological program of the Finnish school, a dual critique of their approach to Luther's theology first in terms of

35. Braaten, "The Finnish Breakthrough," 143.

history and then in systematic terms. My conclusion is that the theology of the *theosis* school develops a theological anthropology which diverges from that of Luther as well as later Lutheranism. The major deficiencies of the theology of *theosis*, from the perspective of Lutheran theology, are its neglect of creation, its failure to grasp Luther's theology of the word, and its inadequate appreciation of the role of Christ's humanity in our justification.

Part of what drives the present study is the conviction that anthropology matters in theology. That is to say, theology must find new ways (or recover and translate old ways) to answer questions about what it means to be human. One purpose of this study, then, is to try to reclaim the doctrine *de homine* as a vital and pertinent dimension of the whole theological enterprise, rather than relegate anthropology to non-theological (or even anti-theological) disciplines. The anthropological suggestions that arise from the studies of the Finnish school, intriguing and stimulating in some respects, ultimately fall short of this goal, in part because they represent a kind of "flight from creation" (to use Wingren's phrase). It is the thesis of this study that reclaiming anthropology as a vital theological discipline will involve a renewed affirmation of the creatureliness of human beings also in terms of redemption, that is, the assertion that our status as creatures is not a limitation to be overcome—as through the deification of the believer—but a gift to be celebrated.

Theosis and Luther Studies

The Finnish School of Tuomo Mannermaa

ECUMENICAL FOREGROUND, PATRISTIC BACKGROUND

THE *THEOSIS* STUDIES OF Tuomo Mannermaa and his school have developed in a decidedly ecumenical context. In recent decades there have been significant discussions between the Orthodox churches and churches in the western tradition, including the Roman Catholics, Anglicans, and Lutherans. Such discussions have resulted in greater awareness in the West of the theological distinctives of the Orthodox tradition, and in a general revival of interest in the theology and worship life of Orthodoxy.[1] Certain anthropological and soteriological elements of the eastern theological tradition are particularly important as background for understanding the concerns and the approach of Mannermaa and the Finnish school. This is true because Finnish theologians, and Mannermaa in particular, have been involved in ecumenical discussions with the Russian Orthodox Church since the 1970's, and this ecumenical context has helped to shape Mannermaa's new approach to the study of Luther's theology.

Theosis, or deification, always prominent in the eastern tradition, has become a key concept in relationships between eastern and western Christendom, and this phenomenon crosses specific confessional lines. The Roman Catholic openness to the eastern tradition may be observed in various aspects of the recent *Catechism of the Catholic Church*, which makes frequent and deliberate use of categories generally associated with

---

1. For a good introduction to the Orthodox understanding of *theosis*, see Mantzaridis, *The Deification of Man*.

eastern Orthodoxy, notably the patristic language of deification.[2] The theological approach of the *Catechism of the Catholic Church* illustrates the broader trend in contemporary ecumenical discussions to focus on the theology of the ancient church fathers. As churches seek not only mutual understanding but theological convergence, patristic theology serves as the point of departure for building consensus.[3]

For some Lutheran scholars, this has meant investigating the patristic roots of the theology of Martin Luther. Wolfgang Bienert has helped identify some specific aspects of patristic theology that are to be found in Luther's own theological works, and he has also pointed to some of the limitations of Luther's patristic sources, which came to him filtered through the framework of medieval Augustinianism.[4] As Bienert points out, "The ecumenical dialog between Lutherans and Orthodox has given important impulses to the study of patristics."[5] One of the scholars in Mannermaa's Finnish school, Jouko Martikainen, has attempted to document Luther's relationship to the patristic tradition of the Eastern Church, especially in formulating his Christology.[6] Martikainen's point of departure is the assumption that "Luther's theology has a certain nearness to eastern theology." This leads him to look for parallels (and possible influence) not only in major church fathers such as Athanasius, Cyril of Alexandria, and Basil the Great, but also in much less well-known figures like Julian of Halicarnassus (one of the disputants in the monophysite aphthartodocetic controversy) and the Syrian sage Aphraates. Bernhard Lohse prefers the term "common Christian heritage" rather than "tradition of the church" in his exploration of Luther's knowledge and use of patristic theology. That choice of terms reflects the ecumenical signifi-

---

2. *Catechism of the Catholic Church.* Cf., as examples of the deification theme, §§260, 460, 1692, 1999. Note the repeated references to 2 Peter 1:4, a reminder that the notion of communion and participation with God is not itself unbiblical. The theology of Orthodoxy and Roman Catholicism identifies "deification" with justification, which distorts the meaning of the biblical expressions.

3. Among the most important documents emerging from the contacts between the Orthodox tradition and Lutheranism are the contribution to *Salvation in Christ: A Lutheran-Orthodox Dialogue*, edited by John Meyendorff and Robert Tobias (Minneapolis: Augsburg, 1992). Cf. especially "Soteriology" and the jointly authored "Common Statement."

4. Bienert, "Patristic Background" and "Aporien."

5. Bienert, "Aporien," 95.

6. Martikainen, J., "*Christologische und trinitätstheologische Aporien.*"

cance of the Reformation attitude toward, and use of, the church fathers. As Lohse shows, Luther was quite familiar and critically engaged with at least some of the fathers. The priority, for Luther and his contemporaries, lies especially with Augustine, but Lohse mentions also Luther's use of Jerome, Gregory I, Bernard of Clairvaux, and William of Ockham.[7] A number of other studies testify to the wide interest in the thematic and historical connections between the theology of the Reformation and that of the ancient fathers, especially as the basis for efforts toward ecumenical understanding.[8]

This ecumenical interest in the theological heritage of the ancient fathers as it relates to the Reformation provides an important element for understanding the theology of Tuomo Mannermaa and the other scholars of the Finnish school. They have been interested primarily in the doctrine of justification, which of course is also the central concern of Luther and the Reformation. What the Finnish school attempts to do is to concentrate on the theme of *theosis*, or deification, especially as it occurs in Luther's writings. For Mannermaa and others, the appearance in Luther's theological works of this typically eastern motif serves an ecumenical function: it provides a point of contact for theological discussion between the Lutherans and the Orthodox. Mannermaa has led the way in re-exploring the theology of Martin Luther in search of themes and ideas which may serve as meaningful points of contact with Orthodox theology. He and others have proposed that there are strong parallels between the Orthodox doctrine of *theosis* (deification) and the Lutheran doctrine of justification, particularly what they identify as Luther's ontological view of the union of the believer with Christ.[9] In fact, the motivation seems to work both ways: just as the contemporary ecumenical contacts have urged closer study of the reformers' appropriation of patristic themes (as explicitly in Jouko Martikainen's work mentioned earlier), so also schol-

---

7. Lohse, "Luther and the Common Christian Heritage." A recent collection of Lohse's studies, *Evangelium in der Geschichte. Band II: Studien zur Theologie der Kirchenväter und zu ihrer Rezeption in der Reformation* (Vandenhoeck & Ruprecht, 1996), was not available at this writing.

8. Cf. two volumes edited by Leif Grane, Alfred Schindler, and Markus Wriedt: *Auctoritas Patrum* and *Auctoritas Patrum II*. For material specifically related to Melanchthon, cf. Fraenkel, *Testimonia Patrum*.

9. The *theosis* theme also presents an opportunity for theological convergence in other ecumenical contexts, such as with the Roman Catholics. Cf. Mannermaa, "*Einig in Sachen der Rechtfertigung?*" and Peura, "*Christus als Gunst und Gabe.*"

ars who have noticed Luther's use of the church fathers have, as a result, become interested in how those patristic themes have been developed elsewhere in Christendom.

Even apart from the ecumenical utility of such studies, Tuomo Mannermaa argues that pursuing *theosis* as a theme in Luther research can help Lutherans themselves recover an important dimension of the reformer's theology that has been neglected in Luther studies. In particular, with reference to the doctrine of justification, Mannermaa believes that the "mainstream" of Luther scholarship has focused too narrowly on what he refers to as the forensic or "ethical-relational" dimension of justification. His assessment of the dominant currents of Luther research over the last century is that the relational conception of justification has been emphasized at the expense of the real-ontological character of Luther's own theology. Mannermaa's program of theological investigation thus pursues its ecumenical interests by seeking to recover what he considers to be a more authentic or genuine Lutheran theology, that is, theology which returns to the insights of Luther himself rather than the theology which came to characterize later generations of Lutheranism. For Mannermaa and those of his school, the "real" Luther is clearly more congenial than, say, the Formula of Concord, which they regard as a one-sided distortion of Luther's own teaching about justification.

THE MEANING OF THEOSIS IN ORTHODOX THEOLOGY

The idea of *theosis* is as foreign to western theology, or at least to Lutheran theology, as it is familiar to Orthodoxy. Western readers generally need a more precise explanation of the term and its implications, for at least two basic reasons. First, for western Christians the strangeness of the notion of *theosis* may result in a distorted caricature of the Orthodox doctrine rather than a nuanced understanding of the real theological issues involved. A critical theological engagement with the soteriology and anthropology that are entailed in the *theosis* theme will require a more detailed knowledge of what is for most westerners at the very least an unfamiliar *modus loquendi*. Secondly, and more directly related to our immediate concern to understand the theological arguments of Mannermaa and the Finnish school, we need to be able to distinguish between the *theosis* doctrine in Orthodoxy and the concept Mannermaa and others find in Luther's theology. Despite their contention that the theme of *theosis* or *Vergottung* offers a crucial point of contact between Lutheran and Orthodox theology, what Mannermaa refers to as *theosis* in Luther's writings is not by any means the same as what is integral to the Orthodox conception of salvation.

It is commonly acknowledged that *theosis*, or deification, is the characteristic way in which the church of the Eastern tradition speaks of man's salvation. The concept, or elements of it, can be traced back to the ancient fathers. The specific vocabulary originated in the work of Irenaeus, and was developed especially by Athanasius and the Cappadocian fathers. But in the tradition of the Eastern Church, the doctrine of man's participation in God was elaborated and given its most definitive systematic shape by Gregory Palamas. A Greek monk and theologian of the fourteenth century, Palamas has had a decisive influence on contemporary Orthodox theologians of differing nationalities. An important part of the so-called "Palamite renaissance" has been a growing awareness of his theology in the West through studies of such theologians as Vladimir Lossky[10] and John Meyendorff,[11] and the publication of English translations of works by Georgios Mantzaridis,[12] and Panayiotis Nellas.[13] The enormous influence of Palamas—especially related to the notion of *theosis*—means that it is inadequate to attempt a dialog with modern Orthodoxy based solely on the earlier fathers like Irenaeus and Athanasius. In Orthodoxy these are generally read through the lens or filter of Palamas. Understanding *theosis* as the dominant theme of contemporary Orthodox theology requires some familiarity with the main points of the theology of Palamas.[14]

Gregory Palamas drew on the Greek patristic tradition which runs from Origen, on through Athanasius, to the Cappadocians and John of Damascus. He affirmed that salvation involved not only the reconciliation of human beings who were estranged from their Creator by sin, but the actual sharing of the divine life with believers through their communion with the triune God. He and other eastern fathers call this participation

10. Lossky, *Mystical Theology.*

11. Meyendorff, *A Study of Gregory Palamas.*

12. Mantzaridis, *The Deification of Man.*

13. Nellas, *Deification in Christ.* Cf. also Metropolitan Hierotheos, *St. Gregory Palamas as a Hagiorite.*

14. For the interest of the Finnish school in the theology of Palamas, cf. Kamppuri, "Theosis." The Mannermaa school have apparently failed to appreciate significant differences between the theology of Palamas and that of Luther, as demonstrated by Flogaus, *Theosis bei Palamas und Luther.*

in the very life of God himself deification, or *theosis*. Man's created nature and being are understood as designed expressly and uniquely for this destiny of deification, so that the human creature is from the beginning "incomplete" and awaiting completion through ontological union with God. Thus the soteriology of Orthodoxy is inseparably related to its anthropology. The creation of man "in the image of God" implied for Palamas that the human creature is "a psycho-physiological whole to whom God brought salvation by his Incarnation,"[15] and who thus reflects God's own being. The "image of God" is variously interpreted by the Greek fathers, but Palamas was well within the Orthodox tradition when he assumed that human beings were created in such a way as to have a certain continuity of being with their Creator. Although discussions of the image tend to emphasize the human intellect, ultimately the concept of the *imago Dei* is "expressed and manifested, as through a prism, throughout the whole of human existence."[16]

There is another way in which theological anthropology is fundamental for understanding the Orthodox view of salvation as *theosis*. An important distinction is made in Orthodox anthropology between "image" and "likeness" (Genesis 1:26–27). For Palamas[17] and the Orthodox tradition, the "image" is identified with the fundamental created reality of human creatures generally, while "likeness" refers not to any actual quality or substance but to human potential for progress toward communion with God and participation in the divine life. The potentiality of the divine "likeness," or similitude to God, represented Adam's original goal and destiny, which he was to have reached through the exercise of his free submission to God's will. Through disobedience Adam lost the power with which he had been originally endowed for communion with God and to have a real part in God's life. Christ, the "enfleshed" divine

---

15. Meyendorff, *A Study of Gregory Palamas*.

16. Mantzaridis, *The Deification of Man*, 16.

17. Although it is not within the scope of the present study to present a detailed analysis of the theology of Palamas, the following editions of his works may be noted in addition to the modern studies of his thought already cited: *Gregorii Acindyni Refutationes duae: operis Gregorii Palamae cui titulus dialogus inter orthodoxum et Barlaamitam* (Turnhout: Brepols; Leuven: University Press, 1995); and *The One Hundred and Fifty Chapters: A Critical Edition*, trans. and study by Robert E. Sinkewicz (Toronto, Ont., Canada : Pontifical Institute of Mediaeval Studies, 1988). A readily accessible English translation of one of Palamas' most important works is Gregory Palamas, *The Triads*, ed. John Meyendorff, trans. Nicholas Gendle.

Logos, restores and repairs this corrupted human nature by joining it to the divine nature in his own person.

Thus the incarnation of the Logos, that is, the joining of the divine and human natures, is the decisive redemptive event in Palamas' theology, as in Orthodoxy in general. The incarnate Logos then becomes the archetype to which restored human nature corresponds, and toward which it is to develop in the process of deification. That is to say, the goal of human nature is beyond merely created human nature, since it is the fusion of the human person with the uncreated divine grace. Genuine humanity, according to Orthodoxy, is necessarily "human-plus," because human nature is intended to be united with the divine nature, a union for which Christ is the example and paradigm. Since he understands Christ as the incarnate Logos and the divine paradigm to be reflected (and, in a sense, *replicated*) in human individuals, "Palamas is particularly eager to speak of Christ as a teacher and as the prototype of the faithful."[18] Salvation is brought about by the incarnation, the hypostatic union of the divine and human natures in the paradigmatic person of Christ, who is unique because his incarnation initiates and makes possible the union of the divine with the human in the persons of believers. Orthodox theology, shaped by Palamas, conceives of deification as "an ontological regeneration of human nature in the hypostasis of the incarnate Logos of God, accessible to every man who participates personally and freely in the life of Christ."[19] Man's free will, directed toward the grace of God, is a necessary cooperative agent in salvation, according to Orthodox theology. Through the cooperation of his will, man is actively involved in the progressive, transformative process[20] by which one gradually becomes increasingly "like" God. This occurs as our *similitudo Dei* is conformed more and more to the true Image, which is Christ. The resource of grace given to man for this task is first of the grace of baptism ("the resurrection of the soul")[21] and then the personal communion with the Holy Spirit, which is made possible by Christ, the New Adam.[22] This communion and participation is essential

18. Mantzaridis, *The Deification of Man*, 28.

19. Ibid., 31.

20. The progressive conception of "justification" (*theosis*) is explored in the theological vernacular of Lutheran theology by Orthodox theologian Konstantinos E. Papapetrou in *Über die anthropologischen Grenzen der Kirche*.

21. Meyendorff, *A Study of Gregory Palamas*, 152–55.

22. Christ's nature marks the return to the original "image and likeness" of original creation, which perfectly reflected God's own nature. There thus existed in Adam, and

to a genuinely human life.[23] That genuine human life is not life *as human creature* but the life that is only complete when the human becomes more than mere creature, through participation in God's own uncreated life. *Theosis* can thus be summarized as transformation through the real communion with, and participation in, the life of God the Father through the Son in the Holy Spirit.

It is also important to recognize that, according to Palamas, the believer is not united with God in such a way that he actually partakes of the divine *essence*. Rather, man is united with and participates in God's uncreated "energies" (*energeia*) in a way that is "supernatural," that is, beyond his created nature.[24] Palamas regarded the notion that man becomes united with the divine *ousia* to be blasphemous; man does not become "God by nature."[25] God's essential nature remains not only unknowable, but even beyond the unknowable; that is, it is unknowable not merely because of human limitations but because God himself transcends all categories.[26] True theology, according to Palamas, must always reckon with this fact of the real and ultimately unspeakable transcendence of God, hence it is "apophatic," a kind of *via negativa* which constantly negates positive statements which would limit God and man's participation in him.[27] This is true *par excellence* of man's deification, which is "a mystical event which takes place within him through God's supranatural [*sic*] power, and as

---

was restored in Christ, "a certain primordial congruence between man's being and God's being." Vladimir Lossky, *Orthodox Theology*, trans. Ian and Ihita Kesarcodi-Watson (Crestwood, NY: St. Vladimir's Seminary Press, 1989), 119.

23. Cf. Meyendorff, "Humanity: 'Old' and 'New.'" Meyendorff refers to the anthropology of Irenaeus (*Adv. Haer.* V), where the "spirit" of human creatures is apparently identical with the Spirit of God. Thus to be human is *by definition* to be united with and participate in God.

24. For a more detailed examination of Palamas' doctrine of divine energies, cf. Meyendorff, *A Study of Gregory Palamas*, 202–27.

25. Pelikan, *The Spirit of Eastern Christendom*.

26. There is an interesting conceptual parallel between this apophatic acknowledgement of the transcendence of God in Orthodoxy on the one hand, and on the other the characteristic confession—or exclamation—of Islam: "*Allahu akbar!*" (God is greater!), which implies not only that God is supreme in comparison with anything else, but that he categorically surpasses all possibility of comparison. For a discussion of the role of transcendence in Muslim piety, cf. Roland E. Miller, *Muslim Friends, The Faith and Feeling: An Introduction to Islam* (St. Louis: CPH, 1995), 40–45.

27. Nellas, *Deification in Christ*, 73.

such is essentially unutterable."[28] Theology remains distinct from contemplation, the latter being primary and having the goal of the soul's direct experience of and participation in the shared divine life and light.[29]

THEOSIS AND THE THEOLOGY OF TUOMO MANNERMAA

The preceding brief discussion of *theosis* and its place in Orthodox theology is intended to provide the background necessary to make sense of the arguments and assertions of the Finnish school in contemporary Lutheran theology. Tuomo Mannermaa has led his group of theologians in an attempt to show that Martin Luther's conception of justification involved an ontological union of the believer with God, a union which, they argue, closely parallels the Orthodox doctrine of *theosis*. Their interest is not restricted simply to Luther's occasional use of specific vocabulary (such as "*vergotten*"), but rather extends more broadly to his understanding of the believer's union with Christ. Claiming a thematic (if not literary) connection with Orthodox theology as developed by Palamas, Mannermaa argues that Luther's view of justification consists in the believer's real[30] participation in Christ, and thus in God himself. Christ himself is really present, and unites himself with the believer, in faith. Mannermaa reacts against any reduction of faith to mere epistemology, as if faith were only a way of knowing, and insists instead that faith constitutes an ontological reality in which Christ is really and personally present. The unity between Christ and the believer that results from this faith-participation is described by Mannermaa and others as a "real-ontic" unity; that is, a fundamental component of the believer's being. Mannermaa and the Finnish school set this conception against what they describe as a purely forensic understanding of justification in which the righteousness of faith is construed as merely, or exclusively, a new *relationship* with God. When justification is understood as *relational*, God remains personally external to the believer, but within the framework of *theosis* God's real presence with and in the believer is what brings about salvation. This means that salvation and justification are described in terms of the believer's essential being; they are *ontological* categories. The exact meaning of *theosis* for

28. Mantzaridis, *The Deification of Man*, 127.

29. Flogaus, *Theosis bei Palamas und Luther*, 77–94.

30. As will be seen, a great deal of Mannermaa's argument hinges on what one counts as "real"—or what one regards as "unreal."

the Finnish school will be explored in greater detail in a moment. What is necessary to recognize at the outset is how Mannermaa and the Finns share with the Orthodox an ontological framework for soteriology.

In contrast to the Orthodox view, on the other hand, Mannermaa and his school do not limit this participation to the divine "energies" as Palamas sought to do; rather they argue that believers participate in God himself, his essential being. They also point out that Luther stressed the divine monergism in this form of deification, whereas the Orthodox tradition has always affirmed the cooperation of the free human will in *theosis*.[31] The union of Christ and the Christian is always "hidden" in this life, because it is not yet completely actualized. Nevertheless, the union manifests itself in a preliminary and partial way through the believer's life of love. Indeed, faith and love constitute the "two natures" of the Christian, corresponding precisely to the divine and human natures in Christ, respectively.[32]

In a foundational essay that sets out the broad features of the theological program of the Finnish school for German and English speakers, Mannermaa outlines many of the ideas and themes of his approach to Luther's theology.[33] Mannermaa attempts to make the case that *theosis* is a legitimate, if for most scholars unfamiliar, theme in Luther's theology. The vocabulary of deification (Latin *deificatio*, German *Vergottung* or *Vergöttlichung*) is used in various places by Luther—even more frequently, Mannermaa claims, than the term "*theologia crucis*"[34]—and the concept is present implicitly even more often in connection with other ideas. Chief among these is the theme of Christ's real presence with and in the believer. Related to this, Mannermaa considers the believer's union

31. Flogaus, *Theosis bei Palamas und Luther*, 403–11.

32. Note that this correlation is itself somewhat counterintuitive, connecting as it does "faith" rather than "love" with the divine nature, as one might have expected in scholastic theology, for instance. The underlying thoughts of Luther here point not to the "essence" of things (i.e., not ontology) but rather to the *orientation* of human existence. Faith is directed toward God and his word, while love serves the neighbor.

33. Mannermaa, "*Theosis als Thema der finnischen Lutherforschung*." Also in English translation: "Theosis as a Subject of Finnish Luther Research."

34. Risto Saarinen agrees with Mannermaa regarding the importance of this theme in Luther's theology, but he also points out that the actual vocables *deifico / vergotten / durchgotten* are not that common in Luther's writings, occurring only "30 times in the Weimar edition." Saarinen, "The Presence of God in Luther's Theology," 9. Simo Peura finds and lists "about twenty" occurrences. Peura, "*Der Vergöttlichungsgedanke*," 172.

with Christ and the "blessed exchange" between Christ and the Christian to be related closely to the idea of deification in Luther's thought. He further argues that a renewed understanding of Luther's use of the concept of *theosis* can illuminate various aspects of the reformer's theology.

Mannermaa identifies three areas of research, each of which has received further attention from Mannermaa himself or from other Finnish Luther scholars. The first of these is a critique of the philosophical presuppositions of Luther research since the mid-nineteenth century, a project that is pursued especially by Risto Saarinen.[35] Next is the task of identifying and analyzing Luther's own use of the distinct vocabulary and ideas of *theosis* as these appear in specific texts. Mannermaa has led the way in this regard. He and others in the Finnish school have attached new importance to various Luther texts, as will be seen in what follows. The third area of research, which has been pursued by Mannermaa and several of his students and colleagues, is an exploration of how an appreciation of the *theosis* theme in Luther's theology can shape the understanding of other structures in his thought, such as the relationship of faith and love in Luther's theology. This last area might be described as a new reading of Luther by means of a hermeneutic of *theosis*. The results of such a new reading of Luther in terms of theological anthropology will be the focus of the next chapter.

The studies produced by the Finnish school make it clear that Mannermaa and his colleagues are not simply interested in *theosis* or deification in a narrow or technical sense. They have pushed the issue to the much more fundamental level of the theological understanding of being itself; that is to say, they have attempted to reclaim a theological vocabulary of ontology. In so doing they have challenged some of the presuppositions that have dominated Luther studies since Albrecht Ritschl, in itself a welcome contribution to Luther studies. The view of the reformer's theology they present is particularly meant to resist what Carl Braaten calls "a neo-Kantianized Luther,"[36] according to which an ontological understanding of faith is excluded *a priori*. As Braaten puts it:

> The Mannermaa school is revising a century of Luther-interpretation which has been dominated by German Protestant theologians, who notoriously read Luther under the spell of neo-

35. Saarinen, *Gottes Wirken auf uns*.
36. Braaten, "Finnish Breakthrough," 143.

Kantian presuppositions. This is true of a long line of German Luther scholarship from Albrecht Ritschl to Gerhard Ebeling. On this basis all ontology to be found in Luther is *verboten*; faith is purely an act of the will with no ontological implications. Faith as volitional obedience rather than as ontological participation is all that a neo-Kantianized Luther would allow. The Finns have found that Luther's texts, when read critically against the background of late medieval philosophy and theology, speak to the contrary.[37]

The Finnish approach to Luther's theology, with its focus on the ontological participation in God as described above, represents a significant departure from most prevailing Luther scholarship. One reason such a conception is bound to sound strange, at least to western ears, as Paul Hinlicky has pointed out, is that the theology of the East, including especially its central affirmation of *theosis*, simply does not address the most fundamental questions in western theology, namely the questions of justice and righteousness.[38] Drawing on the broad characterization dating at least to Albrecht Ritschl,[39] Hinlicky points out that for the eastern fathers, the drama of God's salvation was less about guilt, reconciliation, and forgiveness, than it was revolving around the struggle between the divine life for which man was created and death that had entered and corrupted the world. While Hinlicky is sympathetic to the Finnish school's efforts to integrate the theme of *theosis* into our theological reflection about salvation, he also warns of the danger of attempting to "translate" concepts from one system of thought to another. In the end, it must be remembered that the Orthodox notion of *theosis* is simply set in different theological categories than the generally western preoccupation with righteousness and justification.

Is it possible to describe with more precision what Mannermaa intends with his vocabulary of *theosis*? Despite his frequent use of philosophical vocabulary (such as his common designation "real-ontic" to describe the believer's connection with Christ), a purely "metaphysical" reading of his terms may not grasp the points he wishes to make. Mannermaa maintains that he is not so much interested in a particular metaphysical or

37. Ibid.

38. Hinlicky, "Theological Anthropology."

39. Ritschl: "*Die Begriffe Rechtfertigung und Versöhnung, in welcher Reihenfolge und in welchem Sinne sie . . . verstanden werden mögen, sind Eigentum der abendländischen Kirche.*" Quoted in Kretschmar, "*Die Rezeption der orthodoxen Vergöttlichungslehre.*"

philosophical system as in making certain kinds of theological assertions. Thus he constantly uses the vocabulary of philosophical ontology, while at the same time urging a specifically theological meaning. In a 1993 essay he develops what he considers to be the approach to "theological ontology" most suitable for understanding Luther's theology. Mannermaa takes Luther's Christmas sermon from the year 1514 as a starting point for analyzing the reformer's understanding of "being" in theological terms.[40] According to Mannermaa, even at this early date Luther developed an implicit theological ontology. He attempts to show how Luther appropriated philosophical or metaphysical categories and language, especially from the Aristotelian tradition of the scholastics, without necessarily committing himself to a static, essentialist notion of "substance." Rather, Luther constructs a new *theological* framework for approaching ontology, in which God's own being or essence consists in the inner-trinitarian "movement" by which the Father begets the Son. In God, the "movement" and the Mover are identical: "*motus est ipsa essentia Dei secundum Aristotelem.*"[41] This view of ontology, according to Mannermaa, unites the relational and essential/ontological ("*seinshafte*") aspects of being: the Father begets the Logos, who is one with the Father and yet Another, and thus is related to the Father in love; God's very being consists in this self-differentiation *and* self-relation within the Trinity. In Luther's 1514 sermon, according to Mannermaa, the ontology of the Trinity becomes the pattern for the whole hierarchy of created being. The essence or being of created things, then, reflects or echoes God's own dynamic being. As God's being "is" the *processio verbi*, so also the "movement" of the intellect in the act of intellectual perception constitutes the "being" of the intellect. All other orders of being (rational, sensual, animate, and inanimate) are also understood ontologically to have their "being" according to the same pattern.[42]

Having defined being itself as identical with movement rather than substance, it is a short step to identifying the *esse* of the intellect and the emotions with their object. "Luther describes his strong understanding of participation with the help of the ontological epistemology that comes from Aristotle."[43] This means that the intellect "is" what it perceives.

40. Mannermaa, "*Hat Luther eine trinitarische Ontologie?*"
41. Ibid., 10; quoting WA 1.27.
42. Ibid., 11–12.
43. Ibid., 19.

Although the intellect *potentially* knows (and hence "is") everything, in and of itself it is precisely nothing, mere matter without form. Mannermaa cautions that this line of reasoning must not be confused with a metaphysics of substance, but rather as a way of describing theologically the being of the human *intellectus* and *affectus* as they are directed to God. Ultimately and eschatologically, at least, in the beatific vision, God himself is the "being" of the blessed who see him, so that ontology and relation are united.[44] Mannermaa's point seems to be that, contrary to the notion that Luther simply replaced the philosophical meaning of substance with a new "theological" meaning, the reformer actually maintained both so that "the philosophical categories express precisely theological content."[45]

At times, such as in the essay under consideration here, Mannermaa asserts more than he actually demonstrates. He claims that what he calls "Luther's early theological ontology," as found in the 1514 Christmas sermon, is "determinative" ("*bestimmend*") for all of Luther's theology. But he actually traces its development and implications only in few works, particularly in the second lectures on the Psalms (1519) and the early Galatians commentary (1516–1517). In these, which he considers examples from Luther's "undisputedly reformation period," Mannermaa notes that the platonic principle of "ontological cognition" is at work, expressed in the phrase: *simile simili cognosci*.[46] In order to know God, the human being must become like God; the *similitudo Dei* must be restored in a real (ontological) way for man to attain the beatific vision. This raises the question of whether Luther escaped from scholastic Aristotelianism by resorting or returning to a kind of Christianized (neo-)Platonism. Mannermaa himself does not adequately answer this question, but his insistence on a "real-ontic" understanding of faith and salvation leads the reader in that direction.

When Risto Saarinen comments on the interest of the Finnish school in *theosis* and their ontological assertions about Christ's presence, he explains, "the 'real-ontic' topics do not derive from scholastic metaphysics, and it would be misleading to describe them in terms of philosophical ontology."[47] Nevertheless, Dennis Bielfeldt has attempted exactly such a

---

44. Simply put, this might be expressed as "You become what you see."

45. Mannermaa, "*Hat Luther eine trinitarische Ontologie?*," 18.

46. Ibid., 23–24.

47. Saarinen, "The Presence of God in Luther's Theology," 10.

description, and his conclusions differ slightly from Mannermaa's proposals.[48] Bielfeldt considers no fewer than eight distinct ontological "models" in an effort to identify the most suitable way of describing the reality that underlies both philosophical and theological language about deification. He considers but ultimately dismisses several understandings that rely on the substance-accidence categories of Aristotle and the classical metaphysical tradition, as well as options that are based on the existentialist philosophy of Heidegger. He concludes that the reality described by the Finnish school is most adequately modeled as what he calls a "mystical personal union," according to which the being of the Christian is characterized by two "persons" in one individual.

This model is both analogous to and yet distinct from the hypostatic union in the person of Christ. It asserts a union in which "it is not that the believer just comes to participate in the universal Christ, rather, it is that the particularity of Christ is made really present 'in, with, and under' the particularity of the believer."[49] By this he means that such a mystical (or "metaphysical?")[50] personal union neither relies on the metaphysics of static substances which were operative in scholasticism, nor reduces the believer's connection to Christ to a merely external relationship which seems to characterize "personalist, existentialist Luther interpretation."[51] Bielfeldt's borrowing of sacramental language to describe the manner of the believer's union with Christ is not accidental. The *theosis* posited by Mannermaa and his school is both mediated to believers sacramentally and implies that the Christian's existence is itself a kind of sacrament by which Christ is present to the world.[52] In this respect their view does parallel the theological connection in Orthodoxy between the sacraments and man's deification.[53]

48. Bielfeldt, "Ontology."

49. Ibid., 108.

50. Bielfeldt speaks both ways, unless "metaphysical" is a typographical error; ibid., 110.

51. Ibid.

52. The relationship between *theosis* and the sacraments in both Orthodoxy and the work of the Mannermaa school deserves further study. Cf. Mannermaa, *Der im Glauben gegenwärtige Christus*, 88f. Cf. Pihkala, *"Die Anwesenheit Christi und die Taufe."*

53. Mantzaridis, *The Deification of Man*, 41–60.

PHILOSOPHY AND LUTHER SCHOLARSHIP SINCE RITSCHL

The efforts of Mannermaa and others in the Finnish school promote a new way of reading Luther's theology. They attempt to draw a new map for navigating the complex landscape of the reformer's thought. As mentioned above, a basic component of their theological program is a reaction against a large part of mainstream Luther scholarship. The theologians of the Finnish school particularly take issue with the idea that "the Lutheran approach is anti-metaphysical and practical: it stresses God work *pro me* without making any ontological commitments."[54] This anti-metaphysical position, according to Risto Saarinen, forms a common thread that runs through various different schools of Luther studies.[55] Saarinen traces the roots of these metaphysical presuppositions to the neo-Kantian thought of Hermann Lotze. According to Lotze, a thing can be known only through its effects, never by directly knowing the thing itself. In this view, any real or ontological connection between God and the Christian is excluded on philosophical grounds. The implication of this epistemology for theology, in all of the streams of Luther interpretation examined by Saarinen, is that God is not known by direct experience but only by his effects. God himself always remains fundamentally separate from man and, in a strict sense, unknowable in any direct way. Lotze's philosophy, according to Saarinen, played a great part not only in Albrecht Ritschl's theology, but also in that of Karl Holl and the Luther Renaissance, and of Karl Barth, as well. Ritschl's ethicized Neo-Protestantism is clearly distinct from the approach of Holl, yet there is continuity between them in their common rejection of the scholastic metaphysics of "substance," and their implicit acceptance of Neo-Kantian categories. The dialectical theology of Karl Barth differs from both, yet Barth's notion of "communion of action" ("*Tatgemeinschaft*") closely parallels the focus on the "participation in God's effects" as proposed by the Luther Renaissance.[56] Saarinen and the other Finns call for a critical reexamination of the philosophical and ontological presuppositions of Luther research, especially the mainstream of German scholarship since the middle of the last century. Mannermaa cites and relies on Saarinen's study of how nineteenth-century German

54. Saarinen, "The Presence of God in Luther's Theology," 3.

55. Saarinen, *Gottes Wirken auf uns*, 9–30.

56. Ibid., 230–31.

ontology and epistemology has filtered scholarly understanding of Luther through the lens of a "transcendental effect-orientation."[57]

The consequences of such a philosophical foundation for the interpretation of Luther's theology are far-reaching. Tuomo Mannermaa argues that it imposes on Luther a misleading metaphysical framework that is foreign to Luther's own thought, and thus inevitably distorts some of his ideas. Most notably it fails to explain the full implications of Luther's insistence on the believer's real union with God in Christ. If Saarinen is correct, then Luther scholars since Ritschl have approached Luther deficiently because of their prior assumption that "being" *must* be regarded as *only* "being-in-relation" rather than "being-in-itself."[58] With such a predisposition, says Mannermaa, one can hardly make sense of those places in Luther's writings where he speaks of *theosis* in the specifically technical sense as it was used by the early church fathers. Any real, or ontological, connection between God and man is excluded *a priori* from such a philosophical framework.[59]

THEOSIS AND THE THEOLOGY OF LUTHER

As they explore Luther's theology with a view to the theme of *theosis*, Mannermaa and the other theologians of the Finnish school focus on several of Luther's writings to which they attach particular importance. Mannermaa's starting point is Luther's 1514 Christmas sermon, which was already mentioned above in connection with Mannermaa's essay describing what he calls "theological ontology."[60] The passage that he cites at the center of his discussion is indeed of interest as evidence of how Luther could and did express the *theosis* theme in his early work:

> Just as the word of God became flesh, so it is certainly also necessary that the flesh become word. For the word becomes flesh precisely so that the flesh may become word. In other words: God becomes man so that man may become God. Thus power becomes powerless so that weakness may become powerful. The Logos puts

57. Mannermaa, "Theosis as a Subject of Finnish Luther Research," 41.

58. Of course, Saarinen's critique of Lotze's may be correct as far as it goes but still miss important ways in which Lotze and those in his shadow shared at least superficial similarities with Luther. The question is whether the "real-ontic" categories urged by these Finnish theologians are really better suited for understanding the reformer's thought.

59. Mannermaa, *Grundlagenforschung*, 20–21.

60. WA 1.20–29.

on our form and manner, our image and likeness, so that it may clothe us with its image, its manner, and its likeness. Thus wisdom becomes foolish so that foolishness may become wisdom, and so that in all these things he takes what is ours to himself in order to impart what is his to us.[61]

This sermon is important for Mannermaa's understanding of Luther because he believes to find in it two continuities of special importance to him: continuity with the early church fathers (especially those of the East), and continuity with the rest of Luther's theology.

Regarding the first, continuity with the eastern church fathers, Mannermaa considers the passage just quoted to contain a direct reference to the *theosis* teaching of the early Greek fathers Irenaeus and Athanasius. The Irenaeus passage to which he refers is from the preface of the fifth book of the *Adversus haereses*, where he speaks of "our Lord Jesus Christ, who did, through His transcendent love, become what we are, that He might bring us to be even what He is Himself."[62] From Athanasius Mannermaa refers to the famous formula that Christ "became man so that we might be made divine."[63] Mannermaa does not discuss these formulas from the Greek fathers in any detail, or elaborate on the "different variations and the inner ambiguity of the doctrine of *theosis*" (some points of which were outlined earlier in this chapter), but simply cites them as background for Luther's sermon. He says, "*Vergöttlichung* is presented in this text [Luther's 1514 sermon], with the help of the formulations of Athanasius and Irenaeus, as a union (*unio*) of Logos and flesh, of word

---

61. Christmas sermon (1514), WA 1: 28: 25–32, quoted in Mannermaa, "Theosis as a Subject of Finnish Luther Research," 43.

> ... *sicut verbum Dei caro factum est, ita certe oportet et quod caro fiat verbum. Nam ideo verbum fit caro, ut caro fiat verbum. Ideo Deus fit homo, ut homo fiat Deus. Ideo virtus fit informa, ut infirmitas fiat virtuosa. Induit formam et figuram nostram et imaginem et similitudinem, ut nos induat imagine, forma, similitudine sua: ideo sapientia fit stulta, ut stulta fiat sapientia, et sic de omnibus aliis, quae sunt in Deo et nobis, in quibus omnibus nostra assumsit ut conferret nobis sua.*

62. MPG VII/2.1120. "*Verbum Dei ... qui propter immensam suam dilectionem factus est quod sumus nos, uti nos perficeret esse quod est ipse.*" English translation in *Against Heresies*, V: Pref., in *The Ante-Nicene Fathers*, I: 526.

63. MPG XXV.192. *Autos gar enēnthrōpēsen, hina hēmeis theōpoiēthōmen*. English in St. Athanasius, *On the Incarnation*, tr. & ed. anonymous (Crestwood, NY: St. Vladimir's Seminary Press, 1953), 92f.

and man."[64] Identifying this kind of citation of eastern patristic theology in Luther's writings would help Mannermaa to establish deification as a crucial point of contact between Luther's theology and the tradition of the ancient Greek fathers, and hence with Orthodoxy. When Luther says, "God becomes man so that man may become God," there is certainly an echo of a motif that was long part of the patristic theological vocabulary. Part of Mannermaa's argument is that it was not merely a formal echo but a deliberate appropriation. That is to say, according to Mannermaa, Luther's soteriology of *Vergottung* is largely a simple return to the *theosis* theology of the ancient church fathers, more or less bypassing scholastic theology. This proposition, and the assumption of patristic continuity with which Mannermaa supports it, will be examined later in chapter 3. At this point it is enough to recognize how Mannermaa attaches importance to the 1514 Christmas sermon first of all because he claims that it links Luther with Irenaeus and Athanasius in describing salvation in terms of deification.

The second continuity in Luther's 1514 Christmas sermon that is important for Mannermaa is the continuity with the rest of Luther's theology. For Mannermaa's point is not merely that Luther could and did on occasion make use of vocabulary that was reminiscent of certain Greek fathers, but rather that the theme of deification is foundational to Luther's development and central to his theology. Mannermaa asserts—but does not attempt to demonstrate, at least in the context of his discussion of the 1514 sermon—this centrality, specifically in connection with the Luther text under consideration here. He claims that "the structure that is the object of our interest here permeates every aspect of the reformer's thinking all the way to his final commentary on Genesis."[65] The "structure" in which he is interested is the theme of union or participation between Christ and the believer, expressed in the language of deification. According to Mannermaa, the 1514 sermon is an important watershed in Luther's early writings, and he asserts that "in this text Luther elucidates *the core of his doctrine of justification* with the help of the classical formulations of the doctrine of *Vergöttlichung*."[66] This assertion will be evaluated from a historical perspective later in chapter 3, where Luther's use of the vocabulary

---

64. Mannermaa, "Theosis as a Subject of Finnish Luther Research," 43.

65. Ibid.

66. Ibid., emphasis added.

of deification will be considered against the broader background of his theological development.

In what is perhaps Mannermaa's most influential study, he directs his focus to Luther's Galatians Commentary of 1535.[67] Luther lectured twice on the Epistle to the Galatians, but his commentary published in 1535 (based on his lectures of 1531) has long been recognized as a work of monumental importance for understanding Luther's theology. In it the reformer offers one of his most extensive treatments of the central doctrine of justification, the core of his thought and keystone of all subsequent Lutheran theology. There is no argument that the great Galatians Commentary represents Luther's mature theology, and it is held up by the Formula of Concord as a standard of right teaching specifically on the matter of justification. The Formula's explicit endorsement bolstered the quasi-confessional authority of Luther's Galatians Commentary for later Lutheran theology.

> For any further, necessary explanation of this lofty and sublime article on justification before God, upon which the salvation of our souls depends, we wish to recommend to everyone the wonderful, magnificent exposition by Dr. Luther of St. Paul's Epistle to the Galatians, and for the sake of brevity we refer to it at this point.[68]

On the basis of the 1535 Galatians Commentary, Mannermaa claims to support his contention that Luther equates justification with the ontological union of the believer with Christ, that is, the "real-ontic" presence of Christ in faith. Despite the claim by the Formula that their teaching about justification is in full agreement with the doctrine of justification taught by Luther in his Galatians Commentary, Mannermaa believes that there are significant differences between the theology of Luther and that of "later Lutheranism" (specifically that of the Formula).

> With the introduction of the thought that the presence of the Trinity in faith is not synonymous with the "righteousness of faith," the Formula of Concord relies on the later theology of Melanchthon, to which more or less all Lutheran theology after Luther refers.... In Luther's theology the relationship between jus-

---

67. Mannermaa, *Der im Glauben gegenwärtigen Christus*.

68. *The Book of Concord*, edited by Robert Kolb and Timothy J. Wengert, translated by Charles Arand *et al.* (Minneapolis: Fortress, 2000) (hereafter "Kolb-Wengert"), 573 (SD III 67); *Bekenntnisschriften*, 936.10–18.

tification and God's indwelling in the believer had without doubt been defined otherwise.[69]

This perceived difference between Luther's own conception of justification and that of the Formula leads Mannermaa to ask what is genuinely and normatively "Lutheran" in this critical point of doctrine. Mannermaa makes it clear that he is inclined to follow Luther rather than "the later theology of Melanchthon." His whole theological program is in opposition to that "Melanchthonian" tradition in which justification is "conceived in an entirely forensic way" [*"gänzlich forensisch aufgefät"*], and the *inhabitatio Dei* is regarded as "only a consequence" of that righteousness of faith. Mannermaa regards his preference for Luther as proper and even confessionally defensible in light of the Formula's reference to Luther's Galatians Commentary, where the "beautiful and splendid exposition" offers the "detailed explanation" of the doctrine under discussion in Article III of the Formula. In Mannermaa's opinion, the doctrine of justification in the Galatians Commentary thus has received "a status of final authority" ("*endgültige Autoritätsstellung*") for Lutheran theology. He sees this as legitimizing his efforts to present his understanding of a truly "Lutheran" doctrine of justification based on Luther's teaching, even when his interpretation of Luther stands in explicit distinction to that of the Formula of Concord. Apart from what might be called this "confessional" concern to identify the authentic sources of Lutheran theology,[70] Mannermaa's assertion accents the scholarly interest in clarifying the theology of Luther himself as the point of departure for all subsequent theology in the Lutheran tradition, whether in Lutheran orthodoxy, Pietism, or Neo-Protestantism.[71] In other words, Mannermaa is interested in the scholarly questions about what Luther actually thought and wrote, but he is also concerned with the question of whether what Luther said is true, and hence with the authority of Luther's teaching to shape and guide the theological reflection of Lutherans today.

Mannermaa begins his analysis of Luther's Galatians Commentary by exploring the connection between the doctrine of justification and

69. Mannermaa, *Der im Glauben gegenwärtigen Christus*, 15.

70. Or perhaps it is not too harsh to say that Mannermaa's aim is not so much "objectively" to identify what is authentically Lutheran, but rather is an attempt to defend the legitimacy of his theological position—established, perhaps, on other grounds—within the Lutheran Church.

71. Mannermaa, *Der im Glauben gegenwärtige Christus*, 17.

Christology. On the basis of Luther's adoption of patristic Christology, Mannermaa traces the elements from the Galatians Commentary that are important for his understanding of what he calls the "intersection point" of justification and deification. In the process it becomes clear how Chalcedonian Christology determines and informs Mannermaa's anthropology. He is particularly interested in Luther's use of the early church's Christological tradition. That tradition goes back to Paul's teaching that in the incarnation the Second Person of the Trinity, the divine Logos, became man and assumed the form of a servant. This implies for Luther that the Logos did not assume some kind of "neutral" human nature, but expressly the human nature of a sinner, or as Mannermaa puts it, that "Christ really ("*real*") has and carries the sins of all people in the human nature which he assumes." He bases this assertion on Luther's comments on Galatians 3:13, where he says:

> And all the prophets saw this, that Christ was to become the greatest thief, murderer, adulterer, robber, desecrator, blasphemer, etc., there has ever been anywhere in the world.[72]

Mannermaa speaks of the Logos "communing" with sinful human nature in such a way that He is "submerged" in sin.[73] Luther recognizes that this way of speaking is "highly absurd and insulting" ("*absurdum et contumeliosum*")—but not more absurd or shameful than the crucifixion itself, in which the innocent Christ took on himself all the world's sin and thus became the "greatest sinner," guilty of all sin ("*reus peccatorum totius mundi*").[74] This idea is connected for Mannermaa with what he describes as a central notion of Luther's Christology, namely that Christ is the "greatest person" ("*maxima persona*"). Mannermaa interprets this expression to denote (again in some "real" sense) a "collective person," who unites all human beings in himself, because he vicariously assumed our sinful humanity not for himself but for all actual sinners.[75] He cites

---

72. AE 26:277; WA 40I.433. "*Et hoc viderunt omnes Prophetae, quod Christus futurus esset omnium maximus latro, homicida, adulter, fur, sacrilegus, blasphemus etc., quo nullus maior unquam in mundo fuerit.*"

73. Mannermaa, *Der im Glauben gegenwärtigen Christus*, 25.

74. *Ibid.*, 24, citing WA 40I:436.

75. *Ibid.*, 24–25.

the way Luther depicts the Father's mission to the Son: "In short, be the person of all men, the one who has committed the sins of all men."[76]

Luther describes the conflict between the sin that Christ assumes in the place of all human sinners and his own essential righteousness. Mannermaa reads this as a tension between the two natures of Christ *per se*, which are pit in the deepest opposition to each other imaginable: for the righteous and holy divine nature is united not with a "neutral" human nature (much less with the righteous human nature of Adam before the Fall), but specifically with *sinful* humanity. As Mannermaa says, "Christ as man is 'the greatest sinner of all' and at the same time, in his being as the Logos, he is God, that is, 'perfect righteousness and life.'" For Mannermaa there is an unbridgeable chasm between the two natures of Christ; the difference between the divine and human is exactly equivalent to the difference between God's perfect holiness and human sinfulness, and this chasm is bridged—indeed, swallowed up, overwhelmed, and conquered—in the person of Christ.

Mannermaa misreads Luther at this important point, and this misunderstanding is decisive for his theology. Luther does not speak of Christ's human nature as sinful *per se*, but is instead talking about the gracious imputation of the sins of all human beings to Christ. "In his own person," Christ is perfectly righteous and innocent of sin. "For Christ is innocent so far as His own Person is concerned."[77] Likewise, "[Christ] is a Person of invincible and eternal righteousness."[78] And this "person" who is innocent and righteous is none other than the whole Christ, according to both natures: "the Son of God born of the virgin."[79] The conflict or struggle carried out in Christ is thus the battle between the sin of the whole world, *imputed* to him, and the righteousness of Christ who is both true God and true man. By identifying the "sin" which Christ carried with his human nature, Mannermaa completely changes the meaning of Luther's comments from a statement of the reality of imputation (which is

---

76. "*In Summa, tu sis omnium hominum persona qui feceris omnium hominum peccata . . .*" *Ibid.*, 25, citing WA 40I:437.

77. AE 26:277; WA 40I:434.13. "*Nam Christus, quod ad suam personam attinet, est innocens*" (433.17f), cf. "*. . . quamvis pro sua persona innocentum.*"

78. AE 26:281; WA 40I:439.24. "*. . . eum esse personam invictae et aeternae iustitiae.*"

79. AE 26:277; WA 40I:433.29.

"real" even though hidden from reason and the senses[80]) to an ontological description.[81]

The consequences of such reading this passage of Luther ontologically rather than imputatively become immediately apparent. Saving faith, according to Mannermaa's reading of Luther, is exactly the believer's participation in that triumphant person of Christ. Here again, Mannermaa asserts that Luther has in mind a "real" sharing both in Christ's person and his benefits. "According to the constitutive idea of Luther's theology, the human being has a 'real' share in Christ's person and in the divine life and victory contained in it."[82] Christ gives himself, his own person, to man in the event or moment of faith itself. This presence of Christ is the beginning of God's undoing of sin and its effects in us. "To the extent that Christ reigns in believers' hearts, there is no sin, death, or curse."[83] Mannermaa understands this participation in the most literal, ontological sense. For him justification is a process rather than a fact; the sinner is justified insofar as ("*quantenus*"), rather than because ("*quia*"), he participates in Christ's personal righteousness. And Mannermaa understands that this concept of justification is in conscious distinction to the forensic justification taught in the Formula of Concord. He says:

> For the reformer justifying faith does not mean exclusively the reception of the forgiveness of sins imputed on account of Christ's merit. The Formula of Concord lays special weight on emphasizing this conception. As real participation in Christ, faith means participation in the inauguration "of blessing, righteousness, and life," which happened in Christ. Christ is himself the life, righteousness, and blessing, since God is all this "by nature and substance" [*naturaliter et substantialiter*]. Justifying faith thus means the participation in God's being in Christ.[84]

80. "If you consult your reason and your eyes, you will judge differently," AE 26:285; WA 40I:445.12f. "*Si autem rationem et oculos tuos consulueris, diversum iudicabis.*"

81. Having cited Regin Prenter as a Lutheran theologian who has in some ways paved the way for Mannermaa's work (*Der im Glauben gegenwärtigen Christus*, 18), it is interesting that Mannermaa is nevertheless intent (and perhaps reasonably so) on pursuing what Prenter calls "the dead-end of an ontologically determined doctrine of the two natures." Prenter, "*Der Gott, der Liebe ist,*" 289.

82. Mannermaa, *Der im Glauben gegenwärtigen Christus*, 26.

83. WA 40I.440. "*Quatenus igitur Christus per gratiam suam in cordibus fidelium regnat, nullum peccatum, mors, maledictio est.*"

84. Mannermaa, *Der im Glauben gegenwärtigen Christus*, 26.

Mannermaa links this concept of "real participation" with Luther's theme of the "blessed exchange," which he interprets in literal, ontological categories.

> According to this, Christ makes the sinful person of man his own, and gives man his own righteous person. In this way there occurs between Christ and the believer an exchange of attributes (a kind of *communicatio idiomatum*).

Mannermaa cites Luther's critique of the scholastic view of sin as a quality that clings to human nature until erased by love.

> For the theology of the sophists is unable to consider sin any other way except metaphysically . . . but the true theology teaches that there is no more sin in the world, because Christ, on whom, according to Is. 53:6, the Father has laid the sins of the entire world, has conquered, destroyed, and killed it in His own body.[85]

These words are from Luther's comments on Galatians 2:20 ("I have been crucified with Christ and I no longer live, but Christ lives in me. The life I now live in the body, I live by faith in the Son of God, who loved me and gave himself for me.") From this Mannermaa concludes that Luther's appropriation (and affirmation) of the classic Nicene Christology leads logically to an affirmation of this kind of "real" participation in the divine nature:

> Since faith means the real union with Christ, and since in Christ the Logos is of the same essence with the Father, it follows that the believer, too, shares in a real way in God's essence. That is just what is meant when Luther speaks of Christ as "gift." Christ is not only God's favor, that is, forgiveness, but he is also in a real way the "gift" (*donum*).[86]

The identification of Christ as both the "*favor*" and the "*donum*" of God is the basis of Mannermaa's refusal to separate, or even actually to distinguish, between Christ "*pro nobis*" and Christ "*in nobis*" in his description of justification. In the Formula of Concord the former ("Christ for us") is the external and objective ground of justification *per se*, and the

---

85. AE 26: 285f.; WA 40I.445.24–31. "*Neque enim aliter potest Sophistica Theologia considerare peccatum quam metaphysice . . . Vera autem Theologia docet, quod nullum peccatum amplius sit in mundo, quia Christus in quem Pater coniecit peccata totius mundi, Esa. 53. Cap., vicit, delevit et occidit illud in corpore suo. . .*"

86. Mannermaa, *Der im Glauben gegenwärtigen Christus*, 29.

latter ("Christ in us") is understood to be the gracious gift God gives to those whom he has justified for Christ's sake. This distinction is just what Mannermaa is arguing against, and he uses Luther's 1535 Galatians Commentary to attempt to support his view. He points out that Luther made frequent reference to the classic passage on which so much of the ancient patristic thinking about deification was based, namely 2 Peter 1:4. As Mannermaa says, Luther refers to this passage not only in the 1535 Galatians Commentary, but also in various sermons.[87] For Mannermaa, Luther's repeated reference to this verse reflects the reformer's conception of faith as participation in the divine nature in some "real" or ontological sense, since God in Christ gives himself to the believer to be his righteousness, life, peace, joy, etc. Mannermaa insists that God's divine attributes are never separated from his essence or nature, and are thus also communicated to the believer. He says that faith involves a kind of *communicatio idiomatum*, a communication of attributes, by which the human nature of the believer shares in God's own nature and is "divinized."

In the essay that sketches his program of *theosis* in Luther research, Mannermaa identifies the need to flesh out the centrality of deification by exploring a specific structure in Luther's theology, namely the relationship between faith and love.[88] His purpose is to show how the real, ontological union of Christ and the believer makes sense out of statements that are otherwise problematic. Mannermaa notes that Christ and the Christian are described in exactly the same terms of love directed toward the neighbor, as well as the believer's share in all Christ's honor, benefits, and attributes. This "analogous relationship" between Christ and the Christian is to be explained, according to Mannermaa, by the fact that "Luther does not differentiate, as does subsequent Lutheranism, between the person and the work of Christ."[89] In the context of his study of the 1535 Galatians Commentary, Mannermaa also attempts to describe Luther's theology of love in relation to faith. This he does by comparing Luther's comments to the scholastic system that the reformer rejected, in which the controlling notion was "*fides caritate formata*," faith formed by love. For the scholastics, faith belonged in the realm of the intellect, a spe-

---

87. Mannermaa cites the *Kirchenpostille*, WA 21.458.11–22 (1544).

88. Mannermaa, "Theosis as a Subject of Finnish Luther Research," 44–45. The same theme has occupied some of Mannermaa's students and colleagues, especially Antti Raunio, "Die 'Goldene Regel' als theologisches Prinzip" and "Die goldene Regel."

89. Mannermaa, "Theosis as a Subject of Finnish Luther Research," 46.

cies of knowledge, and as such could not be regarded as the actual arena of man's relationship to God, who is ultimately unknowable. Faith is given its "form," that is, it is brought into full reality, through love. Mannermaa correctly notes that Luther opposed the scholastic program of *fides caritate formata* at several levels, including the conception of faith as merely a sort of knowledge and the idea that grace enables the human being to ascend to Christ through the *habitus* of love. According to Mannermaa's reading of Luther, as we have seen, faith involves the human person in an ontological union with the really present divine Christ. It is thus not the believer's grace-induced love which "actualizes" or informs faith, but rather Christ himself: real faith for Luther is no longer *fides caritate formata*, but *"fides Christo formata."*[90]

> Luther's concept of faith is not rightly understood when one thinks that Christ is merely the object of faith, just as any other thing is the object of human knowledge. Christ's present person is the object of faith, and thus also actually the "subject." Luther says that Christ is the object of faith, indeed, not only the object, but "in faith itself Christ is present" (*in ipsa fide Christus adest*).[91]

Luther's comments on Galatians 2:16 ("a man is not justified by observing the law, but by faith in Christ . . .") are a pivotal passage for Mannermaa as he argues for a more "real" understanding of faith's connection with Christ himself.

> Therefore faith justifies because it takes hold of and possesses this treasure, the present Christ. But how He is present—this is beyond our thought; for there is darkness, as I have said. Where the confidence of the heart is present, therefore, there Christ is present, in that very cloud and faith . . . [J]ust as the sophists say that love forms and trains faith, so we say that it is Christ who forms and trains faith, or is the form of faith. Therefore the Christ who is grasped by faith and who lives in the heart is the true Christian righteousness, on account of which God counts us righteous and grants us eternal life.[92]

---

90. Mannermaa, *Der im Glauben gegenwärtige Christus*, 36, citing WA 40I.229.

91. *Ibid.*, 36f.

92. AE 26:130; WA 40I.229.22–30 (Galatians 2:16). Quoted in Mannermaa, *Der im Glauben gegenwärtige Christus*, 38.

Iustificat ergo fides, quia apprehendit et possidet istum thesaurum, scilicet Christum praesentem. Sed quo modo praesens sit, non est cogitabile, quia sunt tenebrae, ut

In opposition to other enemies, this time not the scholastics but the "sectarians," who taught a false kind of deification, Luther returns to the same theme again. In the theology of the sectarians, according to Mannermaa, the human soul is thought of as moving upward by grace toward God's own transcendence by means of some kind of speculative spirituality. Luther's idea was completely different: for him God's decisive action was to come down to earth in all his fullness in Christ, so that the believer is already "in heaven" because Christ (in whom is the whole fullness of God) is really present. But Mannermaa says that Luther argued that deification is not a matter of speculation but of reality. Citing Luther's comment on Galatians 3:28 ("There is neither Jew nor Greek, slave nor free, male nor female, for you are all one in Christ Jesus"), Mannermaa quotes this passage:

> Hence the speculation of the sectarians is vain when they imagine that Christ is present in us "spiritually," that is, speculatively, but is present really in heaven. Christ and faith must be completely joined. We must simply take our place in heaven, and Christ must be, live, and work in us. But He lives and works in us, not speculatively but really, with presence and with power.[93]

According to Mannermaa, Luther understands justification as living, "real" union with Christ, and this rules out any notion of the law as a way of salvation. Far from offering human beings the opportunity to justify themselves, the law has the opposite effect of burdening and weakening man. The law, indeed, brings man to the true knowledge of himself as sinner, and thus prepares him for God's grace: God kills in order to make alive. Mannermaa quotes Luther again:

---

dixi. Ubi ergo vera fiducia cordis est, ibi adest Christus in ipsa nebula et fide . . . Sicut Sophistae dicunt charitatem formare et imbuere fidem, Sic nos dicimus Christum formare et imbuere fidem vel formam esse fidei. Ergo fide apprehensus et in corde habitans Christus est iustitia Christiana propter quam Deus nos reputat iustos et donat vitam aeternam.

93. AE 26:357; WA 40I.546.23–27. Quoted in Mannermaa, *Der im Glauben gegenwär-tige Christus*, 39.

Ideo vana est Sectariorum speculatio de fide qui somniant Christum spiritualiter, hoc est, speculative in nobis esse, realiter vero in coelis. Oportet Christum et fidem omnino coniungi, oportet simpliciter nos in coelo versari et Christum esse, vivere et operari in nobis; vivit autem et operatur in nobis non speculative, sed realiter, praesentissime et efficacissime.

If the Law does not justify, what is its purpose? . . . [I]t produces in man the knowledge of himself as a sinner . . . Therefore the Law is a minister and preparation for grace. For God is the God of the humble, the miserable, the afflicted, the oppressed, the desperate, and of those who have been brought down to nothing at all. And it is the nature of God to exalt the humble, to feed the hungry, to enlighten the blind, to comfort the miserable and afflicted, to justify sinners, to give life to the dead, and to save those who are desperate and damned. For He is the almighty Creator, who makes everything out of nothing.[94]

Mannermaa takes no note of the echo in this passage of the connection between God as Creator and God as Justifier. For Luther this is fundamental (a point to be consider further in chapter 4). Here Luther simply points to the fact that the function of the law directed at sinners is to "kill" them and reduce them to nothing, to make way for the gospel in which God is the giver of everything. The law excludes any human contribution to justification, being limited to earthly matters.

In his polemics against the scholastics, Luther often emphasizes the *unio personalis* of the believer with Christ. Mannermaa particularly accents some of Luther's comments on Galatians 2:20 ("I have been crucified with Christ and I no longer live, but Christ lives in me"), where Luther (echoing the biblical text at hand) points out how the genuine teaching of faith radically identifies the sinner and Christ. The two become "like one inseparable person" ("*quasi una persona quae non possit segregare*").[95] Mannermaa concludes from his reading of the Galatians Commentary: "there is therefore no doubt that the idea of the 'real' participation in Christ belongs to the essence of Luther's concept of justification."[96]

---

94. AE 26:314; WA 40I.487.30—488.19 (Galatians 3:19). Quoted in Mannermaa, *Der im Glauben gegenwärtige Christus*, 45–46; ellipsis in Mannermaa's citation.

Si lex non iustificat, ad quid valet? . . . Deinde aperit homini cognitionem sui, quod sit peccator . . . Sic ergo lex ministra et praeparatrix est ad gratiam. Nam Deus est Deus humilium, miserorum, afflictorum, oppressorum, desperatorum et eorum qui prorsus in nihilum redacti sunt; Estque Dei natura exaltare humiles, cibare esurientes, illuminare caecos, miseros et afflictos consolari, peccatores iustificare, mortuos vivificare, desperatos et damnatos salvare etc. Est enim Creator omnipotens ex nihilo faciens omnia.

95. AE 26:168; WA 40I.285.25.

96. Mannermaa, *Der im Glauben gegenwärtige Christus*, 51.

Part of the problem with Mannermaa's reading of the 1535 Galatians Commentary is his predetermined concept of what "real" means. For him, "reality" is always an "essential" or ontological category, as in his favorite phrase, "real-ontic." According to this view, nothing that is essentially external to my person is "really" part of my identity, so for Christ's righteousness to "really be" my righteousness I have to be drawn into an ontological connection with Christ, such that he is no longer external to me but is "really present."

But this more or less static realism, which yields a theology in which nothing actually "happens" but everything is decided on the level of "being itself," certainly does not do justice to the theology Luther is expounding in the Galatians Commentary. For Luther, what is "real" is determined exclusively by the word of God. Luther (following Paul!) radicalizes the identity of the human creature as sinner by admitting no measurement or degree, no contribution of the law whatsoever. But this is done to "radicalize" the gospel as the shocking extremity of God's self-giving, unmerited love in Christ. "The Son of God loved me and gave himself for me," says Paul, in words that Luther describes as "sheer thunder and heavenly fire against the righteousness of the law and the doctrine of works."[97] Faith, according to Luther, revels in the new reality created by the word of the gospel, summed up in syllables "*pro me.*" "Therefore read these words '*me*' and '*for me*' with great emphasis, and accustom yourself to accepting this '*me*' with a sure faith and applying it to yourself."[98] The *pro me* of Galatians 2:20 lays claim to the "gave himself" of Christ's suffering and death, not on the basis of any ontological connection but on the basis of a promise attached to history.

The word of the promise charges human sin to Christ and Christ's righteousness to sinners. According to his own essence and identity, Christ is the righteous Son of God, and according to my own, I am "an accursed and damned sinner."[99] But that "reality" is superceded by the reality of the promise, which is the reality of God's gracious imputation. Faith is completely directed to the reality of the word of promise, not to some other reality beyond the word. "There is nothing to be done here but to hear that this has been done in this way, and to take hold of it

97. AE 26:175; WA 40I.294.32f.
98. AE 26:179; WA 40I.299.
99. AE 26:176; WA 40I.295.

with an undoubted faith."[100] The imputed reality of the gospel, this new "ontology of the word," results in a completely different kind of life for the Christian, namely an "alien life" ("*vita aliena*"), the life of Another, just as the Christian's righteousness is *iustitia aliena*: "There is a double life: my own, which is natural or animate; and an alien life, that of Christ in me."[101] The point of this expression is not the location; Christ's life remains my "alien life" even when it is "in me." Mannermaa's "real-ontic" language fails to capture Luther's dynamic understanding of the word in this context; Luther's understanding of the believer's life of faith might better be described as "real-verbal," to express its radical dependence on the "reality" created by the word of the gospel.

THEOSIS, CHRISTOLOGY, AND ANTHROPOLOGY

The concept of *theosis* developed by Mannermaa from his reading of Luther's theology impinges in significant, interrelated ways on both Christology and anthropology. Mannermaa's key idea is that Christ constitutes the righteousness of the Christian, not merely by imputation of his obedience or substitution of his vicarious sacrifice, but by personal identification and ontological union. As he says, "faith means justification precisely on the basis of Christ's person being present in it: *in ipsa fide Christus adest*; in faith itself Christ himself is present."[102] Mannermaa's interpretation of faith and justification in these "real-ontic" terms has two very important implications that shape the way in which anthropological questions are answered.

In the first place, basing justification on the "real" presence of Christ in faith, as Mannermaa does, means that the believer's human essence and existence must be understood in specifically "Christological" categories, rather than in terms of creation. The incarnation of God in Christ becomes the pattern of the believer's own nature. From this it follows that the personal union of the divine and human natures in the person of Christ and the "blessed exchange" between Christ and the sinner must be viewed as analogous concepts.

100. AE 26:161; WA 40I:275 (Galatians 3:19).
101. AE 26:170; WA 40I:287. Cf. WA 2:145 (*Sermo de duplici iustitia*, 1519) for the "*iustitia aliena*."
102. Mannermaa, "Theosis as a Subject of Finnish Luther Research," 46.

The second implication for anthropology relates to how Mannermaa understands the believer's life in tension as *simul iustus et peccator*. If justification *per se* is precisely the union of the human believer with the divine Christ, then it must be asked how this is related to the Christian's sanctification (*Heiligung*). The matter of sanctification, in turn, is intimately connected with the theme of love in Luther's theology.

Another way Mannermaa expresses his central point is by identifying Christ personally as both God's grace (Latin "*favor*") and his gift ("*donum*").[103] As "gift" in the Christian, Christ imparts everything that is connected to divine life.[104] Mannermaa takes this to mean that the Christian shares in the *divine* nature through faith in Christ even while he remains connected to humanity (not to Christ's own human nature, but to human nature in a more general sense) through love for his neighbor. Mannermaa interprets Luther by describing the life of the Christian with language explicitly echoing the church's confession about Christ himself. He explains:

> Since Christ is truly present in faith, the Christian, too, has in a certain sense "two natures" . . . The "divine nature" of the believer is Christ himself . . . the Christian, too takes "human nature," i.e. the misery and burden of his neighbor, upon himself.[105]

This description is problematic, because in it Mannermaa fails to recognize the uniqueness of the person of Christ, and the unrepeatable union of the divine and human natures in him. In fact, this kind of generalizing of the union of the two natures to include all believers was rejected explicitly by the Formula of Concord.[106]

As was mentioned above, Mannermaa describes the union of the divine nature and the human nature in Christ in terms of a tension and struggle within the person of Christ, because he identifies the human na-

---

103. Mannermaa, *Der im Glauben gegenwärtige Christus*, 30–31. Cf. Peura, "*Christus als Gunst und Gabe.*"

104. One difference between the *theosis* theme in Luther and the doctrine as developed in Eastern Orthodoxy seems to be that Luther never made any sharp distinction between God himself (i.e., the divine nature) and his attributes. In contrast, Gregory Palamas built his theological system on a distinction between God's essential nature and his "energies," which are communicated to believers. Cf. Flogaus, *Theosis bei Palamas und Luther*, 77–94.

105. Mannermaa, "Theosis as a Subject of Finnish Luther Research," 48.

106. FC SD VIII:68–70, cf. below in chapter 4.

ture as sinful *per se*. But this tension between the holy righteousness of God and man's sin is, for Mannermaa, the prime Christological datum, the heart of the mystery of the incarnation. At the same time, of course, it is also a basic fact of anthropology, a description of every human person, or at least of every believer's identity. Mannermaa believes that the chasm or conflict between the divine and the human is echoed in the person of each Christian, who is both holy through his union with the divine holiness in Christ's person, and also at the same time a sinner because he shares Adam's fallen humanity. The meaning of the incarnation of the divine Logos is that it establishes the paradigm to which humanity will now conform, as the divine and the human are united.

The "tension" on which Mannermaa focuses is not an ontological rift within the person of Christ, but the mystery of his passion *pro nobis*. It is the scandal of the cross, where "God made him who had no sin to be sin for us, so that in him we might become the righteousness of God" (2 Corinthians 5:21). This is the same outrageous gospel, which imputes our sin to the sinless Christ, which Paul also declares in Galatians 3:13, to which Luther remarked,

> "But it is highly absurd and insulting to call the Son of God a sinner and a curse!" If you want to deny that He is a sinner and a curse, then deny also that He suffered, was crucified, and died. For it is no less absurd to say, as our Creed confesses and prays, that the Son of God was crucified and underwent the torments of sin and death than it is to say that he is a sinner and a curse.[107]

The "absurdity" of the gospel is in the cross, not in the incarnation *per se*.

A similar correlation of the person of Christ and the person of the believer is at work in Mannermaa's examination of the familiar concept of the "blessed exchange." Luther makes frequent use of images in which Christ takes as his own all that we are, namely our sin, death, punishment, etc, and in exchange bestows on us sinners his own righteousness, holiness, and eternal life. Mannermaa, operating from his ontological perspective, describes this motif in Luther as an explic-

---

107. AE 26:278; WA 401:434.29–33.

Sed valde absurdam et contumeliosum est filium Dei appellare peccatorem et maledictum. Si vis negare eum esse peccatorem et maledictum, negato etiam passum, crucifixum et mortuum. Non enim minus absurdam est dicere filium Dei, ut fides nostra confitetur et orat, crucifixum, poenas peccati et mortis sustinuisse, quam peccatorem aut maledictum dicere.

itly Christological paradigm for the human existence of the believer. Mannermaa characterizes the exchange, not as a metaphor for Christ's vicarious atonement and the benefits grasped by faith, but as "a kind of *communicatio idiomatum*" between Christ and the Christian.[108] Note that it is Mannermaa, rather than Luther, who here appropriates the dogmatic language describing the personal union of the two natures of Christ and applies it to the person and life of the believer. He sums up his reading of Luther regarding the Christological pattern and structure of the Christian's human life in this way:

> Justification, according to Luther, is not exclusively a new ethical or juridical relationship between God and man. Where a person believes in Christ, Christ himself is present in faith, in the whole fullness of his divine nature.[109] Luther understands the presence of Christ in such a concrete way that Christ and the Christian form "one person." In the "blessed exchange" man comes to share God's attributes, of which Luther most often mentions "life," "righteousness," "wisdom," "salvation," "power," "joy," and "love."[110]

When he employs the dogmatic vocabulary of *communicatio idiomatum* to describe the new ontological existence of the believer in connection with Christ, Mannermaa is attempting to establish the connection between Christology and anthropology in a way that is new for Lutheran theology. Lutheran dogmatics since Chemnitz has also spoken of the *communicatio idiomatum*, but as a way of expressing the unique point of contact between the divine nature and the human nature in the unique person of Jesus Christ, rather than describing directly what transpires between Christ and the believer. Mannermaa employs the terminology to draw an explicit analogous relationship between Luther's Chalcedonian Christology and the believer's humanity. For Chemnitz, as we will see in more detail in chapter 5, *theosis* was to be predicated not of human beings in general but of the unique humanity of Christ. It was a category and a concept belonging properly to Christology, not anthropology. In Mannermaa's view, however, anthropology is located theologically as a

---

108. Mannermaa, *Der im Glauben gegenwärtige Christus*, 26, 31–33.

109. It is significant that Mannermaa is interested here only in Christ's divine nature, and omits any mention of the believer's union with Christ according to his human nature. This is another similarity with Osiander's position.

110. Mannermaa, *Der im Glauben gegenwärtige Christus*, 92.

sub-locus of Christology, and the two function throughout his theology as unambiguously analogous categories.

Mannermaa himself is certainly aware of this difference between his approach and that of most of Lutheran theology after Luther. He identifies passages in the Formula of Concord as the "classical text on the idea of *inhabitatio*."[111] Nevertheless, Mannermaa believes that the authors of the Formula had already moved away from Luther's own understanding even by distinguishing between the purely forensic, imputed "righteousness of faith" on the one hand, and the indwelling of Christ on the other. The wording in the Formula is as follows:

> In the same way we must also correctly explain the argument regarding the indwelling of the essential righteousness of God in us. To be sure, God the Father, Son, and Holy Spirit, who is the eternal and essential righteousness, dwells through faith in the elect, who have become righteous through Christ and are reconciled with God. (For all Christians are temples of God the Father, Son, and Holy Spirit, who moves them to act properly.) However, this indwelling of God is not the righteousness of faith, which St. Paul treats [Rom. 1:17; 3:5, 22, 25; 2 Cor. 5:21] and calls *iustitia Dei* (that is, the righteousness of God), for the sake of which we are pronounced righteous before God. Rather, this indwelling is a result of the righteousness of faith which precedes it, and this righteousness [of faith] is nothing else than the forgiveness of sins and the acceptance of poor sinners by grace, only because of Christ's obedience and merit.[112]

111. Ibid., 14–15, referring to FC, Epitome, III: 12, 16 and Solid Declaration, III: 54 (see below).

112. FC SD III 54. Kolb-Wengert, 571–2; BSLK, 932–33. The German text reads:

> Gleichfalls muß auch die Disputation von der Einwohnung der wesentlichen Gerechtigkeit Gottes in uns recht erkläret werden. Dann obwohl durch den Glauben in den Auserwählten, so durch Christum gerecht worden und mit Gott versöhnet sind, Gott Vater, Sohn und Heiliger Geist, der die ewige und wesentliche Gerechtigkeit ist, wohnet (dann alle Christen sind Tempel Gottes des Vaters, Sohns und Heiligen Geistes, welcher sie auch treibet, recht zu tuen): so ist doch solche Einwohnung Gottes nicht die Gerechtigkeit des Glaubens, davon S. Paulus handelt und sie iustitiam Dei, das ist, die Gerechtigkeit Gottes, nennet, umb welcher willen wir für Gott gerecht gesprochen werden, sondern sie folget auf die vorgehende Gerechtigkeit des Glaubens, welche anders nicht ist, dann die Vergebung der Sünden und gnädige Annehmung der armen Sünder allein umb Christus Gehorsam und Vordiensts willen.

The Formula carefully distinguishes between what constitutes the righteousness of faith, properly speaking, and the fact that God, who is himself righteousness, dwells in the believer. The Formula does stress the reality of God's divine presence in the believer, but in the precise definition of justification it focuses all attention of Christ's righteousness *pro nobis* and *extra nos*, that is, his obedience to the Father on our behalf according to both his divine and human natures. That obedience is most clearly seen and most fully perfected in his passion, death and resurrection. The writers of the Formula did not regard this distinction as alien to Luther's own theology, but on the contrary cite Luther's Galatians Commentary as the best reference and explanation of the doctrine of justification they were defining.[113] At the same time, they found it necessary to specify more sharply the precise meaning of the "righteousness of faith" largely in response to Andreas Osiander's teaching of "essential righteousness."[114] Osiander's view was (in all important respects) his own version of what Mannermaa and the Finnish school refer to as the "real-ontic" righteousness of God for/in the believer. Reacting against the defining distinctions presented by the Formula of Concord, Mannermaa (largely agreeing with Osiander without mentioning him) argues that the Formula presents a distinction foreign to the theology of Luther himself. In making the distinction between the actual righteousness of faith and the *inhabitatio Dei*, he says:

> . . . the Formula of Concord rests on the later theology of Melanchthon, to which nearly all Lutheran theology after Luther refers. The "making-righteous" [*Gerechtmachung*] is conceived in a completely forensic way, in other words, as the reception of the forgiveness credited on the basis of Christ's obedience and merit. The *inhabitatio Dei* is only a consequence of that "righteousness of faith." Without a doubt, the relation between justification and the indwelling of God in the believer is defined differently in Luther's theology.[115]

In other words, Mannermaa does not accept the way in which the Formula distinguishes between justification and sanctification. For him "the presence of Christ is thus not sanctification attached to the justification as its

113. FC SD III:67.

114. Osiander's teachings on justification, Christology, and anthropology will be discussed in more detail in the next chapter.

115. Mannermaa, *Der im Glauben gegenwärtige Christus*, 15.

consummation, but rather a foundation or precondition of the imputative justification."[116]

Indeed, and this is a very important point to appreciate, Mannermaa does not distinguish in any meaningful way between faith in Christ *pro nobis* and *extra nos* on the one hand, and faith as the presence of Christ's divine nature *in nobis* on the other. This distinction was central to the Formula's understanding of the righteousness of faith (in opposition to Osiandrianism), and the Formula's authors understood it to be crucial in Luther's theology, as well. When Mannermaa ignores or denies this distinction, one result is that he begins to see justification and sanctification as in some sense simply two ways of talking about the same thing: both refer to the single reality of Christ present and at work in the believer through faith.

> It has become commonplace to assert that the idea of justifying faith alone is the center of Luther's thought. This assessment is in need of revision. Justifying faith is, according to the reformer a *fides abstracta*, and abstract faith. It is not the content of the whole of Christian life and doctrine, which only finds expression in the *fides concreta* or *fides incarnata*. Incarnate, concrete faith is always formed by faith together with love. Just such *fides concreta* is the center of the Christian faith....All Christian doctrine, all work and life, is briefly, plainly, and indeed richly contained in two points, faith and love. The *fides concreta*, in which faith and love are united on the basis of the present Christ, recedes into the background when (following Melanchthon's example) the presence of Christ is separated from justifying faith and faith is viewed only as the reception of forgiveness through Christ's merit.[117]

What Mannermaa is proposing is nothing less than a new "center" for Lutheran theology, a center where faith and love are viewed "whole" and together under the category of "*fides concreta*." He says that the believer is "divine" through faith (because Christ is really present in faith itself) and truly "human" through love (because he becomes a kind of "Christ" to his neighbor, "*Christianus Christus proximi*"). The real, ontological presence of Christ—the *inhabitatio Dei*—underlies both faith and love, making these two, in effect, aspects of the same reality.

---

116. Saarinen, "The Presence of God in Luther's Theology," 6.
117. Mannermaa, *Der im Glauben gegenwärtige Christus*, 104–5.

Mannermaa's assertions fail to reflect Luther's own theology adequately, because for Luther these two, faith and love, are quite separate. Faith by definition looks away from itself and toward Christ—not the "Christ-present-in-faith" but the Christ who is present in his word. Following the polarity of "faith" and "works" characteristic of Paul (especially in Romans and Galatians), Luther would put "love" clearly on the side of works, and separate it emphatically from faith. For Luther, faith "is a thing of such magnitude that it obscures and completely removes those foolish dreams of the sophists' doctrine—the fiction of 'formed faith' and of love, of merits, our worthiness, our quality, etc."[118] It subtly but profoundly alters Luther's understanding of faith when Mannermaa makes the "presence of Christ" rather than the external word of the gospel the object of saving faith.

For Mannermaa this change is necessary in order to ground faith in something "real." The word he considers "real" only to the extent that it describes existent realities, i.e., that which is true independently of the word. This is why Mannermaa consistently makes Christ personally the object of faith, in an attempt to ground it in "reality." Thus he says that Christ is the "form" or substance of faith, which he understands to mean that the "real presence" of Christ in the believer makes Christ the real, active subject of the Christian's works of love. While the distinction between the Creator and the creature is not erased, God's own nature comes to define more and more the identity of the human personality of the believer. The connection between Christ and the Christian is so close that they can even be described as one person: "*Itaque Christus et ego iam unum in hac parte sumus.*" ("In this way, therefore, Christ and I are one.")[119] And for Mannermaa, this union has to be "more real" than the word of the gospel alone. For Luther, the word of the gospel was "more real" than any existent thing, more real than any reason or experience, because the word of the Creator is that which makes things out of nothing, and makes them what they are.

This is one way in which Mannermaa's Christology shapes and defines his anthropology.[120] In a sense, the person of Christ as the God-man

---

118. AE 26:169; WA 40I.286.17–20.

119. Mannermaa, *Der im Glauben gegenwärtige Christus*, 49, quoting Luther, WA 40I.283.

120. At least this is how Mannermaa defines the anthropology of Christians; the anthropology of *theosis* suggests that the humanity of believers is of a very different order or kind from that of non-Christians—in itself a rather startling notion.

becomes the model and pattern of restored humanity: the union of deity and humanity in the Incarnation is replicated ontologically in the believer's faith, and the *fides abstracta* takes concrete form in the believer's works of love—with the present Christ as the active subject.[121] The "ontology" of the Christian is thus identical with that of Christ. Mannermaa concludes that it is inadequate, if not simply wrong, to distinguish between how God *declares* the sinner righteous and how he *makes* him righteous.

> The idea of deification, therefore, belongs to the heart of Luther's doctrine of justification. Precisely on this foundation can one understand how the doctrine of justification and the conception of man's sanctification form a unity in Luther's theology.[122]

According to Mannermaa, Luther was familiar with "the forensic dimension of justification," but he denies that Luther's concept was "*purely forensic.*" With emphasis he concludes:

> The idea that *in ipsa fide Christus adest* ["in faith itself Christ is present"] thus makes plain the relationship between "making righteous" [*Gerechtmachung*] and "declaring righteous" [*Gerechterklärung*]. Faith is the foundation of justification precisely because faith means the real presence of the person of Christ, that is, of God's favor and gift. In other words, Christ, who in faith dwells in the Christian, is the Christian righteousness, because of which God imputes righteousness.[123]

The imputation of "alien" righteousness is thus not denied, but in Mannermaa's view the "real-ontic" righteousness of the present Christ is (at least logically) prior to it. Because Christ is present in the believer as divine righteousness, God considers the Christian righteous by virtue of the "real" righteousness of Christ—i.e., his divine nature—in him.

Mannermaa's understanding of justification as *theosis* yields what might be called "Christological" anthropology, in which the incarnation of the second Person of the Trinity establishes the normative model for restored humanity. This view leads us to the second of the anthropological implications of Mannermaa's theology which we wish to examine, namely the notion of the Christian's existence as both righteous and a sinner at the same time (*simul iustus et peccator*). Here Mannermaa contends that

---

121. Mannermaa, *Der im Glauben gegenwärtige Christus*, 55.

122. Ibid., 55.

123. Ibid., 64–65.

his identification of justification with the "real-ontic" union described by the term *theosis* helps make sense of both the "partial" aspect and the "total" aspect of Luther's view of justification.[124] Mannermaa's understanding of Luther's *simul* necessarily considers the Christian as "partially" righteous (in so far as he is united with Christ) and also still "partially" sinful. Mannermaa sets what he sees as Luther's idea of "partial righteousness" over against the more familiar statement that the Christian is, at the same time, both fully a sinner and fully righteous (*simul iustus et peccator*). He cites Luther's reference to Christ as the believer's "yeast," which will gradually permeate the Christian's whole life and ultimately drive out the sinful nature. Mannermaa claims that the yeast image is an important part of the patristic doctrine of *theopoiesis*. He argues that it is the key to understanding Luther's statements about the partial or progressive nature of the Christian's righteousness. By grace the divine nature comes to predominate by means of a more or less gradual process of transformation.[125] As long as the believer is still in the flesh, of course, his being is defined and conditioned not only by Christ who is present in faith, but also by the Old Adam, that is, by his own sinful nature, which is not completely killed and driven out in this life.

But Mannermaa also asserts that "the idea of the real, ontological presence of Christ explains . . . also the total aspect, namely the idea of man as total sinner and totally righteous."[126] This is because the work of sanctification, which begins in faith, is and always remains Christ's own work, as he is present in the believer through faith. Sanctification is an ongoing process, but it is also "total" in the sense that it is wholly worked by Christ. This totality of righteousness in the Christian always remains hidden in this life, since it is never simply observable or perceptible to the senses; but it is nevertheless "real." This is his understanding of Luther's dictum, "we have only the word" ("*solum verbum habemus*"), because only God's word describes the unseen reality of the Christian's righteousness.[127] It is crucial at this point to recognize that in Mannermaa's argument, this "word" is still descriptive, not creative or performative. Such a word sim-

---

124. Ibid., 66–70.

125. In this analysis Mannermaa largely agrees with a recent Orthodox treatment of the same theme by Konstantinos Papapetrou, *Über die anthropologischen Grenzen der Kirche*.

126. Mannermaa, *Der im Glauben gegenwärtige Christus*, 68.

127. Ibid., 85.

ply describes a reality that cannot be seen but is nevertheless "real" in the sense that it is independent of and logically prior to the word. Mannermaa appeals to the Heidelberg Disputation and other writings, in order to show how "deification in Luther is always hidden, according to the theology of the cross, under the form of opposites [*sub contrario*]."[128] The Christian's life and being are thus always *simul* in the sense that they include a hidden reality—namely Christ's own righteousness, life, etc.—which is somehow ontologically present in them, concealed under the external appearances of sin and death.

CONCLUSION

Tuomo Mannermaa has introduced a new approach to the theology of Luther with his focus on the theme of *theosis*, or the "real-ontic" presence of Christ in the believer as the ground and meaning of justification. While Mannermaa intends his studies to serve as bridges between the Lutheran theology and that of the Orthodox Church, significant differences still distinguish the Finnish school's view of *theosis* from that of eastern Orthodoxy (defined largely by the work of Gregory Palamas). Mannermaa claims that Luther's use of the concept of deification links him with the early church fathers, especially those of the East, and that *theosis* remained an important element of the reformer's theology throughout his career. In promoting this new approach to Luther, Mannermaa has highlighted particular works of Luther and given them special theological prominence. The historical dimension of the work of Mannermaa and the *theosis* school of Luther studies will be the subject of chapter 3.

Two aspects of Mannermaa's analysis of Luther should be highlighted, and both of these shed light on the way his idea of deification or *theosis* impinges on the theological understanding of human nature. The first relates to the doctrine of creation, the second to Christology. When salvation is expressed exclusively or primarily in terms of union between the divine and the human, the goodness or wholeness of man's nature *as creature* is, at the very least, left as an unanswered question. In other words, Mannermaa's emphasis on *theosis* moves us toward an exclusively *soteriological* version of theological anthropology. The doctrine *de homine* is shifted from the first article to the second; his theology views human nature as Christological rather than creational. The second

128. Ibid., 199.

aspect of great importance in Mannermaa's analysis relates to the connection between Christology and anthropology. Indeed, the two doctrines cannot be separated theologically. For the Finnish school, in the words of Risto Saarinen, "the reality of Christian faith and life is described in terms of Christology."[129] But the way in which Mannermaa and his colleagues connect anthropology with Christology differs from that of most Lutheran theology since the Formula of Concord. In fundamental ways they echo the ideas of Andreas Osiander, with his teaching of justification by God's "essential righteousness" dwelling in the believer. While refusing to separate God's nature and his attributes (especially his righteousness), Mannermaa emphasizes the person of Christ and pays far less attention to his work, that is, his obedience, death, and resurrection. In the next chapter we will explore in more detail the anthropology that develops out of the Mannermaa school's theme of *theosis*, and we return to the same theme in the final chapter.

---

129. Saarinen, "The Presence of God in Luther's Theology," 5.

2

More Than a Man?

Theosis *and Anthropology according to Simo Peura*

WHILE TUOMO MANNERMAA'S WORK has largely established the conceptual and theological framework for the Finnish school's exploration of the *theosis* theme, other Finnish theologians have developed many of his ideas in various specific areas. We saw at the end of the last chapter how the Finnish school's view of such participation as *theosis* shapes both their Christology and their anthropology. Mannermaa's student and close associate, Simo Peura, explores in particular the Christian's participation in the divine nature of Christ as mediated through word and sacrament. Peura's work is key for understanding the anthropological dimensions of the Finnish *theosis* theology. In several important essays and the published version of his dissertation, Peura works on many themes that are significant in an understanding of the anthropology that underlies the theology of *theosis*. He summarizes what he considers to be the "inner structure" of Luther's doctrine of the deification of human beings.

Peura's first major contribution to the theological program of the Finnish school came with the publication of his dissertation under the title, *More than Human? Deification as a Theme of Martin Luther's Theology from 1513 to 1519.*[1] The first point to appreciate about Peura's major study is his deliberate focus on works from an early period in Luther's theological career, all of which he regards more or less without question as characteristic of Luther's mature reformation theology. He examines the theme of deification in the *Dictata super Psalterium* of 1513–1516, as well as the same 1514 Christmas sermon that attracted Tuomo Mannermaa's attention. From the first lectures on Romans (1515–1516), Peura seeks

1. Peura, *Mehr als ein Mensch?*

to understand deification specifically in the context of Luther's emerging understanding of justification. The latest writings that Peura examines in any detail come from the period of the indulgence controversy and its immediate aftermath: the Heidelberg Disputation, the Leipzig Debate, the Sermon on the Two Kinds of Righteousness, and the *Operationes in Psalmos* are his primary sources. Peura's concentration on these earlier works of Luther tends to attach central importance to statements which belong rather to a formative period in Luther's theological development.[2]

Peura's reading of the early Luther rests on the premise that God's being or essence is identical with his attributes. Peura draws numerous examples from Luther's *Dictata super psalterium* to show how Luther identified God's deity with such attributes as truth, wisdom, goodness, light, power, and life.[3] The attributes of God are also called his "names" (*nomen Dei*), and the "Name" of God is above personified in the Logos, that is, in Christ. On this basis, says Peura, Luther concluded that to be given and receive these goods or benefits is the same as to "have" God.[4] This is how God gives his name, his benefits, and his gifts—in fact, gives himself—to the believer in Christ. When the believer "has" God's mercy, or is given God's name through baptism, he has and is given God himself, because according to Luther, God is not distinguished from his attributes, or *par excellence* from his name.

According to Peura, to "have" God is to be united with him and participate in his divine nature or essence. He draws on Luther's comments in the *Dictata* regarding the familiar theme of the three-fold "coming" of Christ. Christ came to us first in his historical incarnation, born of the Virgin Mary. Daily and continually he comes to us "through grace and his spiritual birth in our souls."[5] And ultimately he will come visibly in glory. Peura says that Luther then used this paradigm of Christ's triple advent as a framework for developing his concept of the *theosis* of human beings. "The pattern of the three-fold coming of Christ now forms the point of departure, in terms of salvation history, for the description of the deifica-

---

2. This point will be explored in more detail in the next chapter.

3. Peura, *Mehr als ein Mensch?*, 47–49.

4. It is worth noting here how different this is from Luther's later explanation, in the Large Catechism, where he focuses entirely on faith: "Therefore, I repeat, the correct interpretation of this commandment is that to have a god is to have something in which the heart trusts completely." Kolb-Wengert, 387 (LC TC 10).

5. Peura, *Mehr als ein Mensch?*, 50.

tion of the Christian."[6] Just as the Second Person of the Trinity assumed human flesh and became not only *deus incarnatus* but also *homo deificatus*, so also by his second, spiritual coming human beings are united with the divine nature in him. This union and participation is already "real," although partial, in this life; it will be completed and fully revealed by Christ's final, eschatological coming.

In the *Dictata* Luther identifies Christ with the Word of God, that is, with God's self-communication. This word of God combined itself with the human nature through the incarnation.[7] Hence God's self-communicating word actually contains the unseen, invisible things of God—that is to say, God himself—in a hidden but real way. Peura bases this conclusion on the fact that there is an ontological connection between the word as "sign" and the thing itself (the *res signata*).[8] The inner, divine word comes to us hidden in the external, human word. But an ontological connection between the two is necessary for Peura's system: "Deification, seen ontologically, presupposes that the word is really *in* the human being. This ontological condition is fulfilled, because the gospel is able to reach the interior of man."[9] Interestingly, Peura cites Luther as applying the law, in contrast, only externally ["*ad nos*"]. Faith, according to this understanding, consists in the proper hearing of this divine word, so that the word, which is Christ himself, is actually in the human heart. Peura's ontological approach determines that such reception and internalization of the divine word must also imply a "real" union between the believer and Christ. Here we see how Peura groups various concepts and expressions together around his central ontological theme:

> Luther's various modes of expression—as, for example, Christ's presence in us, or the Christian's dwelling in God—describe the realization of salvation in the life of the Christian. It is not a matter

6. Ibid., 51.

7. The ambiguity obvious in this discussion between "Word" in the sense of the divine Logos, the second person of the Trinity, and the "word" as Scripture or preaching, is unresolved in Peura's work.

8. Peura, *Mehr als ein Mensch?*, 60. Whether this "*ontologische Zusammengehörigkeit*" of the sign and the conceptual signified can really be maintained and demonstrated for Luther, given his background in the Nominalism of Ockham and Biel, is another matter altogether, and one which Peura does not address as such. In fact, Peura devotes very little attention to Nominalism as an influence on the language and categories of Luther's early theology.

9. Ibid., 62.

simply of the divine effect in the human being [this in opposition to the Lotzean, neo-Kantian metaphysics of Ritschl *et al.*], but rather the fact that God himself is in the human being and has and brings salvation when he unites himself with human beings. This union of God and man is precisely the deification of man.[10]

The initial and definitive union of God and man occurs in the incarnation. But the ambiguous connection between the incarnate "Word" and the "word" of the gospel comes into play again, as the union of the divine and human is replicated in those who hear and believe the gospel. "This makes possible the spiritual fellowship with God, when man hears the word and God unites himself with the spirit of man through faith and love."[11] According to Peura's reading of Luther here, the union of God and man in the incarnation of Christ serves as the formative pattern or paradigm according to which the deification of believers then can occur. This makes the incarnation of Christ more a salvific paradigm than a salvific event: its importance is realized only, or primarily, when it is replicated in believers. This is accented by Peura's emphasis on the "real," or ontological, nature of justification, salvation, and Christ's presence in faith. He, like Mannermaa, is reacting especially against the neo-Kantian metaphysics of Ritschl, and after him much of modern Luther scholarship. In deliberate rejection of a reduction of salvation to mere "effect," Peura insists that

> Luther also illustrates this real, ontological participation with the help of various metaphors . . . These figures of speech already indicate that the *unio cum Christo* is for Luther a real, ontological, and almost "physical" union, and that he understands participation realistically in the sense of an ontological "continuum." . . . Only with an ontological understanding can one explain Luther's assertion that what is said of the origin (Christ) can also be said participatively of the saints. It depends therefore on the real, ontological participation that that which is true in respect to Christ can also be true in a similar sense of the saints.[12]

From such statements it is clear that Peura is advocating a particular way of reading Luther, namely through an "ontological lens," in which the metaphors and figures of speech are to be taken in the most "real" sense possible. What Peura is demonstrating, in fact, is not so much that

10. Ibid., 68.
11. Ibid.
12. Ibid., 72.

this is the only possible way to understand Luther, but rather that these early works of Luther can be read in a way consistent with this ontological preoccupation. While he says that his use of the term "ontological" is intended to be a reference to being as such and ontology in general, without commitment to any particular system of philosophical ontology,[13] Peura's repeated insistence on "real" participation and union makes it clear that he favors some form of philosophical realism as the correct framework and background for understanding Luther's theology.

Within that system, believers are holy and "saints" exactly through their direct participation in God's own holiness. This implies that they are to be conformed to Christ, in whom they are united to God.

> The conformity with Christ now means that Luther understands the justification of the Christian by analogy to the two natures of Christ. God, to whom belong the invisible things, took on visible flesh in the person of Christ. The same thing happens, according to Luther, in the Christian.[14]

The believer, in union with Christ, becomes an echo or reiteration of the paradigm of the incarnation; if there is a difference between the union of the two natures in Christ and in the believer, Peura does not mention it. Justification is an "essential" sharing in the attributes of God, and hence in God himself.

> Salvation is realized in man in such a way that God justifies him through his [God's] own righteousness, or makes him wise through his own wisdom. Thus the essential attributes of God become attributes of man on the basis of the participation. Since these attributes are God himself, justification understood in this way implies the deification of man.[15]

Peura goes on to say that what constitutes the righteousness of the believer is exactly God's own divine righteousness: "It is always a matter of one and the same righteousness by which God himself is righteous and by which he makes the Christian righteous."[16] Here there is no mention of Christ's vicarious work, his suffering and death, as the source of the

13. Ibid., 49, note 10.

14. Ibid., 73f.

15. Ibid., 74. As we shall see later, there is a similarity here to the doctrine of "essential righteousness" as taught by Osiander.

16. Ibid.

Christian's righteousness or justification, but the focus is instead squarely on God's own essential righteousness and the believer's participation in that righteousness. That participation makes the Christian actually and "really" righteous, and thus acceptable to God. However, the Christian's righteousness, though real, is nevertheless inchoate and partial: as long as they are still in this life, sin continues to cling to them. As a defense against this remaining sin, the believer needs Christ's perfect righteousness as a shield. "The deified human being must remain under Christ's protection, because he has only been made righteous in part."[17] The real, ontological participation and deification of man is also necessarily *partial*: Peura goes so far as to describe Christians as "partially gods" in this life.

It is not entirely clear from reading Peura's discussion whether the deification of the believer is "hidden" because it also involves the believer in the cross, i.e., the human nature of Christ and therefore his sufferings (as Peura says elsewhere), or whether it is because the "partial" righteousness and "deification" of the Christian are still such small portions of his being that they do not become visible. In other words, is it possible that certain people progress in their participation sufficiently in this life that their "real" divine character becomes evident and observable? It seems unavoidable that, as soon as one speaks in categories of "partial" righteousness or a gradual *profectio* of sanctification, that it must be possible—at least in principle—to distinguish the greater saints already in this life, at least in a tentative or preliminary way. This, of course, is part and parcel of the Orthodox and Roman Catholic doctrine of the saints. Peura does not say, but it is not unreasonable to suppose that his view would be consistent with that of Luther himself during the period of his career under consideration. Peura simply concludes that the participation, which as he understands it is synonymous with deification, is not yet the complete fulfillment. That fulfillment awaits the final joy of the church triumphant.

DEIFICATION IN LUTHER'S EARLY WORKS

Having examined the theme of deification (sometimes referred to as participation in God, or union with Christ) in the *Dictata super psalterium*, Peura turns (as Mannermaa did) to Luther's 1514 Christmas sermon.[18]

---

17. Ibid., 79.

18. Cf. Mannermaa, "Theosis as a Subject of Finnish Luther Research," 37–48; and "*Hat Luther eine trinitarische Ontologie?*," 9–27.

It is somewhat remarkable that this early sermon of Luther's has come to occupy such a central place in the studies of the Finnish school. The reason is probably, as Peura points out, that here Luther addresses the theme of the incarnation, and of the Christian's resultant participation in God's nature, in terms of philosophical ontology. Peura's treatment of this sermon adds some detail but little of substance to the analysis of Mannermaa, except perhaps to reinforce the Finnish school's interest in what may be called the "ontology of language," the close and "real" connection between the linguistic signs and the realities thus signified. Since Christ is identified as the word of God, this interplay of sign and *res* was not merely semantics but a burning issue of theological reflection as well. Peura makes the connection with the incarnation of the Logos this way:

> The incarnation of the inner word of God is important because it creates the ontological connection with the external word. So when God binds himself to the external word, his inner word becomes a visible word in unity with the flesh and the humanity. According to Luther, God reveals in the visible word what Christ has thought. ...Above all, it is a matter of the unity of the inner word with the word-made-flesh. On the basis of this unity, the *verbum externum Dei*, that is, the incarnate Christ, is God.[19]

Like Mannermaa, Peura sees in Luther's sermon a kind of "ontological perception,"[20] drawn from Aristotle, by which the hearers of the word in some sense "become" what they hear. And precisely this, rather than the historical incarnation of the Logos, is of prime importance for Peura (as it seems for Luther in 1514).[21] Luther, utilizing the four-fold method of biblical interpretation that he inherited from the medieval tradition, identifies also the tropological sense of the text. The result is that, in keeping with the tropological sense of the *Quadriga*, "what is said about Christ is applied to the believer."[22] Given that hermeneutical approach, it is not surprising that Luther's expressions of *theosis* closely parallel his description of the incarnation: the same Scripture is to be interpreted in analo-

---

19. Peura, *Mehr als ein Mensch?*, 88.

20. See the previous chapter for Mannermaa's use of this idea.

21. Remember that when he spoke of the "triple advent" of Christ in 1514, Luther's real interest was in the second, or "spiritual" coming of Christ to be born in the believer's heart, of which he says, "*sine quo primus [scil. quando incarnatus est filius dei] nihil prodest.*" WA 4.305, quoted in Peura, *Mehr als ein Mensch?*, 51, note 14.

22. Peura, *Mehr als ein Mensch?*, 93.

gous ways according to the different levels or senses. Thus, "the *deificatio hominis* occurs corresponding to the incarnation of the word. The created human being receives the word through faith, and is thus united with the word"[23] The union of man with the word and with God, and thus also his participation in God's attributes and nature, are seen by Peura as "real" and ontological, that is to say, they involve the very being and inmost existence of the believer, and are not to be understood as mere external relations or effects. Even so, Peura attempts to avoid the misconception that *theosis* involves some kind of transformation of substance in the human creature. Again, the model for human ontology is the *unio personalis* of the God-man Christ. Just as the incarnation did not transform one nature into the other, but united them inseparably but without confusion in one Person, so through faith (understood precisely as such "real" participation, not as trust in the external word of promise) the believer is connected to and participates in the divine nature. This happens in a real way, according to Peura, but nevertheless does not negate the believer's humanity.

In Luther's lectures on Romans (1515–1516), Peura follows the theme of justification and love. Especially important for Peura in this connection is the thought that justification is the equivalent of personal ("real, ontological") conformity with Christ, and this involves the union of the believer with Christ through love. Such conformity, however, is always "hidden" as God performs his "alien work" by reducing the human person to nothing. This is the necessary preparation for deification, or for receiving God himself. However, this *reductio in nihilum* is not to be understood in any sense as a *self*-preparation, but a *passio* through which God makes man *capax Dei*. The man merely suffers and is "done to" to reduce him to the nothing that can receive God and his gifts.[24] When man has been thus reduced, God gives himself (not merely his benefits, attributes, or effects) to man by giving him his Word.

Peura here argues that "word" for Luther through 1519 always meant both the historical incarnation of Christ *and* the spiritual coming of Christ to the believer. "In his early writings," writes Peura, "Luther uses the *terminus technicus* of deification in the context of the historical incarnation as a description of the doctrine of the two natures: Christ is thus at the

23. Ibid., 96.

24. For a more extensive exploration of this idea of the *reductio in nihilum*, cf. Juntunen, *Der Begriff des Nichts bei Luther.*

same time *deus incarnatus* and *homo deificatus.*"[25] When the Word (which is identical with Christ) is in the believer, the believer is united with it and "becomes" the Word. "The presence of Christ means that the triune God takes up residence in the Christian." This presence of the incarnate Logos in the believer is directly and intimately connected with man's justification. "The justification of man consists in this, that because of Christ who is present [in him] he is *both* declared righteous *and* made righteous." The believer's union with God is not merely relational or external, but means that the Christian has his being in God. Nevertheless, maintains Peura, "this understanding of being implies *no* static-material metaphysic. God is God in that he brings forth his word, and man is man, even if deified, in that he *participates* in this word. . . . What is *personaliter* in Christ is *participative* in us." Peura documents how Luther uses traditional philosophical terminology (*forma-materia*) or Aristotelian categories (e.g., "*simile simili cognosci*") to describe this union with God.

God's proper work of justification climaxes in deification. "The indwelling of Christ through faith means precisely deification." Here Peura's central text from Luther is the saying, "*homo enim homo est, donec fiat deus.*"[26] (*AWA* 2:305). His point is to show that true Christian anthropology ultimately requires that man be *more than man*, in fact that he be deified. This deification involves a "real-ontic" change in man through the *unio cum verbo*. Peura says that this does not involve a *change* in substance, but rather something like a union of two substances. This cannot be adequately explained in the terms of scholastic categories, even though Luther does use terms such as "substance" and "accidence." The real-ontic change in man is nevertheless only partial and incipient in this life, and is evidenced especially in love. Peura tries to show that Luther closely connects his idea of deification with love. The divine virtues of love (and it must be remembered that God's attributes are not separate from his very being; Luther, says Peura, does not distinguish the *person* from the *work*

---

25. Peura, *Mehr als ein Mensch?*, 296. Of course, it must be noted that Luther here speaks specifically of Christ, not the individual believer; this distinction is strangely unimportant to Peura.

26. AWA 2:305.18–19 (Luther commenting on Psalm 5). However, in his comments a few verses earlier, Luther seems to present almost the opposite view, and focuses his attention rather on the "descent" of God into human form "in order to restore us to knowledge of ourselves," AWA 2:226.5–10.

of Christ) are "incarnated" in the believer, and thus the believer is himself deified.

According to Peura, Luther understands deification as occurring *under the cross*, and here he investigates Luther's *theologia crucis*, particularly drawing on the *Resolutiones disputationum de indulgentiarum virtute* (1518) and the *Operationes in Psalmos* (1519). He identifies three different but related aspect of the theology of the cross as it relates to his main idea of deification. First, God's work of deifying the believer presupposes God's alien work of reducing him to nothing. This is because man's sinful nature is centered in selfish love, and God's work in him begins with its destruction. Thus the human *deificatio* requires a prior *passio*. Second, deification, while it is already "real" in this life, is nevertheless hidden and not perceptible to the senses. The union with Christ is the same as God's infusion of grace into the believer, and this involves a transformation, but the transformation is concealed under the form and appearance of its very opposite. "Man can thus not see and perceive his new condition, because only sin is evident." And third, *theosis* involves the believer in a life-long way of the cross, a *resignatio ad infernum* from which God ultimately (but only after death) raises him up. The Christian's life is an unfinished process or *profectio*, as the sin that remains in man is gradually driven out, and this happens through suffering and death. As Risto Saarinen summarizes, "the ongoing restitution process is not sanctification in a naïve sense, but rather a process of mortification."[27] Such a formulation is not problematic in itself, but it blurs a crucial distinction when this "process of mortification" is identified with justification, as Peura attempts to do.

What this understanding of justification as deification means for a theological conception of man becomes clear in consequence of what has been said. For Peura, true human nature, or at least the human nature restored in Christ, surpasses the merely human, because it is united with the divine. Peura asserts that "deification understood in terms of the theology of the cross means that man is, through grace, as Luther concludes, 'more than a man.'" This, of course, is no cause for boasting, but rather for selfless love of God and neighbor. But the "incarnation" of God's love in the Christian results in a new being that is, in some important sense, *more* than a human creature. He reaches such a conclusion because the presence of God's love is in a real way—and for Peura, "real" always means

27. Saarinen, "The Presence of God in Luther's Theology," 7.

"ontological"—the presence of God himself. The continual renewal of deification is *not merely* the restoration of man's original state, but involves something "more," which cannot be more precisely defined. But the birth of love in the believer is the signal that he is united in an ontological way with God himself.

According to Peura, Luther's teaching about deification is not adequately explained or understood when the being of God and that of man are conceived of in exclusively relational (or cognitive) terms, as if the one were and remained outside the other. Again it becomes clear that he is reacting against the philosophical presuppositions of Ritschl, but he generalizes his comment as if it applied equally to all of Lutheran theology since Melanchthon. "The exclusively ethicizing [*ethisierende*] interpretation is likewise inappropriate, because it takes into account neither the participation in the divine nature as the ground of justification, nor the accomplished real-ontic change as the ground of love." Luther thus must not be understood as representing the modern personal-relational "effect theory."[28] This seems to demonstrate again how Peura (like Mannermaa) fails to grasp Luther's theology of the word, the promise of the gospel, and faith.

Peura says that Luther cannot be understood "relationally," but neither, according to Peura, can Luther's concept of deification simply be explained in terms of the medieval substance metaphysics. Peura suggests that Luther's ontology (at least during the rather early period which he examines) might be described as "ontology under the cross." He says that such ontology seems to imply a way of being that "stands in strong tension with a human understanding: deification as being in God through participation in him is a being in one's own nothingness."[29]

In any case, for Peura this hidden ontology of "more-than-man" in some way moves beyond "mere" creatureliness. It is not much of an exaggeration to describe it as the *negation* of man-as-creature, since it necessarily involves the reduction of the human self (i.e., the created self) to exactly "nothing." Risto Saarinen calls attention to the connection between Peura's anthropology and the concept of the divine image in man, saying that the "anthropological view of the human being as God's image is outlined with the help of the notion of participation. The soteriological

---

28. Cf. Saarinen, *Gottes Wirken auf uns.*
29. Peura, *Mehr als ein Mensch?*, 302.

process aims at making a person a 'better image' of God than Adam was in Paradise."[30] *Theosis*, that is, participation in God, refers to the eschatological consummation of the process which begins in this life, and the final end of the process takes human beings beyond being mere creatures. Peura cites the provocative dictum of Luther: "*Homo enim homo est, donec fiat deus . . .* —man is man as long as he is made God." But the sentence continues in Luther's echo of the mystics' love of self-annihilation: "For where does he arrive who hopes in God, except at his own nothingness?"[31] The human self who is mere creature must be reduced to nothing in order for the new self-in-Christ to emerge who is *mehr als ein Mensch*.

THEOSIS AND THE IMAGE OF GOD

We have been examining Peura's efforts to reassert an ontological understanding of salvation that differs not only from the nineteenth-century neo-Kantian metaphysics of Ritschl but also from the Lutheran understanding of justification since the adoption of the Formula of Concord. Underlying his theological program are definite presuppositions about the nature and destiny of man, in other words, a framework of theological anthropology. Peura elaborates on these presuppositions by taking note of Luther's analysis of two Biblical texts that are essential to his understanding of *theosis*: Genesis 1:26–27 and 2 Peter 1:4.

> Luther's understanding of participation, and at the same time his doctrine of *theosis*, can thus also be clarified through the analysis of his interpretation of the mentioned Bible texts [Genesis 1:26–27; 2 Peter 1:4]. In doing so it is helpful to investigate Luther's view of the constitution of man, received in creation and fallen from the innocence of man's original state: the *imago et similitudo Dei* (Genesis 1:26–27). It is to be generally assumed as a presupposition for participation, that the human being in creation received a nature which can also participate in God, because he is the image of God.[32]

Following the lead of some of Luther's comments in the Genesis Commentary, Peura asserts that human beings were created in such a

30. Saarinen, "The Presence of God in Luther's Theology," 7.

31. AWA 2:305.20–21: "*Quo enim perveniat, qui speat in deum, nisi in sui nihilum?*" This is a key passage for Peura, and he quotes it often.

32. Peura, "*Die Teilhabe an Christus bei Luther*," 122.

way that it was their nature to participate in God and live in intimate fellowship with him. This, he says, is the meaning of the "image of God" in which Adam was made. Such participation constituted the spiritual life of man in his original state and distinguished him from all other creatures. Nevertheless, Adam's life in God was by grace, since he lived in the dependence of faith rather than as some sort of "self-existent, autonomous being independent of his creator. . . . Adam did not have immortality and participation in God *simpliciter*, but only from his grace."[33] Luther departs from the scholastic idea that the original state of man included not just perfect human nature, but also an additional, supernatural gift of grace (*donum superadditum*). Instead, he believes that "both the image of God and the resemblance (likeness) of God are contained in the creaturely nature and constitution of human beings."[34] The scholastics distinguished between the two parallel terms in Genesis (*imago* and *similitudo*), associating one with man's natural being and the other with the *donum superadditum*. Luther rejects the distinction between the natural and the supernatural in his interpretation, but he still distinguishes the two terms and understands them as referring to two different realities. He regards the "image" as consisting in the highest powers of the soul, such as the intellect, the will, etc. The "likeness," on the other hand, means the actual, God-pleasing operations and orientations of these powers. Both belonged to human nature as originally created by God. Adam's "original righteousness" (*iustitia originalis*), far from being viewed in the scholastic way as something added to man from outside his nature, was for Luther rather a co-natural quality of his created being: it was an "essential righteousness." Peura says that Luther grounded the first humans' dominion over other creatures in their created nature as including the "image and likeness" of God.

Having thus sketched Luther's conception of the original state of human creatures in the image and likeness of God, Peura proceeds to show how the *Urstand*, the original condition of human creatures, included a certain openness to something even better.

> In view of the anthropological questions of the doctrine of justification, however, Luther's view is important, according to which man's original state was not yet his final state, despite its blessed-

33. Ibid., 125.
34. Ibid., 126.

ness, excellence, and goodness. The restitution of the believer, who lives *post peccatum*, is thus more "complicated" and therefore more than just a restoration of the original state.[35]

Such a description of sin as a "complication" in God's intention for humanity certainly minimizes sin. To more fully understand the "more complicated" matter of the restitution of fallen human creatures, Peura turns first to consider Luther's construction of what the original state would have been and become if there had been no sin. He says that Luther considered Adam's original condition as good in itself, but not a final or permanent condition. Unlike the angels, the first humans lived a "life in between" (*vita posita in medio*), because their nature included not only original righteousness but also the possibility of sin. According to Peura,

> it was possible for Adam to remain in that life for which he was created, and later to be transported to immortality which could not be lost. It was of course also possible that he would fall into sin and lose his immortality. Adam's blameless state was thus open to a change in two opposite directions.[36]

Thus, for Luther (at least according to Peura),[37] the original condition of humans contained essentially the potential for transition to something better. Adam and Eve's path to the ultimate "angelic life" that awaited them would involve a process of obedience, and only after that would God translate them from the intermediate state in paradise to their ultimate immortality.[38] The point is that the original created life in Eden would have ended in any case, and if there had been no fall into sin the end of earthly life would have been a smooth and harmonious transition to a state of confirmed righteousness and immortality. Peura says that the ultimate life was to be a "spiritual" life free of all the limitations imposed by bodily existence. Their life in paradise was to involve a kind of "progress" (*profectio*) or gradual improvement. And the period of the *profectio* also meant that the first humans had to wait some time before God transferred them to final immortality. This illustrates how humans in their original state were bound by time, and therefore lived in hope. Peura concludes

35. Ibid., 132.

36. Ibid., 133.

37. Peura's discussion here follows Luther's comments in AE 1:55ff; WA 42:41ff (Lectures on Genesis, 1535).

38. Peura, *Mehr als ein Mensch?*, 134.

from all this that "the participation [in God] in the original state would have led, even without the fall into sin, to the likeness to God which is realized in eternity."[39] Such likeness is conceived by Luther as the original goal (*finis principalis*) of human beings.[40]

With the fall of the first humans into sin, this impacted their human nature. The damage to human nature does not mean that man's natural abilities are lost altogether, but that these abilities have been corrupted and have forfeited their integrity.[41] The human will and reason were corrupted, so that human beings no longer loved God and knew him rightly but, on the contrary, began to hate God. The disruption of their fellowship with their Creator also resulted in an inability to know the rest of creation correctly. The effect of sin was that first the *similitudo* and then the *imago Dei* were lost.[42] The restitution of what was lost through sin therefore means the re-creation of that image in man, which, as we have seen, for Peura implies ontological participation in God. This re-creation also includes the fact that the ultimate state to which Adam looked forward *before* the fall, that "spiritual life" which would be free from the limitations of time and space, is now the hope of Christians as well. Thus "the restitution is not a matter of simply re-establishing and renewing the original condition," but sets believers on the way toward the "better *imago*" for which Adam, too, hoped.[43] In this sense, then, "Christ makes our condition even better than Adam's was in paradise."[44] Peura points out that this is because "the original state was not a final and static condition, but one open to change."[45] According to Peura, Luther's anthropology is directly connected to his soteriology:

> Thus in Luther, the conception of human beings in their original state as imago et similitudo Dei, and of the loss of the image in the fall into sin, and of the restitution in Christ are strictly presupposed, so that the reformer, as a consequence, speaks explicitly of a participation in the divine nature which happens in Christ.[46]

39. Ibid., 137.
40. Ibid., 138.
41. Ibid., 138f.
42. Ibid., 138. WA 42.248: "*Sed per peccatum tum similitudo tum imago amissa est.*"
43. Ibid., 142f.
44. Ibid., 143.
45. Ibid., 143.
46. Ibid., 147.

As examples of such a conclusion, Peura refers to the *Resolutiones*, the 1519 Galatians Commentary, and the Sermon on the Two Kinds of Righteousness. The pivotal verse for Peura's "real, ontological" understanding is 2 Peter 1:4 ("Through these [God's glory and goodness] he has given us his very great and precious promises, so that through them you may participate in the divine nature and escape the corruption in the world caused by evil desires"). Peura's central argument is that both Luther's anthropology of the original human condition and his anthropology of the final restoration involve the human creature in an ontological participation in the divine nature. Such participation amounts to a release or escape from the false loves of mere creaturely existence, as the divine nature in Christ conquers and absorbs the sinful human nature, initially and partially in this life but ultimately and completely in the resurrection.

> The release from destructive love, under the power which man holds rather to God's goods than to God, means that man is reduced to nothing. He has thus "released" himself from himself and from the creature in terms of that spoiled love, and therefore stands outside the realm of the creaturely. Since there is no third thing between the creature and God, it follows from what has been said that man comes to God and is in God.[47]

CHRIST AS "GRACE" AND "GIFT"

In a more recent essay, Peura concentrates on the identification of Christ as both "grace" and "gift" in Luther's theology.[48] Among other works, Peura here draws especially on Luther's "Against Latomus" (1521). Following Mannermaa's lead, Peura argues that "gift" in this context refers to the real, ontological presence of Christ, as well as to related concepts which derive from Christ's presence (such as renewal, vivification, the new birth, sanctification, etc.). In Peura's parlance, "gift" denotes the real, ontologically "effective" aspect of justification, which is identified with Christ himself but actually located in the believer. "Grace," on the other hand, refers to the declarative imputation of forgiveness for the sake of Christ's merit and death; it is forensic and external to the believer. "Grace" is, according to this view, necessary but not yet "real" until it is actualized by Christ's

47. Ibid., 160.
48. Simo Peura, *"Christus als Gunst und Gabe."*

real presence in the believer. "Grace" and "gift" presuppose each other: one is never possible or certain without the other. This is because they both reflect the reality of the *unio cum Christo*, which in turn involves the believer in a process of *conformitas Christi* lasting until the resurrection on the Last Day.[49]

Peura, like Mannermaa, turns to Luther's writings in search of an "authentic" Lutheran theology as an explicit alternative to most of the Lutheran theological tradition, especially to the Formula of Concord. In particular Peura laments the Formula's emphasis on forensic justification and what he sees as the consequent neglect of the concept of "gift."

> In the history of Lutheranism, the relationship of grace and gift has usually been interpreted on the basis of the Formula of Concord. The Formula followed Luther's conception, that grace and gift should be differentiated, in such a way that the gift was almost reduced to a *minimum in loco iustificationis*.[50]

That emphasis on the forensic nature of justification before God, and the accompanying shift away from the concept of "gift" in the FC's understanding of justification, is regarded by Peura as an unacceptably one-sided distortion of Luther's doctrine. What Peura finds inadequate in the Formula's doctrine of justification is its more exclusive focus on the external word of declarative righteousness, the pronouncement which is identified especially with absolution.

> In the Formula of Concord justification (*iustitia fidei coram Deo*) is related only to God's favor [*Gunst*], that is, to the righteousness imputed forensically by God. Justification thus corresponds materially to absolution, that is, the declared forgiveness of sins.[51]

Peura regards the Formula's conception of forensic justification as inadequate because it does not reflect what he considers to be Luther's own view, in which Christ himself is both "grace" and "gift" in the believer's *unio cum Christo*. The FC does not deny any of those things Peura

---

49. Ibid., 353–55.

50. Ibid., 344.

51. Ibid., 344. In fact, in this regard the Formula is following the insight Luther reached at least as early as 1518, as a result of his struggles over the theology of indulgences and the sacrament of penance. Cf. WA 2:630–33 (*Pro veritate inquirenda et timoratis conscientiis consolandis . . .* , 1518). Cf. Jared Wicks, "*Fides sacramenti—fides specialis*: Luther's Development in 1518." *Gregorianum* 65 (1984), 53–87.

includes under the concept of "gift" (*renovatio, vivificatio, inhabitatio Dei*), but distinguishes between them and justification *per se*. From this distinction Peura then (rightly) concludes that these latter benefits are no longer an integral part of justification, as he insists they were for Luther, but merely necessary consequences of the imputed righteousness.[52] Having thus characterized the Formula of Concord's doctrine, he draws an important—if dubious—conclusion: "This therefore means that God is *not* present precisely when the sinner is declared righteous because of Christ's obedience."[53] This result is unacceptable for Peura. In his view, the "authentic" Reformation doctrine of justification is better represented by Luther himself than by the FC, because Luther speaks of the forensic-declarative and the effective-ontological aspects together, and in such a way that the believer "really" participates in the divine nature. Peura says:

> In my opinion the FC [Formula of Concord] does not present Luther's understanding of grace and gift entirely correctly. The reformer understands gift in a much broader sense than does the FC: even the renewal of man itself (*renovatio*), that is, the effective aspect, belongs for Luther to the *locus iustificationis*. The renewal is thus not only to be understood as a consequence of forensic imputation. God renews the sinner in justification in such a way that he lets man participate in his divine nature.[54]

According to Peura, the doctrine presented and defined by the Formula's distinctions, which has shaped practically all of subsequent Lutheranism, stands in need of correction. He and the rest of the Finnish school seek such a corrective by appealing to Luther's own theology as the "authentic" basis for Lutheran theology.

> Finnish Lutheranism is presently rather concerned with the question of the extent to which Lutherans churches want to align their ecumenical efforts with the theology of the reformer [i.e., Luther]. Too often contemporary Lutheranism tends to use modern theological categories, or to build rather on the distinctions of the FC than on the theology of the reformer.[55]

---

52. Peura, "*Christus als Gunst und Gabe*," 345.

53. Ibid.

54. Ibid., 346.

55. Ibid., 358.

Peura points out that the Formula's emphasis and accent arose especially out of the historical controversy surrounding the theology of Andreas Osiander. This brings us back again to the relationship between Osiander's ideas of justification, Christology, and anthropology, and those of the Finnish school, a connection we encountered earlier. Peura believes that the distinctions of the FC fail to address Osiander's real error, which was not his basing of justification on the indwelling of God, but rather a Christological failure.

> It must be kept in mind that the problem with Osiander does not actually relate to his assertion that the indwelling of God also belongs to justification. Osiander's problems lie rather in the christological presuppositions of this assertion. In contrast to Luther, Osiander divides the human nature and the divine nature of Christ, and as a consequence of this the *unio personalis* in Christ is lost. Because of this, the man Christ, his obedience, and everything he did as man on the cross, has only an instrumental role both in redemption and in justification.[56]

It is this connection with the theology of Osiander which we must next address in our pursuit of Peura's theological anthropology.

OSIANDER AND THE *THEOSIS* THEOLOGY OF THE FINNISH SCHOOL

Peura discusses the theology of Osiander in more detail in a 1996 essay.[57] Since the second half of the sixteenth century, Lutheran theology has recognized that Osiander's concept of justification includes elements of "deification" of the Christian through union with God's essential righteousness, as well as an emphasis on defining justification as "making righteous" [*Gerechtmachung*] as opposed to mere[58] "declaring righteous" [*Gerechterklärung*]. At least since the acceptance of the Formula of Concord it has also been asserted that Osiander's view differs in important respects from that of Luther. In Peura's opinion, however, the relationship between Osiander's and Luther's theology has not been

---

56. Ibid., 345.

57. Peura, "*Gott und Mensch in der Unio.*"

58. The tendentious and pejorative use of "mere" characterizes both the Osiandrian and the Finnish comments regarding forensic justification. Much mischief is done with such abuse of a mere "mere."

sufficiently clarified. Article III of the Solid Declaration, he suggests, is chiefly concerned to "legitimize" imputed, forensic justification, and fails to address the main points that distinguish Osiander from Luther. Peura attempts to re-read Osiander's theology and identify what might be called "genuine Osiandrian" theology and compare that to his reading of "genuine Lutheran" theology (which he understands as primarily the theology of Luther's own writings. Peura's interest in Osiander is appropriate, indeed necessary, since there are important general similarities between Osiander's theology of "essential righteousness" and the Finnish school's contention that some idea of *theosis* lies at the heart of Luther's understanding of the gospel. Peura recognizes the implication that, if one accepts the Finnish re-reading of Luther, then one must also reexamine— if not rehabilitate—Osiander as well.

> But how are we to understand the relation between Luther's and Osiander's teachings on justification, when it is shown that "making righteous" and deification are also contained in the Wittenberg reformer's doctrine of justification? In the first place it seems that the problem with Osiander's doctrine of justification does not relate first and foremost to his conception that justification rests on God's essential righteousness. The heart of the problem lies rather in *what* Osiander means with his concept of "essential righteousness" and *how* the believer comes to share in this righteousness.[59]

In an effort to clarify these points about Osiander's teaching and the ways in which it may have differed from Luther's own, Peura sets out to explain Osiander's understanding of "union" (*unio*). According to Peura, the notion of "union" is definitive for Osiander's theology, first Christologically as the union between God and man (*unio personalis*) in the person of Christ, and then anthropologically as God unites himself with the sinner through faith (*unio cum Deo*). The anthropological *unio* that defines each Christian's existence explicitly reflects and parallels the Christological *unio*. Peura's argument is that the theological decisions Osiander makes regarding the person of Christ therefore have direct consequences also for his doctrine of man and justification. As a result, and despite Osiander's appeal to Luther during his controversy in Königsberg, his Christology ultimately divides him from Luther in ways which are not

59. Peura, "*Gott und Mensch in der Unio,*" 35.

identified or addressed when the Formula of Concord rejects Osiander's doctrine of "essential righteousness."

As Peura sets out to compare the views of Luther and Osiander regarding the "union" of God and man (whether in the person of Christ or in the believer), he relies upon Tuomo Mannermaa's analysis of Luther, especially his treatment of the 1535 Galatians Commentary. He starts with the assertion: "Luther's doctrine of justification has as its foundation the Christology of the early church."[60] According to this, he says, the incarnation is identical with Christ's humiliation and *kenosis*: the divine Logos became not only a man but a sinner, the "greatest sinner," whose character as "collective person" actually absorbs all sin in himself. This means that Christ unites in his own person the extreme tension and opposition between God in his pure holiness and man in his sinfulness. The *unio personalis* holds these two conflicting natures together in Christ, and also makes possible the final resolution of the struggle, for the attributes of the divine nature "absorb and conquer sin and death."[61] The unity of Christ's person also results in the *communicatio idiomatum* by which the attributes of each nature are predicated of the whole person. For Peura, of course, this is an anthropological as well as a Christological truth; he takes it as a synonym for the "blessed exchange." Christ's work of salvation is therefore to be seen as the work of the whole Christ, in the union of the divine and human natures. According to Peura, this occurs in such a way that the person and work of Christ are not divided. "The merit of Christ on the cross and his righteousness are essentially the same righteousness which belongs to God in his essence and Christ in his person. This righteousness is received through faith as a gift."[62]

Christ unites the divine holiness and human sin in his person, and this same union, according to Peura, is then worked in each person, through faith, as a gift. This involves, according to Peura, a divine-human union in the person of each believer which parallels and derives from the *unio personalis* in Christ. "Justification happens when the Christian becomes one with Christ by means of faith (*unio cum Deo*), and this union corresponds to the Christological union."[63] Significantly, as he

60. Ibid., 36.
61. Ibid., 38.
62. Ibid., 39.
63. Ibid., 40.

turns his attention from Christology and the *communicatio idiomatum* to justification and the *unio cum Deo*, Peura abandons Luther's Galatians Commentary and relies instead on the Hebrews Lectures (1517–1518). In that much earlier work, Luther regarded the *iustitia Dei* as both the divine righteousness with which God himself is righteous, and also the grace by which he justifies human beings, which he equated with the theological virtues of faith hope and love.[64] This leads to a central point in Peura's argument: God's own righteousness becomes "in a certain way" (*"in gewisser Weise,"* *quodammodo*) the righteousness of the believer's heart. Peura cites Luther:

> ... [F]aith so exalts man's heart and transfers it from itself to God that the heart and God become one spirit and thus in a way are the divine righteousness, the "formative" righteousness, as they call it, just as in Christ the humanity, through the union with the divine nature, became one and the same Person.[65]

Of great interest is the preceding context and the first part of this very sentence, which Peura omits. In context, Luther explicitly rejects the notion that this is God's "essential righteousness" in the believer, and this of course undermines the entire point Peura is trying to make:

> But this righteousness [i.e., justifying faith, the mercy or salvation of God] is the righteousness about which it is written in Rom. 1:17 that it is from faith, as is stated that in the Gospel "the righteousness of God is revealed from faith to faith." *This is erroneously explained as referring to the righteousness of God by which He himself is righteous*, unless it were understood that faith so exalts [etc.] ...[66]

Peura's ellipsis here is very misleading; Luther is explicitly distinguishing the righteousness of faith from God's essential righteousness.

But Peura proceeds: he argues that this sharing of God's righteousness to be—"*quodammodo*"—the believer's own righteousness is to be

64. Ibid., quoting WA 57H:187: "... *quod 'iustitia' sit ipsa grati, qua iustificatur homo, id est fides, spes, charitas* ..."

65. AE 29:188; WA 57H:187.17—188.3. Quoted in Peura, "Gott und Mensch in der Unio," 41.

> ... *quia fides ita exaltat cor hominis et transfert de se ipso in Deum, ut unus spiritus fiat ex corde et Deo ac sic ipsa divina iustitia sit cordis iusticia quodammodo, ut illi dicunt 'informans,' sicut in Christo humanitas per unionem cum divina natura una et eadem facta est persona.*

66. AE 29:188; WA 57H:187.

explained in terms of the "union": first of the *unio personalis* of the two natures in Christ, but then especially of the *unio cum Deo* (or *Christo*) in which the person of the believer reflects and in some way repeats the paradigm of union in Christ's person.

> In the same way that the attributes of Christ's divine nature communicate with the human nature on the basis of the unity of the person, Christ's righteousness communicates with the sinful human being on the basis of the Christ-union brought about by faith, and forms the righteousness of his heart. Union with God thus means that the Christian, just like Christ, has "two natures."[67]

The heart of the Christian's existence is therefore this individual iteration of the *unio personalis* as Christ becomes the believer's "divine nature." The description of the Christian can no longer really be characterized as "anthropology," since a believer is necessarily and by definition *"mehr als ein Mensch."*

PEURA'S SUBSTANTIAL AGREEMENT WITH OSIANDER

Despite his criticism of Osiander for separating the two natures in Christ's person and deriving the Christian's righteousness exclusively from union with the divine nature, Peura seems to fall prey to exactly the same error. Here again he follows Mannermaa. When the Finnish theologians speak of the Christian's "two natures" as a result of union with Christ, then Christ is always depicted as the "divine" nature of the Christian. "Salvation is thus grounded in the Christ-union: in it the Christian is one with Christ and participates in the *divine* nature."[68] The omission of the human nature from this and similar expressions of the Finnish school's concept of union with God through faith is both consistent and significant. Since, for Peura and Mannermaa, Christ's human nature is (strictly speaking) only *sinful* human nature, it contributes nothing to the righteousness which Christ is and accomplishes for us. Indeed, the human nature Christ assumes is in reality rather something to be overcome and defeated in the struggle for our salvation. Peura agrees with Mannermaa on this point, even after criticizing Osiander for a similar idea. Christ is our righteousness precisely because his divine nature is able to "conquer and absorb" the sin and death that are inherent in the human nature. His victory is the triumph of

---

67. Peura, *"Gott und Mensch in der Unio,"* 41.

68. Ibid., 45.

the holy over the sinful—which, in fact, means the divine over the human. The only meaning Christ's *human* nature has for the Christian in this *unio* is that it places the Christian under the cross, but in saying this Peura clearly uses "cross" as a metaphor for the experience of the Christian, not in reference to the work of redemption accomplished in history through Christ's own suffering and death. Especially for Peura, the deification of the believer is never apparent to the senses, but always hidden under the opposite experience of suffering.

> Participation in Christ is always also sharing in his cross, that is, assumption of the form of a servant (*forma servi*) corresponding to the example of Christ. . . . The cross therefore belongs to the Christians life not only as an 'alien work' of God preceding justification, but also remains an integral component of his life in faith. . . . In Luther's theology participation in God and participation in the cross of Christ form two sides of the same thing.[69]

Participation in Christ's cross also involves the Christian in the need and misery of his neighbor: by means of love, the believer's human existence is also located and directed outside himself. This parallels Mannermaa's statement that the believer's "divine nature" is Christ (with whom he is united by faith), while his "human nature" is his neighbor (with whom he is connected by love).[70] This new "ecstatic" (in the sense of an escape from self) existence redirects the believer's life away from self-seeking ambition or self-glorification. According to Peura, this is what Luther means by his claim that the Christian becomes *human*.[71]

There are definite similarities between Peura's interpretation of Luther's view of the *unio* between God and man and the ideas of Osiander. Despite such parallels, however, Peura argues that Osiander did not share the basic concepts that shaped Luther's doctrine. In his effort to clarify Osiander's position, he turns first to a 1525 work, "The Great Nuremberg Counsel," where Osiander begins with the presupposition of God's fundamental incomprehensibility and unknowability.[72] Only God can really

69. Ibid.

70. Mannermaa, "Theosis as a Subject of Finnish Luther Research," 48.

71. Peura, "*Gott und Mensch in der Unio*," 46, referring to WA 21:78.13–23Ref & date for this WA ref.?.

72. Here again is the theme of an "apophatic" approach to theology, which we saw earlier in the theological world of Orthodoxy and the *via negativa* of the western mystical tradition.

know himself, and this self-knowledge of God is precisely the Logos or Son of God. This is the "Word of God," which for Osiander is never identified with a physical, audible word. "God's Word is an inner, spiritual Word. The external, spoken word can bring forth the Word of God and point to it as a sign. But God's Word remains all the while an inner and singular Word, just as there is also only one single, entire divine essence."[73] The outer word can and does carry out the instrumental function of passing on and rendering intelligible the true, divine, inner Word, but the two are never really united. This becomes an especially important point when it is remembered that Osiander explicitly identifies the "inner Word" with Christ's divine nature. His refusal to join the inner and outer "words" is not a matter of linguistic metaphysics, but rather a theological decision about Christology. As Peura puts it:

> In Osiander's understanding, the inner Word is precisely one with the divine nature of Christ. On the other hand, the human nature, the mere flesh and blood, *only* has meaning in the transmittal [Vermittlung] of the inner Word. For in order to be able to speak the inner wisdom of the Father, Christ needs a mouth and a body, that is, a human nature. Nevertheless Osiander is no Docetist; he simply instrumentalizes the human nature of Christ. There exists no inseparable union between the natures in the sense of classical christology.[74]

Osiander's Christology distinguishes emphatically between the two natures of Christ, at the expense of the unity of his person and the *communicatio idiomatum*. Indeed, as Peura rightly points out, Osiander regards it as the express task of Christology to specify which nature is active in every work or attribute of Christ. Although he affirms the unity of the person of Christ as his point of departure, he is not willing—as Luther was willing—to predicate of *both* natures the whole of Christ's being and work.[75] Luther could and did say that the newborn child in Bethlehem's manger is the Creator of heaven and earth.[76] For Osiander such a statement must be regarded as theologically false, since the work of creation is only to be attributed to the divine nature, and the humble birth only to the human nature. Osiander's goal in Christology is to identify carefully what

73. Peura, "*Gott und Mensch in der Unio*," 47f.

74. Ibid., 49.

75. Cf. WA 56.343.20ff.

76. As, for instance in the 1535 Galatians Commentary, WA 40I:415f.

Christ has done as God and what He has done as man.[77] And in making such distinctions, Osiander expressly states that what one nature does is *not* done by the other nature:

> So also, when one says, "Jesus Christ, true Son of God, shed his blood for us and died for us," I consider it a good, right, and Christian way of speaking. But when I ask a theologian, according to which nature God's Son shed his blood and died, then he must answer and say to me: according to his human nature he shed his blood and died, and by no means according to his divine nature.[78]

What this means, of course, is that Osiander denies the *communicatio idiomatum* in any meaningful sense of the term: Christ's suffering and death on the cross were the work of his human nature and expressly *not* of his divine nature. Likewise, the works of the divine nature are explicitly separated from the human nature:

> Since Christ has become righteousness for us, and Christ is a name of the whole, undivided person, in whom both the divine and human natures are united, so the question now is, according to which nature is he our righteousness? In the same way one asks, according to which nature he died. Here is now my true, correct, and clear answer: he is our righteousness according to his divine nature and not according to the human nature . . .[79]

In Osiander's view, the attributes and works of the divine nature are never really shared with the human nature. In fact, Osiander's Christology ends up dividing the person of Christ through this strict separation of the natures. A consequence of this division is that also Christ's person and work are ultimately divided: "since the person is our righteousness, it follows undeniably that no work of this person can be our righteousness."[80] This means for Osiander that the righteousness of Christ by which we are justified and the merit of his suffering and cross are two entirely separate

---

77. Peura, "*Gott und Mensch in der Unio*," 53. Peura refers also to Theodor Mahlmann, *Die neue Dogma der lutherischen Christologie. Problem und Geschichte seiner Begründung.*

78. Peura, "*Gott und Mensch in der Unio*," 54. Peura bases his citation of Osiander on Theodor Mahlmann, *Das neue Dogma der lutherischen Christologie: Problem und Geschichte seiner Begründung* (Gütersloh: Gerd Mohn, 1969) 96–97. Osiander's tract "Von dem einigen Mittler" is in AOG 10:78–300.

79. Ibid.

80. Ibid., 55.

things: the former is attributed to his divine nature alone, while the latter is exclusively a work of the human nature. Peura correctly points out that for Osiander, Christ's atoning death on the cross was a necessary preliminary to actual justification. Through his vicarious sacrificial death, Christ turned away God's wrath and made possible forgiveness for sinners. This atonement and forgiveness, however, are not yet justification in the strict sense of the word, which is the union of the believer with Christ, who is our righteousness according to his divine nature. The role of Christ's human nature in that justification is purely functional or instrumental: its purpose is only to create a connection between God and man. The human nature transmits or communicates the divine righteousness, just as the spoken "outer word" can communicate the divine "inner Word," without being identified with it. "The actual justification is the merit of the divine nature and is grounded in its attributes."[81] Thus the human nature of Christ is the instrument by which the divine essence is communicated to human beings, but Christ's humanity does not contribute to or constitute the Christian's righteousness in any real way.

Peura's assessment of Osiander's Christology is substantially correct, as far as it goes, but his suggestion that the Formula failed to grasp Osiander's real point is unconvincing. Osiander's separation of the two natures of Christ, and his attribution of the Christian's righteousness of faith to the divine nature alone, are indeed rejected by the Formula of Concord. The union of the two natures and the communication of attributes are treated in detail in Article VIII. Osiander's exclusive focus on the divine nature of Christ as the source of the righteousness of faith is also rejected in the Formula, along with the opposite (but related) error of Stancaro that Christ is our righteousness only according to his human nature.

> Against both parties other teachers of the Augsburg Confession have preached unanimously that Christ is our righteousness not only according to his divine nature and also not only according to his human nature, but according to both natures. As God and as human being he has redeemed us from all sin, made us righteous, and saved us through his perfect obedience. Therefore, they have taught that the righteousness of faith is the forgiveness of sins, reconciliation with God, and that we are accepted as children of God for the sake of Christ's obedience alone, which is reckoned

81. Ibid., 57.

as righteousness through faith alone, out of sheer grace, to all who truly believe. Because of this they are absolved from all their unrighteousness.[82]

According to the Formula, therefore, the undivided person of Christ is the righteousness of the Christian, because Christ rendered complete and perfect obedience to the Father vicariously on our behalf according to both his divine and human natures.

Peura devotes careful study to Osiander's Christology in an effort to demonstrate how Osiander differed from Luther. Peura does *not* take issue with Osiander's concept of the deification of the believer through union with Christ, which, according to Peura, Luther shared. The target of Peura's criticism is Osiander's faulty Christology. However, Peura's study of Osiander's doctrine does not really consider Osiander's important "Disputation Concerning Justification,"[83] in which the Christological decisions (correctly highlighted by Peura) form the background for Osiander's soteriology. In Osiander's theses it becomes clear that for him Christ is our righteousness (Thesis 18), not in the sense that his righteousness is reckoned or accounted to us by imputation—such imputation is not very significant to Osiander (Thesis 22)—but ontologically and actually, because we are united with Christ (Thesis 19). Furthermore, the righteousness of Christ by which we are made righteous is not the righteousness of his obedient suffering and death, that is, not the righteousness achieved and completed on the cross, but rather his essential divine righteousness which is his from all eternity: "But he [Christ] is not righteous because he has fulfilled the law, but because he is born from eternity as a righteous Son of the righteous Father" (Thesis 27). This, significantly, is a point with which Peura would agree.

This fact has profound implications for the way Osiander understands salvation. If Christ's eternal, divine righteousness is the key to our salvation, then the decisive act in the history of salvation is the incarnation *per se* rather than the passion, death, and resurrection of Christ. Osiander attributes to the human nature of Christ the same relationship to the divine nature as the external word has to the true, divine Word which is to be born in the hearts of believers, and the similarity is not coincidental. What he did in the days of his human flesh can only be of secondary

---

82. Kolb-Wengert, 562f (FC SD III.4).
83. AOG 9:422–47.

importance: already at the moment of the incarnation the righteousness by which we are made righteous was already complete. The righteousness of God himself—not only of the Son, but also of the Father and the Holy Spirit—is precisely the righteousness that dwells in believers (Thesis 28). The incarnation is the key salvific event for Osiander, because it becomes paradigmatic for our union with God: in Christ's incarnation we see the divine united with the human, as it is also to be united in us.

This is particularly clear in the way Osiander misquotes 1 John 4:2–3. In its original form and context, this passage affirms the historical reality of the incarnation in opposition to some kind of Docetism. But Osiander uses the passage instead to support the indwelling of the divine righteousness, by inserting key phrases that change the meaning: "Every spirit that confesses that Jesus Christ came *in this way, and still comes* in *our* flesh, is from God. And every spirit that does not confess that Jesus Christ came *in this way in our flesh* is not from God" (Theses 67–68). In so doing Osiander shifts the center of theological attention away from the specific Incarnation of the Son of God in history, to a view of the incarnation as the pattern according to which God and his divine righteousness are joined with our human nature.

While Peura may conclude that Osiander's error actually lay in his Christology, the fact remains that the Formula of Concord rejects not only Osiander's Christology but also the concept of justification contained in his "Disputation Concerning Justification." Specifically denied is the way he based justification on the indwelling of God himself and his essential, divine righteousness. The antitheses in FC SD III specifically target the attempt to link the *inhabitatio Dei* with Christ's obedience as part of justification. There the authors "unanimously reject and condemn" the following teaching:

> That faith looks not to Christ's obedience alone, but to his divine nature, as it dwells in us and works in us, and that through this indwelling our sins are covered up in God's sight.[84]

This antithesis seems to be a very apt and pointed description of precisely what the Finnish theologians are urging: a faith that looks not solely to Christ's obedience, but also to his divine nature dwelling and working in us. That Peura and Mannermaa pursue this with more intellectual agility, and within a more sophisticated metaphysical framework, than Osiander

---

84. Kolb-Wengert, 573 (FC SD III.63).

did does not alter the fact that the categories of their theological discourse resemble Osiander's far more than those of the Formula of Concord.

Peura claims that Osiander was wrong because the "essential righteousness" he taught was only that of Christ's divine nature, and not of the whole Christ in both natures. This amounts, according to Peura, to separating the natures of Christ and instrumentalizing the human nature. Such a limitation of the righteousness of Christ—and hence the righteousness of the Christian—is rejected by the Formula of Concord. There the obedience which Christ rendered *pro nobis*, according to both natures, is called the righteousness of faith. This view makes both natures of Christ, united in the one Person, simultaneously important and indispensable.

Yet Peura, like Tuomo Mannermaa, also attaches supreme importance to the believer's participation specifically in Christ's divine nature. At times, in an effort to establish a parallel between the incarnation of the Logos and the *unio cum Christo*, they assert that the believer, like Christ, has "two natures." According to this model, Christ constitutes the Christian's *divine* nature: there is no indication that his human nature is involved in any "essential" way in the Christian's justification and righteousness. Despite his criticism of Osiander for dividing the natures of Christ and attaching the righteousness of faith only to the divine nature, Peura winds up committing himself to the same separation, because when justification is understood as *theosis*, only Christ's divine nature is decisive.

Peura and Mannermaa do not identify Christ's righteousness *pro nobis* as the merit of his active and passive vicarious obedience, as the Formula does. Instead, they focus on the ontological union of God with Christ's human nature, as both the inauguration and the paradigm of the believer's union with God. In the case of justification, they are concerned especially with who Christ *is*, and much less so with what he has *done*. It is possible to read Mannermaa and Peura and their discussions of justification, and still be left to ask why Christ's passion and death are particularly important, not to say necessary, in the whole affair. They portray Christ's benefits and merit for us not in terms of *action* but of *being*. This puts them in much closer sympathy to the theology of Osiander than Peura would like to admit.

At the same time, while wanting to distance himself somewhat from Osiander, Peura (like Mannermaa) wants to retain Osiander's assertion that justification is not purely forensic, that is, not merely synonymous with absolution or forgiveness of sins, but "real" and ontological. He wants to make sure that when God calls the sinner righteous, it is a statement which is "really" and descriptively true. This of course was also one of Osiander's objections to forensic justification, and the reason he reacted so heatedly to what he considered to be putting a "legal fiction" in the mouth of God. But Luther understood that forensic justification is "as real as it gets," because it is grounded in God's own creative word which calls reality into being.

It is Peura's desire for a justification that is "really" and descriptively true that moves him to shift attention away from Osiander's identification of justification with God's "essential righteousness" and turns instead to the questions of *what* that righteousness is and *how* the Christian comes to participate in it.[85] While he says that the Formula of Concord tries to "legitimize" imputative (forensic) justification, Peura in fact undertakes the task of legitimizing a notion of "essential righteousness" imparted through *theosis*. This implies, if not a complete rehabilitation of Osiander, then at least the attempt to salvage key elements of his system which has previously been rejected by the Lutheranism of the Formula of Concord. The difficulty for Peura and the Finnish school is that the elements of Osiander's theology most congenial to their program of *theosis* were explicitly condemned by the Formula.

LUTHER AND LUTHERAN THEOLOGY TODAY

Peura's concerns, like Mannermaa's, are not simply historical but relate directly to contemporary ecumenical interests. In other words, Peura is urging a re-reading of Luther's theology in such a way that it opens new possibilities for *rapprochement* between Lutherans and other confessions, especially Roman Catholics and Orthodox.

> As we have noted, it is possible in Luther's theology to connect logically the forensic and the effective aspects of justification on the basis of the ideas of the *unio cum Christo* and the *inhabitatio Christi*. When these ideas receive attention, Lutherans can assert in ecumenical conversation with Catholics—without losing what is specific to the reformation—that the Christian is made righteous and comes to share in the divine nature. It is perhaps not altogether unimportant that this can be expressed on the basis of the genuine, authentic Lutheran tradition.[86]

85. Peura, "*Gott und Mensch in der Unio*," 35.
86. Peura, "*Christus als Gunst und Gabe*," 361.

That Peura regards Luther's writings up to 1519 as examples of "the genuine, authentic Lutheran tradition," in preference over the Formula of Concord, reveals his somewhat tendentious definition of that tradition. What Peura seeks is a Lutheranism in which the distinctions made by the Formula are not normative, in which questions once answered may be reopened.

> Although the Lutheran understanding of effective righteousness is not identical with the Catholic doctrine of *fides charitate formata*, it is nevertheless more promising to aim at ecumenical consensus with Catholic theology on the basis of Luther's seminal ideas. It is our task as Lutheran theologians to set these ideas of the reformer in the foreground of the ecumenical dialogue. Otherwise essential aspects of our own tradition are forgotten, and at the same time we ourselves are driven into such a narrowness from which it becomes difficult to find a possible way to agreement with representatives of other churches in the truths of faith.[87]

Peura's depiction of the proper task of Lutheran theologians ought not to go unchallenged, since the task of a theologian is not to champion the views of Luther or anyone else, but to explicate and enunciate the gospel in all its articles. This is a task of confession, of intellect in service to faith and in pursuit of truth. The path of confession can divide as well as unite, since it makes differences clearer and more distinct. The task of a theologian may drive him to a sharper focus—to a kind of narrowness, if you will—and it ought to be the narrow precision of accuracy and definition of which an open mind is capable. It need not be the narrowness of sectarian exclusiveness Peura apparently fears. The narrowness of precision will be our object in the following chapters, as we first consider the historical matrix of the Finnish school's re-reading of Luther, and then move on to consider some of the implications of the anthropology of *theosis*.

---

87. Ibid., 362.

3

Theosis in Luther's Theology?

A Historical Assessment

THE ARGUMENTS AND CONCLUSIONS of the Mannermaa school outlined in the preceding chapters need closer critical attention and
analysis, and this needs to be approached from several directions. In
this chapter our concern will be historical. Of course, the Mannermaa
school's re-reading of Luther does not arise in the first place out of purely
historical concerns, but rather in the context of their ecumenical dia-
logues, especially with the churches of the Orthodox tradition. This fact
is important for an understanding of their program of research, since the
reader must keep in mind that Mannermaa, Peura, and their colleagues
approach Luther consciously in search of what may be called, without being tendentious, "ecumenical resources." That is to say, they are deliberately
looking for elements in the reformer's theology that can serve as points of
contact and possible convergence in the dialogue with Orthodox theology. This is not necessarily a criticism; any theology which is not merely
sectarian will offer such points of contact to initiate discussion with other
traditions, and these "points of contact" are not limited to antitheses and
anathemas. But it is important that the points of contact be genuine and
real, and not merely superficial similarities. In the case of the Mannermaa
school's Luther studies, a consequence of their particular ecumenical
concerns seems to be that they have been too ready to identify some of
the reformer's ideas and vocabulary with concepts and categories from
the Orthodox tradition. As even an ally of the *theosis* school's ecumenical
agenda has pointed out, there is a real danger of simply "translating" ideas
from one tradition to another.[1] The theologians of Mannermaa's school

---

1. Hinlicky, "Theological Anthropology," 55ff.

run into precisely this danger when they neglect the actual historical context out of which the Luther material they cite arose.

It was earlier remarked in the discussion of Tuomo Mannermaa's theological program (chapter 1) that Mannermaa's interpretation of Luther's theology depends on two kinds of continuity. The first is continuity between the ancient church fathers, especially those of the East, and the theology of Luther. The second is continuity between certain early expressions and formulations of Luther and the later development of his thought. Both of these assertions of continuity are subject to historical investigation. It is the argument of this chapter that both are simply inadequate as means to understanding Luther's theology in its historical context. Our examination of the studies of Mannermaa and Peura raise concerns regarding their historical approach and method, concerns which should inspire caution regarding their conclusions. After considering these fundamental historical questions in this chapter, the following two chapters will concentrate on the systematic theological implications of the *theosis* theme, as it impacts the interrelated doctrines of anthropology and Christology.

The first point of historical concern has to do with the inattention of the Finnish scholars to the antecedents and sources that influenced Luther's thought, especially in his earliest work. That is to say, they at times read Luther's early writings without meaningful reference to the historical context in which they were written. This same innocence of historical rigor further leads them to assert connections between Luther's thought and the theology of the eastern fathers, for instance, that are simply not supported by the evidence. Questions of the sources and influences of Luther's theology can be extremely helpful for an accurate understanding of his thought, but such questions are not answered by assuming or asserting Luther's reliance on the early Greek fathers. That kind of direct connection would be, no doubt, useful for the ecumenical agenda that underlies much of the Mannermaa school's work, but the facts turn out to be more interesting and more complex. Our first task in this chapter will be a critical examination of Luther's alleged Eastern sources, and that needs to be followed by an attempt to trace the actual historical antecedents of the expressions and themes in Luther's writings which have captured the interest of scholars such as Mannermaa and Peura.

Secondly, and more importantly, the Finnish theologians frequently ignore or minimize crucial developments in Luther's theology over the course of his career. In other words, Mannermaa and his school assume a profound and important continuity within Luther's theology from the beginning of his career to the end. There is little appreciation in their studies of the most profound turning points in Luther's theology, and little engagement with the whole scholarly debate about the shape and significance of the reformer's theological development. In short, their approach is practically a-historical: both the 1514 Christmas sermon and the 1535 Galatians Commentary are adduced to support their claims, and both works are regarded as (or simply assumed to be) equally typical of Luther's theology. Of course, if it were actually true that Luther's understanding of justification remained essentially the same in those two works, it would be a fact of enormous historical and theological importance, and a convincing proof of such a thesis would revolutionize Luther studies. But Mannermaa and his colleagues do not provide us with any such proof. The historical concern with how Luther's theology developed, or with the various influences and insights that shaped it, or at what point his distinctive and genuinely evangelical grasp of the *iustitia Dei* comes to dominate his theology—all this is conspicuous in the Finnish studies by its absence. This is a very broad area of study in itself, and it will not be possible to provide a comprehensive review of the research in the scope of this chapter. We will have to confine ourselves to an assessment of some of the specific claims made by the Mannermaa school with regard to the theological continuity of various Luther texts, a process which will lead us to analyze the theme of deification in Luther in the light of his theological development. The results of this survey will provide at least an outline of Luther's mature, evangelical anthropology, in contrast to that proposed by the Mannermaa school.

LUTHER'S EARLY THEOLOGY: SOURCES AND INFLUENCES

In Search of a Point of Intersection

The goal of Mannermaa's study "*In ipsa fide Christus adest*," is to make the case for what he calls "the point of intersection between Lutheran and Orthodox theology." Mannermaa believes he has identified this "point of intersection" in Luther's doctrine of the believer's union with Christ, which Mannermaa equates with the "righteousness of faith." Mannermaa's central point is that Luther's concept of *unio* has much in common with the Orthodox doctrine of deification in Christ. This supposed intersection rests on the first of the continuities mentioned above, the convergence of Luther's theology with certain elements of the patristic notion of *theosis*. Here Mannermaa indicates that he is not the first to focus on the connection between justification and deification. In particular, he mentions that Regin Prenter had already alluded to the similarity between Luther's doctrine of justification and the orthodox teaching of *theopoiesis*. He also refers to the work of Georg Kretschmar as one who previously noted Luther's use of deification language.[2] On the other hand, according to Risto Saarinen (who laid the framework for this element of the Finnish school's program), scholars in the school of Karl Holl have been influenced by Lotze's Neo-Kantian metaphysics, which restricts the "union" between God and believers to a harmony of wills, and understands God's "presence" in the believer only in terms of divine effects rather than divine being. Operating within such a metaphysical framework, Luther scholars since the last century have tended to emphasize the exclusively forensic understanding of justification in Luther's theology. In Mannermaa's view, this "neo-Kantian" reading of Luther's theology which arose in the nineteenth century is somehow congruent[3] with the development which characterized Lutheranism, at least as it was played out in the generation following Luther's death. Thus the forensic nature of justification is emphasized especially in the Formula of Concord, along with the careful distinction (not separation) between such justification and the believer's union with Christ.[4]

Mannermaa focuses attention first of all on Luther's insights into the connection between Christology and the theology of faith. This connec-

2. Mannermaa, *Der im Glauben gegenwärtige Christus*, 18. Mannermaa refers to Kretschmar, "*Kreuz und Auferstehung.*" It is significant to note that Kretschmar, like Mannermaa, approaches his study of Luther specifically for purposes of ecumenical discussions with the Russian Orthodox Church.

3. It would be plausible, perhaps, to argue that these ideas are congruent or similar, but surely they are not identical. Mannermaa and the other Finnish scholars do not, in fact, distinguish between what they call "Melanchthonian" doctrine of forensic justification that triumphed in the Formula of Concord and the "Lotzean" influence, based on Kant's metaphysics, on which they blame the "ethicized" direction of Luther research for the last century. Of course, it may be true that Holl and the whole Luther Renaissance fall under the long shadow of Lotze: but what about the Formula of Concord? If there is no significant difference in this point between Melanchthon and Lotze, between the Formula and the Luther Renaissance, that would be a startling fact. And if there are significant differences, why do they not seem to matter for the Finns?

4. FC SD III.54 (*BSLK*, 932f).

tion was also a prominent feature of the theology of the ancient church fathers. Mannermaa points out that Holl, Hirsch, and Vogelsang identified the connection between Christology and faith, although their primary interest was not the patristic roots of these ideas.[5] Wilhelm Maurer and the Finnish scholar Lauri Haikola are cited as some who have specifically explored the connections of Luther with the theology of the early church fathers.[6] Mannermaa particularly takes Maurer's work as a starting point for his own work: he identifies the foundation of Luther's theology as the Christological thinking of the early church.[7] The continuity of Luther's theology with the whole catholic tradition (and particularly with patristic theology) is certainly a subject that begs further study. Indeed, such patristic connections may even prove to be decisive for the task of interpreting Luther in an ecumenical context.[8] There is a sense in which the ancient church fathers offer "neutral ground" on which to engage in theological conversations without immediately resorting to the mutual polemics of the more recent past. Since Mannermaa and the Finnish theologians have approached their Luther studies, at least initially, in the setting of ecumenical dialogue with the Orthodox churches, patristic elements in Luther's theology become highly significant for them.

The Question of Luther's Acquaintance with the Fathers

From the above it becomes clear that an important assumption for Mannermaa's Luther studies is that Luther knew and used the works of the ancient fathers, and adopted certain theological themes from their writings. To be specific, Mannermaa gives the impression that Luther's Christology and soteriology were shaped under the more or less direct influence of Irenaeus and Athanasius. This premise is open to serious debate. Of course, Mannermaa qualifies his assertion somewhat when he says:

5. Mannermaa, *Der im Glauben gegenwärtige Christus*, 18–19.

6. Ibid., 17–19.

7. Ibid., 22.

8. Witness the considerable interest and enthusiasm surrounding the publication of a new commentary series drawing precisely on the tradition of the ancient fathers: the Ancient Christian Commentary on Scripture, from InterVarsity Press. It is significant that the impetus for this project, so similar in some ways to the medieval *Glossa ordinaria*, comes largely from evangelical protestant theologians. They, perhaps more than their Roman Catholic brethren, feel a sense of historical rootlessness.

Despite the fact that Luther's theology contains his own concept of deification, one should nevertheless be careful not to simply equate this with the patristic, Orthodox doctrine of deification. This study ["*In ipsa fide Christus adest*," in *Der im Glauben gegenwärtige Christus*], according to its purpose, has merely been able to conclude that Luther's theology contains a concept analogous to the Orthodox doctrine of *theopoiesis*, a concept that is provocative for the doctrine of justification and for the reformer's whole theology.[9]

In some other contexts Mannermaa is not as careful. His pioneering essay, "Theosis as a Subject of Finnish Luther Research,"[10] was one of the first products of the Finnish school to appear in English, and lays out the program for the Finnish school. In this essay he describes what he regards as "the core of the patristic doctrine" (42) with brief citations from Irenaeus and Athanasius (cf. above, in chapter 1). He then states that Luther's early Christmas sermon presents the reformer's own understanding of deification (*Vergöttlichung*) "with the help of the formulations of Athanasius and Irenaeus" (43). That is to say, Mannermaa not only claims to detect some similar ideas in Luther's theology and in the early fathers, but also asserts that Luther even makes use of formulations which he borrows from the fathers. The continuity he sees between Luther's idea of *unio* and the *theosis* doctrine of the early church fathers, and especially with those of the East, is an important element in the Finnish theological program. Mannermaa's case for that continuity depends on some kind of direct dependence of Luther on the ancient fathers.

As a matter of fact, the question of Luther's acquaintance with and use of the ancient fathers, and especially the Greek patristic tradition, is probably much more complicated than Mannermaa assumes. The resurgent interest in the ancient church fathers was certainly an important part of the intellectual climate at the beginning of the Reformation. This revival of patristic studies, as much a feature of humanism as it was a theological reaction against scholasticism, included some attention to the Greek fathers such as Origen, but most of the attention was focused on Ambrose,

---

9. Mannermaa, *Der im Glauben gegenwärtige Christus*, 93. Reinhard Flogaus has carefully documented the very substantial differences between *theosis* as it is conceived by the Finnish school and the doctrine in the theology of Orthodoxy in *Theosis bei Palamas und Luther.*

10. In *Pro Ecclesia*, Vol. IV, No. 1, 37–48.

Jerome, Augustine, and the like.[11] As Wolfgang Bienert points out, "Only seldom does Luther refer to the Greek fathers. Apparently, he rarely encountered them, and when he did it was only in Latin translation."[12] The ancient church father *par excellence*, whom Luther (as all other theologians of the West) knew best and favored most, was Augustine. But Bienert finds no evidence that he was directly familiar with the writings of eastern fathers such as Irenaeus, with whom Mannermaa and the Finnish school would connect his thought.

Other scholars have also studied and documented with some precision this crucial point of Luther's use of and attitude toward the church fathers. Two studies by Bernhard Lohse are particularly helpful here. In "Luther and the Common Christian Heritage," Lohse briefly describes the theological traditions which exerted a demonstrable influence on Luther, especially in his early years. He identifies six: the Ockhamist tradition (mediated especially through Gabriel Biel), Augustine, von Staupitz, the German mystics, Humanism, and Bernard of Clairvaux.[13] Some of these, such as the Nominalism of Ockham and Biel or the monastic tradition of Bernard, were simply part of Luther's formation as a student in Erfurt and as an Augustinian monk. With regard to others, notably Augustine and the German mysticism of the *Theologia Deutsch*, Luther deliberately devoted serious and independent study. But what must be noted from Lohse's work is the fact that Luther was firmly rooted in the theological tradition of the western church. Eastern Greek fathers such as Irenaeus or the Cappadocians simply did not play a significant role in the formation of his thought. The Roman Catholic scholar Peter Manns, who is sympathetic to the approach of the Finnish school, also studies Luther's roots in the church fathers. He argues that, rather than asserting that Luther somehow reclaimed the pristine theology of the early (eastern) church, it may be more appropriate to speak of Luther's return to the "monastic" theology of the later western fathers, especially that of Bernard. Nevertheless, Manns agrees that Luther's theological "discovery" involved a return to something in the western tradition that had been obscured

---

11. Leif Grane provides an interesting sketch of the function of patristic study and patristic argument in the period up to 1520. Grane, "Some Remarks on the Church Fathers."

12. Bienert, "Patristic Background," 265.

13. Lohse, "Luther and the Common Christian Heritage," 15.

through scholasticism.[14] Thus Manns confirms the idea, sketched also by Lohse and Bienert, that Luther stood firmly in the western church, and was not acquainted with (let alone dependent on) eastern fathers such as Irenaeus in more than a very limited way, if at all.

A second study by Lohse concentrates on Luther's attitude toward Athanasius. Here again one of Lohse's contributions is to illustrate how limited was the reformer's direct knowledge of the theology of the Alexandrian champion of Nicene orthodoxy.[15] Luther apparently first became acquainted with Athanasius through a late fifth-century dialogue written by Vigilius of Thapsus (or perhaps only an excerpt of that work dating from the Carolingian period), as well as through the work of Hilary of Poitiers. Lohse summarizes:

> ... [O]ne must say that Luther hardly had any first-hand knowl-
> edge about Athanasius. Athanasius is an authority for Luther as
> a champion of the orthodox trinitarian doctrine; but the exact
> contours of Athanasius' theology would not have been known to
> Luther.[16]

Lohse makes the point that Luther was always concerned to defend the fundamental articles of faith, specifically the doctrines of the Trinity and of Christology. It was in the context of his interest in these doctrines that Luther turned to Athanasius as a model. The Alexandrian bishop was for Luther the archetype of the true Christian bishop as a defender of the orthodox faith. The defense of orthodox trinitarian dogma was specifi-cally an issue when Bugenhagen published an edition of works attributed to Athanasius in 1532, for which Luther penned the preface. The occasion for such an edition was the teaching of the anti-trinitarian Campanus, who was active in Braunschweig in late 1531.[17]

Lohse's study of Luther's relationship to Athanasius helps us evalu-ate Mannermaa's assertion of continuity between Luther and Athanasius regarding the concept of *theosis*. Lohse does so partly by highlighting

14. Manns, "*Zum Gespräch*."

15. Lohse, "Luther und Athanasius."

16. Ibid., 101.

17. Ibid., 100.WA ref? Lohse shows how Luther's esteem for Athanasius comes to the fore when he fought against the *Schwärmer*, many of whom were anti-trinitarian. Luther's initial struggles against the scholastic theology of Rome did not involve disagreements about the fundamental articles of Nicene orthodoxy, and thus did not occasion a specific appeal to Athanasius.

those aspects of Athanasius' life and work which were most important to Luther, but more importantly by pointing out the limits of Luther's first-hand acquaintance with Athanasius' writings. As Lohse states,

> Luther did not study the writings of Athanasius thoroughly. Luther did not even have an exact knowledge of Athanasius' theology. What impressed him about Athanasius were his orthodox doctrine of God and his christology, as well as his unrelenting struggle against Arius."[18]

In his conclusion to this same study, Lohse himself notes how such a study of what Luther actually knew and said about Athanasius should temper enthusiasm for the program of the Finnish school:

> Within these limits, it seems, one would have to view also the conception of deification which has been strongly emphasized by Finnish research. While a more detailed discussion is not possible here, let it be said that there is certainly a "*theosis*" idea in Luther, but that it can hardly called the center of Luther's reformation theology. Nevertheless, this "*theosis*" idea is important to the extent that it can correct a purely ethical conception of the doctrine of justification."[19]

Bienert also echoes the same point about the limits of Luther's direct knowledge of Athanasius' writings. He says, "Luther knew only a few of the authentic writings of Athanasius, and even these only in Latin translation."[20] The reason for this is that no Greek edition of Athanasius' works existed before the beginning of the seventeenth century, and the earlier Latin collections did not distinguish between what was authentic and inauthentic. Luther's knowledge of Athanasius was thus incomplete at best, and perhaps unreliable in detail. This does not by any means imply that Luther was not a good scholar, within the limitations of his age, but it does imply that a degree of historical skepticism is appropriate when Mannermaa and the Finnish school assert connections between Luther's theology and that of the Greek fathers.

One specific instance illustrates well why caution is needed, and is of particular interest in evaluating the connection that Mannermaa attempts to make between the patristic doctrine of *theosis* and Luther's

18. Ibid., 114.

19. Ibid., 114f.

20. Bienert, "Patristic Background," 267.

pivotal insight into justification. Luther was apparently unfamiliar with precisely that work of Athanasius to which Mannermaa refers. According to Bienert, "Luther did not know the foundational writing of Athanasius (*De incarnatione Verbi*) and . . . he also knew other writings of the Alexandrian only through secondary translations."[21] Nevertheless, Luther revered Athanasius because of his close association with the defense of Nicene orthodoxy against the Arians. His remarks frequently express "a particular respect for the defender of the ancient church's doctrine of the Trinity, even if they are not based on knowledge of the original writings of Athanasius."[22]

The point of this example is certainly not to belittle Luther's competence as a scholar. Indeed, as Lohse puts it, "in the sixteenth century there was hardly any other theologian who was more acquainted with the Christian past than Luther."[23] Rather, the point of this example of Athanasius is that one cannot conclude, from patristic references or even occasional citations in Luther's writings, that the reformer was thoroughly acquainted with the writings of a particular church father. One must not suppose that Luther as a scholar and theologian had access to complete and reliable collections of patristic texts. An average theological library of today, or even a pastor's private bookshelf, may easily contain a better supply of full and reliable texts of the eastern fathers than a European university in the late Middle Ages. As we have seen, it is by no means clear that Luther was acquainted first-hand with the great theologians of the East, at least not in any detail. His knowledge of their work was much more likely to have been acquired somewhat piecemeal, as transmitted through the medieval *florilegia* which were available to monks and theologians of his time. Obviously Luther knew and used the church fathers, but he turned most often and most naturally to the fathers of the Western church: Augustine, Bernard, and the German mystics. To a very large extent, he received their theology "filtered" through medieval writers and secondary sources. The standard theological texts of the time such as Peter Lombard's *Sentences* or the *Glossa ordinaria* set many patristic quotations in a systematized context for Luther and his contemporaries, rather than providing them with complete works. In the face of these facts, it is im-

21. Ibid., 270.
22. Ibid., 268.
23. Lohse, "Luther and the Common Christian Heritage," 17.

plausible to assume, as Mannermaa does, a direct or facile connection between the patristic theological tradition that shaped Orthodoxy and the writings of a German Augustinian monk who pitted himself against scholasticism in the early sixteenth century. This improbability is reinforced by the fact that there is another explanation readily at hand for the appearance of deification as a motif in Luther's early writings.

In other words, it is probably a mistake to account for Luther's deification language, as Mannermaa does, by assuming that Luther relied directly on the patristic literature. Granting (as Lohse, for example, does in a passage cited above) that there is a "*theosis* theme" in some of Luther's writings, the source of such language and its place in Luther's theology need to be evaluated differently. One could, for example, conclude that the notion of deification in Luther had some entirely different source, or that the expressions were in some way an original and independent development in Luther's theology. In either case, the connection and thematic unity which Mannermaa supposes between Luther and such fathers as Athanasius and Irenaeus is no longer quite as clear as he would like us to believe. What we know of the sources of Luther's theology leads us to conclude that the language of *Vergottung* would have appeared in his vocabulary quite independently of any alleged dependence on the Greek patristic tradition.

Luther and the Mystics

Mannermaa and his school have identified a theme in some of Luther's writings which revolves around the concept of deification (German "*vergotten*," "*vergöttern*," or similar terms), and they have attempted to interpret it in relation to the ancient eastern fathers. A different explanation is both more natural and more adequately documented. This is the demonstrable interest shown by Luther in late medieval German mysticism and the influence on his thought by such figures as Johannes Tauler and the author of the *Theologia Deutsch*.[24] We have already noted that Lohse identified the German mystics as a formative theological influence on the young Luther, and one that attracted his interest and deliberate study.[25] We now consider this in more detail.

24. *Theologia Deutsch*.
25. Lohse, "Luther and the Common Christian Heritage," 15.

Luther became acquainted with the sermons of the late medieval German Dominican preacher and mystic Johannes Tauler[26] (ca. 1300–1361) quite early in his career, having purchased a copy of the 1508 edition of Tauler's works. Tauler's thoughts on patience and suffering seem to have influenced Luther's own lectures on Romans (1515–1516), at least to judge from Luther's notes,[27] and Tauler probably also lay behind Luther's distinction between the "inward" and "outward" life of the Christian.[28] When Luther came across the anonymous work which came to be called the *Theologia Deutsch* (hereafter *Theologia Deutsch*) in 1516, he was so impressed with its simple wisdom that he published it with a brief foreword under the title "A Spiritually Noble Little Book." This seems to have been Luther's first publication, appearing in December 1516. From his own notes in the margins of his copy of this book, we know that Luther highlighted the description of *"ein vergotter mensch,"*[29] but there is little indication what Luther understood the phrase to mean at the time. Luther also noted the similarities between this book and the theology and language he had encountered in Tauler. "Recently this little book was found without title or name. But to the best of our judgment the material is almost the same as that of the enlightened Doctor Tauler."[30] His enthusiasm for this example of "pure, solid, ancient" theology in German prompted Luther to send a copy of the *Theologia Deutsch* to his friend Spalatin, with a letter warmly recommending the anonymous book itself as well as Tauler's sermons.[31] A second, more complete edition was then printed in 1518, with a longer introduction. By that time Luther was embroiled in the controversy about indulgences, and appealed to the *Theologia Deutsch* as proof that the evangelical insights he had begun to defend were not new or original to him, but had ancient roots. He also delighted in its vernacular simplicity, so unlike the technical language of the scholastics.

26. Tauler, *Predigten*. Selected sermons available in Tauler, *Sermons*.

27. WA 56:378. AE 25:368. Cf. also Luther's comments on Romans 8:26, compared with his marginal notes in his copy of Tauler, WA 9:102.17–27.

28. WA 56:229. AE 25:213.

29. WA 59.18.30. (Luther's marginalia to the *Theologia Deutsch*, ca. 1520). The passage on which he is commenting is *Theologia Deutsch*, 130, cap. 41.

30. WA 1:153. *"dan dißmall ist das buchleyn an titell unnd namen funden. Aber nach müglichem gedencken zu schetzen ist die matery faßt nach der art des erleuchten doctors Tauleri."*

31. WABr 1:79.58–64. AE 48:35f.

"I thank God that I hear and find my God in the German tongue," writes Luther, "whereas I, and they with me, previously did not find him either in the Latin, the Greek, or the Hebrew tongue."[32] The same year (1518), Tauler surfaces again in Luther's *Explanation of the Ninety-Five Theses*, in connection with the punishments suffered by the soul in this life.[33] Luther later (1521) cites the mystic again as a source who speaks about purgatory, and Tauler's authority seems to persuade Luther to accept purgatory in spite of finding no firm proof in Scripture.[34] Luther's interest in Tauler may have dwindled later in his life, but it did not disappear altogether. As late as 1544, in his famous lectures on Genesis, Luther returns to a quotation from Tauler in reference to the theology of the cross. The Christian endures suffering patiently, trusting in God's promise despite every kind of cross, affliction, and misfortune. Such patient endurance is rejected by the ungodly, but it is nevertheless God's way of working and must not be despised. As Tauler puts it, "Man should know that he has done great damage if he does not wait for God's work." True, Luther qualifies his citation of Tauler here by observing that "he does not speak in terms of Holy Scripture but employs a strange and foreign way of speaking."[35] But it is clear that, to the very end of his life, Luther regarded Tauler as a legitimate voice of the gospel and one of his spiritual predecessors.

Franz Posset has shown that the mystical tradition of Tauler and the *Theologia Deutsch* traces its roots back to Bernard and Augustine, and thus belongs to the western tradition rather than being dependent in any direct way on the Greek fathers.[36] Luther was unquestionably familiar with these two theologians in Latin, but his encounter with the notion of the *"vergottet"* human nature was probably mediated through Tauler and the *Theologia Deutsch*.[37] This does not necessarily mean that Luther simply adopted the whole mystical framework which Tauler and the *Theologia Deutsch* attributed to (Pseudo-)Dionysius. In fact, Posset points out that Luther appropriated the *"vergotten"* vocabulary while explicitly rejecting

---

32. WA 1:379.8–10; cf. AE 31:76.

33. WA 1:557.25–32. AE 31:128f.; cf. WA 1:586.18f. AE 31:178.

34. WA 7:450.16–18; cf. AE 32: 95.

35. AE 7:133. WA 44:397.13f. *"Extat vox Tauleri, quanquam non loquitur in terminis scripturae sanctae, sed alieno et peregrino sermone utitur…"*

36. Posset, "'Deification,'" 105–7.

37. Ibid., 107f.

the Pseudo-Dionysian background in Tauler.[38] The appeal for Luther was the way in which Tauler and the *Theologia Deutsch* emphasized the passive reception of God's transforming grace, and the rejection of human efforts to attain a higher spiritual state or salvation by human activity. Deification in the tradition of Tauler was passively worked upon the human being through the activity of the Holy Spirit. Posset suggests that these medieval German mystics were "the most likely sources for Luther's concept of 'being deified.'"[39] Significantly, in precisely the early Christmas sermon where Mannermaa claims to hear echoes of Athanasius or Irenaeus, Posset identifies the formulation as more likely deriving from Augustine, or even an echo of the *Theologia Deutsch*.[40] What is more, such a connection by no means ascribes to Luther the Neoplatonic ideas of Pseudo-Dionysius, which undoubtedly had influenced Tauler and the *Theologia Deutsch*. As Posset puts it, Luther seems to have read Tauler "in such a way that he begins to filter Dionysius out and take Augustine in."[41] The process may have been gradual, since by his own account Luther was initially attracted to Dionysian mysticism, as expressed especially in the *Dictata*,[42] but later rejected it as harmful and destructive to true faith, particularly because of its platonizing tendencies.[43]

What finally separated Luther from the Dionysian elements (even in authors he generally approved and used) was his growing emphasis on the centrality of faith, and on God's word of promise as the object of faith.[44] Posset's conclusions largely agree with those of Karl-Heinz zur Mühlen, who differentiates between Dionysian, Latin, German, and "exegetical" streams of medieval mysticism, each with varying influences on

38. Ibid., 110f.

39. Ibid., 124.

40. Ibid., 113. Cf. *Theologia Deutsch*, 74: "*Da vmmbe nam got menschlich natur ader menschheit an sich vnd wart vormenscht vnd der mensch wart vorgotet.*" This would assume, however, that Luther became familiar with the *Theologia Deutsch* some two years before it was printed in December of 1516. Though this is not impossible, there is no other documentation to support such a hypothesis.

41. Posset, "'Deification,'" 112.

42. WA 3:3728ff, 124.32ff. Cf. Karl-Heinz zur Mühlen, "Mystik des Wortes: über die Bedeutung mystischen Denkens für Luthers Lehre von der Rechtfertigung des Sünders," Zeitwende 52 (1981)" 209ff.

43. WA 30I:389.18—390.5; cf. WA 6:562.8–10.

44. Cf. WA 6:516.30–32.

Luther's own theology.[45] According to zur Mühlen, the German mysticism of Tauler and the *Theologia Deutsch* was helpful to Luther in formulating his doctrine of the righteousness of God, by which man is justified and ultimately transcends himself. Luther, in his lectures on Romans, similarly taught that justification depends on an "alien righteousness" to which a person is directed outside of himself. But in contrast to Tauler, Luther describes this as happening not through the mystical "divine love" (*amor divinus*) but through faith. This concentration on faith Luther correlates not directly to Tauler's "inner word" but rather to the external, preached word.[46] Likewise, Luther's selective appropriation of the Latin mysticism, especially his occasional use of Bernard's "bridal mysticism" (*Brautmystik*), demonstrates a shift away from the "inner" to the "outer" word. "What bridal mysticism connects to the inner word as the Bridegroom of the soul, Luther connects to the external word, to the promise of the Bridegroom."[47] Thus, zur Mühlen argues, it is appropriate to talk about Luther developing a "mysticism of the word" (zur Mühlen's phrase), not with reference to an inner, uncreated word accessed by direct contemplative experience, but rather as a designation for the creative power of the external word of God's promise, through which God gives and bestows everything on the believer.[48] This, of course, is no longer "mysticism" as generally understood, but the term accents the way in which the external word in Luther's thought came to replace the inner illumination or direct experience of God in the mystical tradition.

Steven Ozment has also studied the relationship between the thought of Tauler (and Jean Gerson) and that of Luther, specifically in the area of their respective approaches to theological anthropology. He concludes that Luther learned from Tauler, especially from Tauler's theme of *resignatio* or passive obedience (being acted upon by God rather than acting). However, in his marginal comments on Tauler's sermons,[49] Luther parts

45. zur Mühlen, "*Mystik des Wortes*," 206–25.

46. Ibid., 222f.

47. Ibid.

48. Ibid., 224. In much of his analysis, zur Mühlen follows the earlier work of Erich Vogelsang, "*Luther und die Mystik*."

49. Ozment, following Johannes Ficker and A. V. Müller, dates these comments as roughly contemporary with Luther's *Dictata* and the lectures on Romans (i.e., perhaps in late 1515), which allows him to interpret those better known writings in the light of the Tauler notes and *vice versa*. This is related to Ozment's rather early dating of Luther's fundamental evangelical insight. Cf. *Homo Spiritualis*, 1 (note), and 215 (note).

company with the fourteenth-century preacher precisely on the point of anthropology as it relates to man's salvation. Tauler affirms a basically tripartite structure of the human person, of which the highest and noblest element is the human "*gemuete*" (or "*grunt der selen*"). He then relates the life of the "spiritual man" to this "*gemuete*" (the equivalent of Gerson's *synteresis*), which is an innate, interior, and ontological connection between man and God. For Luther, as evidenced by his notes, the focus for spiritual existence is not any interior, anthropological reference, but faith.[50] This orientation around faith is a radical departure from the mystical system of Tauler, even as it retains some formal parallels and occasionally uses similar vocabulary. When the *homo spiritualis* "depends upon faith" ("*nititur fide*"), the object of that faith is the antithesis of all anthropological reference, for it lies outside the human person. Thus Ozment identifies a fundamental shift in Luther's theological anthropology, away from that of the previous mystical tradition, a shift which creates "a chasm between his theological thought and that of Tauler and Gerson, which is quite incapable of being bridged."[51] Chasm there may be, but there is also a clear and well-documented connection between Luther and the mystical thinking of Tauler and Gerson, with whom he interacted. Heiko Oberman suggests that Luther's attitude toward medieval mysticism was part of a larger trend in the late Middle Ages which he labels "the democratization of mysticism," and that terminology borrowed from the mystics should not necessarily be read with full mystical-theological freight when such authors are cited. "What is retained of such an author as Bernard of Clairvaux or Hugo of St. Victor is often his piety, not his mysticism. . . . [T]he traditional mystical terminology is appropriated for the description of the Christian life of the average believer."[52] Something of this kind may also have operated in Luther's vocabulary of "*vergotten*." Oberman argues for a "non-ontological" reading of Luther's use of language usually associated with the mystics ("*excessus*," "*raptus*," etc.):

> Again, as we noted with *excessus*, *raptus* does not mean an ontological transformation but a transformation of *affectus* and *fiducia*,

---

50. WA 9:103.39–41. "*homo sensualis qui nititur sensu; rationalis qui nititur ratione; spiritualis qui nititur fide.*"

51. Ozment, *Homo Spiritualis*, 214.

52. Oberman, "*Simul Gemitus et Raptus*," 140.

of our love and trust. Hence we do not argue that Luther is a mystical theologian because of his use of these terms.[53]

Oberman, like Ozment, Vogelsang, and zur Mühlen, helps us account for both continuity and discontinuity between Luther and medieval mysticism.

What we have established here briefly (and certainly not exhaustively) is that Luther knew and used the late medieval German mystical tradition represented by Tauler and the *Theologia Deutsch*, without necessarily adopting all aspects of their mystical ideas. These seem to be the most probable sources for the "deification" concept and vocabulary in Luther's early theological development. Despite this rather obvious and well-established connection, theologians of the Finnish school have declined to pursue this direction in their studies. Tauler and the *Theologia Deutsch* are almost completely ignored in their work. Simo Peura, in his study of the anthropological aspect of Luther's early soteriology, mentions Tauler only in a brief footnote: "Although it would be important in itself, it is not our task here to establish to what extent Tauler's [sic] *Theologia Deutsch*, medieval monastic or scholastic theology influenced Luther's understanding of deification."[54] The probable cause of this neglect of the rather obvious connection with late medieval German mysticism on the part of the Finnish school lies in the ecumenical context and motivation of their studies. "Points of intersection" between Luther and the eastern fathers would clearly serve as important resources for theological dialogue with the Orthodox churches, in a way that elements of medieval German mysticism would not. But while the relationship of Luther to the German mystics, and especially his appropriation of their vocabulary of deification, may not directly further the ecumenical goals which underlie the Finnish school's *theosis* studies, a clearer understanding of that relationship is nevertheless fundamental for a genuinely historical understanding of Luther's early theology.

Before we shift our attention from the sources of Luther's early theology to his later development, we should note that if one accepts Tauler and the *Theologia Deutsch* as the most direct sources of Luther's early language of deification, a modified case could still be made for the "point of intersection" sought by Mannermaa and the Finns, or at least for an

---

53. Ibid., 150.

54. Peura, *Mehr als ein Mensch?*, 6, n. 20.

indirect but significant connection. It could be argued that the Orthodox conception of *theosis* ultimately inspired the German mystics whose writings influenced Luther, and that they formed his link with the eastern tradition. The probable connection here is the figure of Pseudo-Dionysius, the Neoplatonist writer whose sermons were both well-known and extremely influential on the whole mystical tradition in the West,[55] and who was mentioned by name both by Tauler and in the *Theologia Deutsch*. Of course, this avenue of argumentation is somewhat problematic for explaining the theme in Luther, since Luther himself was harshly critical of Dionysius. In order to build a case in support of that thesis, it would be necessary first to document the influence—or, at least, prove real common ground—between the Greek fathers and the German mystics, and then to ascertain that Luther meant the same thing as the mystics when he spoke of *Vergottung*. Neither of these has been attempted, let alone accomplished, by the Finnish school. Indeed, there is considerable doubt about the first, namely the connection between the Orthodox tradition and, say, Tauler. What is clear is that the theme of *theosis / deificatio / vergotten* in medieval western mysticism needs to be explored more fully.[56] Regarding the second step in the reasoning, that Luther not only appropriated vocabulary but also adopted the conceptual framework of Tauler and the *Theologia Deutsch*, some significant work has pointed to the conclusion that this was not, in fact, the case.[57]

LUTHER'S DEVELOPMENT

The last section examined historically the Finnish assumption of continuity between Luther's theology (in particular his concept of *theosis*) and the Greek patristic theology of Orthodoxy. In this section we turn our atten-

55. For the relationship between Luther and Pseudo-Dionysius, see Paul Rorem, "Martin Luther's Christocentric Critique of Pseudo-Dionysian Spirituality," *Lutheran Quarterly*, XI n.s., no. 3 (Autumn 1997), 291–307.

56. On this connection cf. three essays in the collection *The Church, Mysticism, Sanctification and the Natural in Luther's Thought* (Philadelphia: Fortress, 1967): Oberman, "*Simul Gemitus et Raptus: Luther und die Mystik,*" Hägglund, "Luther und die Mystik," and Iserloh, "*Luther und die Mystik.*"

57. Cf. Ozment, zur Mühlen, Posset, as above. Cf. the following essays in *The Church, Mysticism, Sanctification and the Natural in Luther's Thought* (Philadelphia: Fortress, 1967): Hägglund, "Luther und die Mystik," Iserloh, "*Luther und die Mystik,*" Oberman, "*Simul Gemitus et Raptus: Luther und die Mystik.*" Also Vogelsang, "*Luther und die Mystik.*"

tion to the other kind of continuity posited by the school of Mannermaa and Peura, namely the continuity of Luther's ideas throughout his career as a theologian. We shall approach this task in three stages. First, we shall examine a number of characteristic passages in which Luther uses the language of deification most explicitly, and attempt to understand these passages in their context. Second, we need to consider how Luther's use of *theosis* terminology relates to what scholars have suggested about the reformer's theological development. Our specific interest in this regard is Luther's so-called evangelical breakthrough. How did Luther's new grasp of the gospel alter and shape his earlier use of the terms associated with deification? Finally, we will identify what we consider to be the salient points of Luther's mature, evangelical anthropology, and set this in contrast to the proposals of the Finnish school.

Luther's Use of Vergotten / Deificare

There can be no argument about the fact that "deification" as a theme or concept does crop up in Luther's writings. The Finnish scholars, although not the first to take note of this element in the reformer's theological language, have drawn attention to a number of occurrences. Mannermaa and others of his school have argued that the theme plays a much more significant part in Luther's theology than has been generally supposed. As Reinhard Flogaus has pointed out, the actual body of texts in which Luther uses the specific terms of deification (German "*vergotten*" or Latin "*deificare*") is rather limited, though research about theme should not necessarily be limited to the exact terms.[58] What follows in this section is a survey of numerous passages from assorted works of Luther in which he employs various related verbal forms, in either German or Latin. The choice of passages is not meant to be exhaustive, but representative. In each case we will place the passage in the context of Luther's own theological development, and comment on the significance of his usage.

Several interesting passages from Luther's first lectures on the Psalms, the *Dictata*, reflect this theme of deification. The first applies this notion particularly to Christ himself:

> Christ is our psaltery and zither . . . psaltery because he is God incarnate and zither because he is deified man . . .[59]

58. Flogaus, *Theosis bei Palamas und Luther*, 37–38.
59. WA 3.319.35: "[*Chr est psalterium nostrum et cithara nostra . . .*] *Quare psalterium*

Such a Christological reference does not in itself lend any support to the Finnish theme of the deification of believers. Rather, this passage should be understood as an expression of Luther's orthodox Christology, in harmony with the ancient church, which includes his affirmation of the *communicatio idiomatum* in the unique person of Christ. Luther's rather frequent use of *deificatus* (or the German *vergottet*) as a predicate for Christ's human nature simply does not provide any support to the Finnish school's thesis that some element of *theosis* was central to Luther's doctrine of justification. It is rather an expression of the so-called *genus maiestaticum*, which is taught also in the Formula of Concord.[60]

Luther's gloss of Psalm 82:6 from his first lectures on the psalms offers his explanation of the divinity ascribed to believers in the Psalm, in which he points out that this applies not "naturally" but "*per adoptionem.*"

> I said, you are gods, because you are born of God through the Holy Spirit, not by nature. And you are all sons by adoption of the most high God the Father. But you others, unbelievers, just as one, Lucifer, the first of the original fallen angels, will fall into the eternal damnation of eternal death.[61]

This passage seems to have in view a transformation of human nature through re-birth or divine adoption. It is instructive to compare this gloss with a later comment from Luther about the same passage, this time dating from 1530. A very different perspective on Luther's conception of "deification" emerges.

> One might wonder why He calls such wicked people, whom He rebukes so harshly, "children of God," or "of the Highest," since it is the holy and believing people who are called children of God in Scripture. Answer: It is just as great a wonder that He calls these wicked people by His own name, gods; indeed, calling them gods is even more than calling them children. But it is all in the word: "I have said." As we have often said, the Word of God hallows and

---

ipse ex hoc, quia ipse est deus incarnatus, et cithara, quia est homo deificatus, ut sic dicamus ..." (scholae Ps. 56 (57), ca. 1513–1516).

60. FC SD VIII.67–70.

61. WA 3.619.19ff (re: Psalm 81).

Ego dixi ad vos qui estis boni: dii estis, quia ex Deo nati per spiritum sanctum, non per naturam: et filii per adoptionem excelsi altissimi Dei patris omnes. Vos alii autem increduli sicut unus, primus, lucifer, de principibus angelis apostatis cadetis in eternam damnationem morte eterna.

deifies everything to which it is applied. Therefore those estates that are appointed by God's Word are all holy, divine estates, even though the persons in them are not holy. Thus father, mother, son, daughter, master, mistress, servant, maid, preacher, pastor—all these are holy and divine positions in life, even though the persons in these positions may be knaves and rascals. So, because He here founds and orders the office of ruler, the rulers are rightly called "gods" and "children of God" for the sake of the divine office and the divine Word; and yet they are wicked knaves, as He here calls them.[62]

In this remarkable passage, Luther connects the notion of "deification" exclusively with the word of God, and not with the nature or "essence" of any person or thing. The "divine" status of persons or offices or anything else consists solely in the connection to the word. Here Luther construes the sense of "deify" in a very different way than the "real-ontic" union urged by the Finnish school. In a sense, Luther is more pragmatic, and more "real," since he has here become anchored to the concrete realities of human existence as creatures. In this mature, evangelical view, such human existence is properly connected to God—"deified"—precisely to the extent that it is concretely played out in the divinely ordered (divinely "spoken") sphere of very *human* activity: parents, children, masters, servants. The "divine" character of such people has nothing to do with overcoming or transcending who they are as human creatures, but depends directly on what God says. God's word blesses, sanctifies—even *deifies*—precisely in the midst of created human life.

---

62. AE 13:71. WA 31I.217.4–17

Das möcht einen wundern, warumb er solche böse leute, die er so hart schilt, dennoch Kinder Gottes odder des Höhesten heisst, weil Gottes kinder ynn der schrifft die heiligen, gleubigen leute heissen? Antwort. Es ist auch wol so gros wunder, das er solche böse leute mit seinem eigen namen Götter heisst. Ja es ist wol mehr, das er sie Götter heisst, denn das er sie kinder heisst. Es ligt aber alles ynn dem wort 'Ich had gesagt'. Denn wir nu offt gesagt, das Gottes wort heiliget und vergöttet alle ding, dazu es gesetzt wird. Darumb heissen solche stende, so mit Gottes wort gestifftet sind, alles heilige, Göttliche stende, ob gleich die personen nicht heilig sind, Als Vater, Mutter, Son, Tochter, Herr, Fraw, Knecht, Magd, Prediger, Pfarher etc sind alles heilige, Göttliche stende und möchten doch drinnen wol die personen buben und schelcke sein. Also weil Gott die Oberkeit hie mit seinem wort stifftet und fasset [= anordnet], heissen sie billich Götter und Gottes kinder umb des Göttlichen standes und Gottes worts willen und sind doch böse buben, wie er hie klagt und schilt.

Luther's *scholia* on Romans were mentioned above as reflecting a certain influence of Tauler's sermon's, particularly with reference to the distinction between the "inner" and "outer" man. A similar expression occurs in Luther's comments on Romans 7:18 ("I know that nothing good dwells in me, that is, in my flesh . . ."), again highlighting the contradictory realities that comprise human existence.

> Therefore we must note that the words "I want" and "I hate" refer
> to the spiritual man or to the spirit, but "I do" and "I work" refer
> to the carnal man or to the flesh. But because the same one com-
> plete man consists of flesh and spirit, therefore he attributes to the
> whole man both of these opposing qualities which come from the
> opposing parts of him. For in this way there comes about a com-
> munication of attributes, for one and the same man is spiritual and
> carnal, righteous and a sinner, good and evil. Just as the one and
> the same Person of Christ is both dead and alive, at the same time
> suffering and in a state of bliss, both working and at rest, etc., be-
> cause of the communication of His attributes, although neither of
> the natures possesses the properties of the other, but are absolutely
> different, as we all know.[63]

Luther does not use specific deification vocabulary in this passage, but speaks first of the human person as a union of contraries, and then cor-relates the dual nature of the Christian (carnal and spiritual) with the two natures in the person of Christ. It should be noted that this analogous reference to the "communication of attributes" in the human person is not the same as the framework proposed by Mannermaa, according to which Christ himself forms the "divine nature" of the Christian. Rather, in the Romans *scholia* just cited, Luther proposes a kind of *genus idiomaticum*, by which the attributes of both "parts" of man (i.e., his spirit and his flesh) are both predicated of the "one complete man" ("*unus homo totalis*").[64]

---

63. AE 25:332. WA 56.343.18–23.

Ideo Notandum, Quod hoc verbum 'Volo' et 'odio' ad spiritualem hominem seu spiri-tum, 'facio' autem et 'operor' ad carnalem seu ad carnem refertur. Sed quia ex carne et spiritu idem unus homo constat totalis, ideo toti homini tribuit vtraque contraria, que ex contrariis sui partibus veniunt. Sic enim fit communio Ideomatum, Quod idem homo est spiritualis et carnalis, Iustus et peccator, Bonus et malus. Sicut eadem persona Christi simul mortua et viua, simul passa et beata, simul operata et quieta etc. propter communionem Ideomatum, licet neutri naturarum alterius proprium conueniat, Sed contrariissime dissentit, vt notum est.

64. Here the contribution of Ozment is particularly relevant, since it makes a ma-jor difference in one's understanding of Luther at this point—as early as the Romans

In other words, the anthropology of the believer is "duplex," since it includes these two contraries in one single person. Unbelievers have no such complexity or contradiction in their persons.[65]

In a sermon on the festival of SS Peter and Paul (June 29) 1519, Luther preached on Matthew 16:13–19 ("Who do you say that I am?"). This was delivered at the castle in Leipzig, where Luther had traveled to take part in the debate with Eck. A passage from this sermon contains a striking image of the Christian as "more than man," a phrase which figures prominently in Simo Peura's work.

> Therefore Jerome well says concerning this Gospel that it should be noted how Christ asks his disciples what men are saying of him and then afterwards asks them what they say of him, just as if they were not men. For it is true that man helped by grace is more than a man; indeed, the grace of God gives him the form of God and deifies him, so that even Scripture calls him "God" and God's son. Thus a man must be extended beyond flesh and blood and become more than man, if he is to become good.[66]

Luther seems to have in mind such passages as Psalm 82:6 ("I said, 'you are "gods"; you are all sons of the Most High.'"). Whatever else is to be said about this passage from Luther's sermon,[67] it has to be noted that Luther is still operating with many of the categories and terminology he inherited from the medieval tradition; immediately after this passage, he tells the congregation to "do what lies in them" (echoing the Nominalist "*facere quod in se est*").

In 1521, while at the Wartburg, Luther took time out from his translation of the Bible to compose his response to Latomus. In one passage

---

lectures—whether the *homo spiritualis* should be understood as strictly dependent on faith, as in Luther's marginal notes to Tauler.

65. Cf. WA 56:343.23f.

66. AE 51:58. WA 2.247.37—248.2.

Drumb spricht wol sanct Hieronymus uner diß ewangelium, das zu merken sey, wie Christus seine jünger fragt, was die menschen von yhm sagen, und darnach, was sie von ym sagten, sam sie nit menschen weren. Dann war ist es, das der mensch mit gnaden beholfen mehr ist dann ein mensch, Ja die gnad gottis macht yn gotformig und vergottet yn, das yn auch die schrift go und gottis sun heist. Also mus de mensch uber fleisch und blut ausgezogen werden, soll er frum werden.

67. And it must be pointed out how unconvincing the claim is about Christ first asking what "men" say and then what the disciples say, implying that they are "more" than men!

WHO DO I SAY THAT YOU ARE?

he again makes use of the "*deus incarnatus—homo deificatus*" theme, and once again the referent is explicitly Christological. That is, with reference to the person of Christ it is possible to speak of "incarnate God" and "deified Man," in a way that is not appropriate when talking simply about God or man in general.

> He who wishes to discuss sin and grace, law and gospel, Christ and man, in a Christian way, necessarily discourses for the most part on nothing else than God and man in Christ; and in doing this one must pay the most careful attention to predicating both natures, with all their properties, of the whole Person, and yet take heed not to attribute to this what belongs exclusively to God or exclusively to man. For it is one thing to speak of the incarnate God, or of the deified man [*homine deificato*], and another to talk simply of God or of man.[68]

Here *homo deificatus* is a reference to Christ and the union of the divine and human natures in his person. As noted above (with reference to the passage from the *Dictata*, WA 3.319), the specifically Christological use of deification terminology does not support the Finnish assertion that *theosis* plays a central role in Luther's soteriology (or anthropology). In the context, Luther's argument against Latomus is in answer to the charge that Luther's doctrine makes "sin" no longer "sin," since sin does not condemn a person who is "in Christ." But, answers Luther, it makes all the difference in the world whether one is talking about sin *per se*, or sin *in Christo*, i.e., the effects of sin for a person who has faith in Christ. The difference has nothing to do with changing the nature of the thing (whether "sin" or "man") into something else, but rather depends on Christ's work as man's substitute. This shifts the referent for *deificatus* from the human person himself to a location external to him, namely Christ. Thus it does not describe a new quality of man at all, but rather states that the Christian's identity is, in fact, extrinsic to himself, located in Christ.

---

68. WA 8.126.23–28 (*Rationis Latomianae confutatio*, 1521).

Nam qui de peccato et gratia, de lege et Euangelio, de Christo et homine volet Christianiter disserere, oportet ferme non aliter quam de deo et homine in Christo disserere. Ubi cautissime observandum, ut utramque naturam de tota persona enunciet cum omnibus suis propriis, et tamen caveat, ne quod simpliciter deo aut simpliciter homini convenit, ei tribuat. Aliud enim est, de deo incarnato vel homine deificato loqui, et aliud de deo vel homine simpliciter.

In a sermon on Genesis 28 (Jacob's dream of the ladder), Luther interprets the text using the allegorical method he inherited from the medieval tradition.

> First the angels ascend, that is, the priests ought first to be good themselves, having been tested by many trials, enlightened in spirit. They should first be deified, and then become men again.[69]

This passage illustrates well the continuity between Luther's "deification" language and the western mystical tradition, in particular what zur Mühlen refers to as "exegetical mysticism." In the passage Luther depicts the movement up to union with God (which is "deification," "*ersthlich vergottet seyn*"), followed by descent to humanity again ("*darnach wiederumb menschen werden*"). As such it is very reminiscent of some of Johannes Tauler's sermons, in which he describes the movement of the soul upward into union with God, and then back again into the world. For Tauler the vehicle of such spiritual movement is prayer, in particular the "heavenly" prayer taught by the Lord himself. Tauler describes the movement induced in the soul by the Lord's Prayer:

> This true prayer . . . is a genuine ascent to God, a lifting of the spirit upward, so that God may in reality enter the purest, most inward, noblest part of the soul—its deepest ground—where alone there is undifferentiated unity. . . . [T]his state of the soul cannot be compared to what it has been before, for now it is granted to share in the divine life itself. . . . And from this height such men descend again into all the needs of Christendom . . . their charity embraces every man's need . . .[70]

This spiritual ascent in Tauler is closely echoed in Luther's phrase, "*sollen ersthlich vergottet seyn*," and the subsequent descent to address the needs of the fellow man parallels Luther's "*darnach wiederumb menschen werden*" in the passage just cited. This sermon of Luther seems to be a good example of how he appropriated the German mystical tradition of Tauler and others, especially in his earlier work. A few years later, a sermon on Ephesians 3:19 (". . . that you may be filled up to all the fullness of God")

---

69. WA 9.408.16f. "*Angeli primum ascendunt, idest Sacerdotes primum ipsi sint boni, experti multarum tentationem, illuminati in spiritu. Sollen ersthlich vergottet seyn, darnach wiederumb menschen werden.*" The sermon dates from 1519 or 1520.

70. Tauler, *Sermons*, 89–90.

led Luther to return both to the idea of deification and, incidentally, to the image of the ladder which he had used as late as 1520.

> Therefore the summary of this wish is that we should increase in faith, so that it becomes strong and powerful, and love becomes warm and sincere. And also that we be filled "with all the fullness," that is a Hebrew way of saying "filled in every way." He fills us and makes us full of God and showered with all gifts and grace, and filled with his Spirit, who encourages us, and enlightens us with his light, and lives his life in us. His blessedness makes us blessed, his love awakes love in us. In short, that everything he is and is able to do, be fully in us and work powerfully, so that we become completely deified, not piecemeal or merely having some piece of God, but all the fullness. Much has been written about how man should become deified. They have made ladders on which one is to climb up to heaven and many such things. But it is all purely piecemeal. But here the true and nearest way to advance is shown, so that you become full, full of God, so that you not lack anything, but have everything in one fell swoop ["auff eynen hauffen"], and everything you speak, think, do—in short, your whole life may be entirely divine.[71]

This passage seems to negate the very idea of "partial" deification, or of an oscillating movement into and out of union with God. Rather, Luther emphasizes here, all such talk is useless, since the gospel bestows the totality of God and his blessings to the believer, who becomes "completely deified" ("gantz vergottet") and "entirely divine" ("gar Gottisch"). It is not at all clear what sort of ontological freight such expressions can be made

71. WA 17I:438.12–28.

Also ist kurtz die summa dises wundschs, Das wir ym glawben zunemen sollen, auff das er starck und krefftig, die liebe hitzig und brunstig sey. Und wir so erfullet werden 'mit allerley Gottes fulle', das ist auff Ebreische weyse soviel geredt: das wir erfullet werden auff alle weise, damit er voll macht und voll Gotes werden uberschuttet mit allen gaben und gnade und erfullet mit seynem geyst, der uns mutig mache und mit seynem liecht erleucht und seyn leben ynn uns lebe, seyne selickeit uns selig mache, seyne liebe yn uns die liebe erwecke, Kurtz umb, das alles, was er ist und vermag, ynn uns vollig sey und krefftig wircke, das wir gantz vergottet werden, nicht eyn partecken odder allein etliche stuck Gottes habt, sondern alle fulle, Es ist viel davon geschrieben, wie der mensch soll vergottet werden, da haben sie leytern gemacht, daran man gen hymel steyge und viel solchs dings, es ist aber eytel partecken werck, hie ist aber der rechte und nehiste weg hynan zu komen angezeygt, das du voll voll Gottes werdest, das dirs an keynem stuck feyle, sondern alles auff eynen hauffen habist, das alles, was du redist, denckist, gehist, summa: deyn gantzes leben gar Gottisch sey.

to carry for Luther in the 1520s, since his purpose is not to define the structure of human existence but to express the totality of God's gift. This "total" aspect of salvation makes "ladder" images useless, since they imply both incremental progress and human effort toward the goal, both of which are what Luther calls "*eytel partecken werck*" and inconsistent with the totality of the righteousness of God.[72]

In a sermon on Matthew 3, Christ's baptism, from 1526, "*vergottet*" is again employed, this time as a term to express the "blessed exchange" between Christ and the believer.

> . . . and again with the same words He pours both Himself and Christ His dear Son over us and pours Himself into us and draws us into Himself, so that He becomes completely human and we become completely deified.[73]

Here again, man is not "*vergottet*" in a process of spiritual progress, but "*gantz und gar.*" And again, it is far from clear how much "ontology" one should read into the expression. The expression "become completely deified" is used as a synonymous parallel with the phrase "draws us into himself." Christ takes as his own what we are and gives us all that he is, not partially or fractionally but completely and comprehensively. The theme of the *commercium mirabile* should not be pressed to support a particular "real-ontic" version of metaphysics.

In fact, we can document that Luther's use of "*vergottet*" and related terminology moved further and further away from some kind of realist ontology of essential, mystical union. In another sermonic passage from 1530, "*vergottet*" is used to describe a servant who is completely certain whose servant he is, and who therefore gladly does his duty. That kind of certainty is Luther's picture of genuine faith, but can hardly be identified with some kind of ontological union. The Christian, as God's "*knecht,*" confidently knows and serves his Master. Such faith characteristically connects to the content of the First Commandment, as the source and heart

---

72. Posset suggests that Luther's target was the speculative system of someone like Birgitta of Sweden. ("'Deification,'" 121, esp. note 109) He may have had such writings in mind, but Luther's own earlier use and later rejection of the "ladder" image seems to indicate that something had changed in his thinking during the early 1520's.

73. WA 20.229.33. ". . . *und widderumb mit den selbigen worten beyde sich selbs und Christum seynen lieben son ausschuttet uber uns und sich ynn uns geust und uns ynn sich zeucht, das er gantz und gar vermenschet wird und wyr gantz und gar vergottet werden*" [1526].

of all other commandments. As surely as the servant's obedience flows from certainty about whose servant he is, so disobedience and disloyalty flow from uncertainty, which is the essence of unfaith. The confident, believing servant is "*vergottet*," while the uncertain, unbelieving servant is not "*vergottet*." Luther concludes, "Thus we see that all sin must flow from unbelief."[74] From the context it seems unlikely that "*vergottet*" here refers to any kind of "real-ontic" union between the servant and his master: rather it has to be understood as a synonym for "believing."

During Bugenhagen's absence from Wittenberg (from November 1530 to March 1532), Luther added to his other duties the burden of preaching twice a week in the city church. At the Saturday services he continued Bugenhagen's exposition of the Gospel of John. These sermons, as well as Luther's sermonic commentary on the Sermon on the Mount (preached at the Wednesday services), were edited and printed by Johannes Aurifaber in 1565.[75] A number of passages from Luther's comments on John 6 utilize the vocabulary associated with deification. Several of these passages deserve our attention. In the 14th sermon, Luther speaks of the "spiritual eating and drinking" as a metaphor for believing. At first glance the passage seems to speak vividly in terms of the believer's own deification through connection with Christ:

> The word "My" is definitive and determines the distinction [i.e., between the flesh of Christ and all other flesh]. He wants to say: "I am placing flesh and blood before you; eat and drink it, that is, believe it. [For here the term 'to eat' signifies to believe.] If you touch my flesh, you are not touching simple flesh and blood; you are eating and drinking flesh and blood which makes you divine. It does not make you flesh and blood, but it has the nature and strength of God." As I remarked before, sugar water is no longer mere water; it is sugar water, and it does what sugar does.[76]

74. WA 32.96.13,16. "*Daher sehen wir, das alle sunde mussen aus dem unglauben fliessen.*"

75. The fact that none of the manuscript transcriptions from which Aurifaber produced his printed edition survives, and the uncertainty about the accuracy of his editorial practice, combine to urge caution in building too much on individual words from the text of these sermons. Cf. AE 23:ix–xi.

76. AE 23:122. WA 33.188.15ff.

> . . . *gleube es, den essen heisst alhier gleuben, gleube an das fleisch undt blutt, den so du mein fleisch ergreiffst, so ergreiffstu nicht schlecht fleisch undt blutt, Sondern issest undt trinckest fleisch undt blutt, das göttert, das ist: es gibt die art undt krafft*

The American Edition here translates "*göttern*" as a transitive verb, "make divine," and supplies "you" as the direct object. Similarly it renders the parallel "*fleischern*" and "*bluthern*" as transitive verbs and likewise supplies "you" to complete the thought. But this is misleading. The German lacks the direct object in both sentences, and this is because the verb "*göttern*" (as well as the following "*fleischern*" and "*bluthern*") should be taken as intransitive, with the meaning "act and work in a divine [or fleshly or blood-like] way, have a divine effect."[77] The final sentence in the paragraph uses the verbs "*wessern*" and "*zuckern*" in exactly this way, as the context makes clear. Sugar water no longer "*wessert*," i.e., it no longer acts like plain water, but rather it "*zuckert*" and "gives and works the power which sugar has." It would be absurd to suppose that this last verb should be supplied with a direct object, and be understood in the sense of transforming the taster into sugar. It is just as unnecessary to apply such contortions to "*göttern*."

Not only does an intransitive translation of "*göttern*" fit the grammar of the German better, but it also agrees with the context, in which Luther is not really interested in highlighting the change produced in believers as a result of faith in Christ. Rather, he wants to distinguish this "flesh and blood" of Christ, i.e., his human nature, from ordinary human nature. He emphasizes the saving power of Christ's unique person, not the transformation of Christians. As is well known, Luther declined to interpret John 6 sacramentally, with a narrow focus on the Eucharist. His exegesis is rather Christological, emphasizing the necessity of attaching faith ("spiritual eating and drinking") to Christ's human nature ("flesh and blood"). The power of that human nature derives from its personal union with the divine nature, and this union is unique to the person of Christ. Christ's "flesh" (human nature) thus has the ability to do divine things which no other human person has the power to do, such as give eternal life, forgive sin, deliver from the devil and death, and—in short—to save.

> This also applies here. This flesh does not have the qualities of flesh. When you eat this flesh, it will not strengthen your flesh. It will not give birth to sin in you, or to a bad conscience or death, as other

---

der gottheit, es fleischert oder bluthert nicht, Sondern es hat die artt und krafft so gott hat, gleich wie ich droben gesagt habe, das Zuckerwasser nicht mehr wessert, Sondern es zuckert undt gibt undt wirckt die krafft, so der Zucker hat. Also alhier auch, dis fleisch fleischert nicht . . .

77. One may also understand the term qualitatively, as in the very next paragraph, where "*fleischern*" is translated "have the qualities of flesh"—but *not* "change into flesh."

flesh does; but it will imbue you with godlike power ["*durchgöt-tern*"], with godlike virtues and works. It will wipe out your sin; it will deliver you from the devil and death; it will free you from all wretchedness.[78]

This also accounts for the way in which Luther stresses Christ's word "My": no other human person, no matter how holy, has the power to do the divine works and impart the divine benefits which are done and imparted by Christ's human nature. This fact is missed by all heretics who denied either Christ's true human nature or its genuine union with the divine nature. This uniqueness of Christ's person makes even (and especially!) his human nature a necessary anchor for true Christian faith.

> Yes, if it were true that Christ were a man such as you and I are, then it would be plain flesh, and the word "My" would have to be deleted. But since Christ adds this word, you find that it is a deified flesh ["*ein vergöttert fleisch*"], impelling you and me to say: "I know not where to find God, either in heaven or on earth, except in the flesh of Christ."[79]

From this we conclude that the real location of "deification" for Luther in this passage is not the Christian at all, but the person of Jesus Christ, where *his* human nature, in a way unparalleled by any other, shares in the qualities of God, and thus has saving power for us who believe in him. Deification is thus a category more appropriate to Christology than to anthropology, and actually describes the *genus maiestaticum*, the sharing of the divine attributes with Christ's human nature. This assertion about Christ's human nature makes his humanity the unique and absolutely certain place where the true God can be found. Through its union with the divine nature, *that* "flesh," the human nature of *Christ*, is deified (*vergöttert*). God is not to be sought or found anywhere except in this very person, Jesus Christ, born of the Virgin and crucified.[80]

The incarnation, including the idea of the deified humanity of Christ, is the heart of the "hiddenness" of God, since God does not reveal himself to us directly. For Luther this had become a key to understanding

---

78. WA 33:188.30–40.

79. WA 33:189.20–30. Cf. Luther's use of "*vergöttern*" and similar terms in WA 33:193.14–24; 194.21—195.8; and 202.23–34, all in direct reference to Christ's human nature as uniquely "deified" and thus wielding divine power to save.

80. Cf. WA 33:190.33–37.

how God acts among us. God "hides, covers, and conceals" himself in the humanity, the flesh and blood, of Christ. And God's hidden way of revealing himself flows from the incarnation to all his ways of dealing with us: the word, the "*mundtliche predigtampt*," baptism, Lord's Supper. As God approaches and encounters us in all these ways, the paradoxical paradigm of the incarnation shows itself repeatedly, as God "must conceal Himself . . . in order that we may recognize Him." What makes such divine concealment not merely obscure but actually and effectively revelatory is the fact that in every case the outward forms which God uses are connected to God's word of promise.[81] This returns us once again to the centrality of the word of God in Luther's theology, not simply as a source of reliable information about God, but as God himself at work as Creator, Redeemer, and Sanctifier.

The way in which the concept of "*vergotten*" for Luther comes to hinge exclusively and completely on God's word of promise is illustrated well through some material from his 1534 sermons on baptism. When speaking about the water of baptism, Luther stresses the all-important function of God's word attached to or mixed with the water.

> I the Father, I the Son, I the Holy Spirit give this water. It is not simply water, but deified water [*durchgottet wasser*], because it and my name are not far apart. It is not watery water, but divine, heavenly water, in which there is deity itself. So do not look at it as water, but wherever someone is baptized, here is poured out water mixed with God's name. . . . Thus is baptism the water is deified [*durch Gottet*], saturated with God's name.[82]

The water of baptism is called "deified" not because of any substantial change or because it has been transformed in and of itself, but strictly because God's name and word have been attached to it. God's name and word work with God's own power.[83] Hence "because of the Name and the Word it is made a divine water, heavenly, living, deified, spiritual water."[84] These passages need to be read in light of the wording of the Small Catechism: "Baptism is not just plain water, but it is water included

81. Cf. WA 33:189.33—190.19. See Trigg, *Baptism*.

82. WA 37:264.25–34.

83. WA 37:265.5f.

84. WA 37:265.23f. ". . . *propter nomen et verbum fit divina aqua, celestis, viva, durchgottet, durchgeistert wasser*."

in God's command and combined with God's word." The force, then, of "*durchgottet*" applied to the water in baptism should not be understood in an ontological sense, but rather it simply means "water connected (in some way) to God." The term itself does not necessarily convey exactly what sort of connection is to be understood, but in the light of Luther's catechetical explanations about baptism elsewhere, it is reasonable to take "*durchgottet*" in this context as meaning "God-connected water," and the connection is that of God's word of command and promise. This usage of Luther referring to the "deification" of the water of baptism should be kept in mind when evaluating Luther's use of similar vocabulary ("*durchgottet*" / "*vergottet*") when referring to individuals; that is to say, it connotes a connection and relation to God mediated through his word of command and promise.[85]

In sermons on John 14–15 dating from the late 1530's, Luther again describes the Christian as "*durchgottet*," and the context is very revealing for his understanding of justification and the place of the concept of "deification." The Spirit, he says, does two things in the heart of the Christian.

> First, that their hearts be certain and sure that they have a gracious God; and second, that they help others through prayer. The first part makes them reconciled to God and provides them with everything they need. When they have that, then they should afterward become gods and the world's saviors through prayer.... For when a Christian begins to know Christ as his Lord and Savior, through whom he is redeemed from death and brought into his kingdom and inheritance, then his heart is completely deified, so that he would gladly help everyone, for he has no higher joy than in this treasure: that he knows Christ.[86]

Here Luther speaks of a Christian as "deified" because of the "divine" zeal he has for interceding for others and for sharing the gospel with others, by which his own will is in tune with Christ. "Deification" is not so much a term to describe the believer's restored and renewed relationship to God, but rather refers to the resultant relationship to other people, expressed by a zeal to help the neighbor and pray for him. This is precisely the distinction between justification and sanctification pressed in the Formula

---

85. Cf. WA 37.642.21; 649.12. Also WA 46.173.26 (1538), another reference to baptism as "*vergottet*" or "*durchgottet*" water.

86. WA 45:540.5–17.

of Concord. The "second work" of the Spirit, in this text called "*vergotten*," follows the recognition of Christ as Savior. Significantly, this second work, which Luther does not shrink from calling a kind of deification, is directed not "upward" to God (as, for instance in the system described in Tauler's sermons) but "outward" to the neighbor. Far from constituting the believer's ground of confidence before God or forming his righteousness *coram Deo*, this concept of deification strictly follows after faith in the God who has already justified the sinner for Christ's sake, and its whole sphere of activity is *coram hominibus*. Calling this "deification" signals that it is a work of the Spirit who is actually present in the believer's heart, but there is no reason to suppose that this is identical with the sinner's justification, least of all in the sense of an "ontological" transformation of the Christian. In this text Luther argues that the believer already has "everything he needs," and that his subsequent life becomes directed to the need of his neighbor, and especially to the propagation of the gospel.[87]

This connection of the idea of "*vergotten*" to the Christian's life in service to his neighbor is very important for another reason, namely that it redirects the focus of religious life outward into the Christian's vocation in the world. This stands in sharp contradiction to the medieval mystical tradition, which valued the contemplative, inward-focused life above all. For Tauler, to mention only one example, union with God could only be attained, if at all, through the necessary exercise of disciplined prayer, and this meant that it required a life removed from the ordinary obligations and distractions of daily life. Indeed, work in the world in service of others was part of the downward counterpoint of the soul that had ascended (even briefly) to union with God. For Luther the Christians' vocation in the world, far from being a distraction or an obstacle to their spiritual life, is precisely the place where they show themselves to be truly spiritual and "*vergottet*."[88]

Of particular importance for grasping Luther's idea of justification (and his anthropology) is his commentary on Galatians published in 1535. Tuomo Mannermaa makes extensive reference to certain sections of this work in his *Der im Glauben gegenwärtige Christus*, which was the main seminal work for subsequent studies from his students and like-minded colleagues. The Formula of Concord also claims to be in agreement with

87. Cf. WA 40I.576.21–25.

88. Such an understanding of "*vergotten*" corresponds to a "horizontal" (functional or vocational, rather than ontological) orientation of the *imago Dei* in Genesis 1.

Luther's work on Galatians, and cites it as the clearest exposition of what the Formula wants to teach concerning justification. Since the Finns appeal to the Galatians commentary *against* the Formula, while the Formula itself appeals to the same work *in support* of its exposition of the righteousness of faith, it is obviously crucial to come to some clarity about what Luther says there, if we are to evaluate the basic assertions of the Mannermaa school.

In his preparatory notes for the 1531 Galatians lectures (on which the published commentary of 1535 was based), Luther connects "works" with "deification" and with creation. He writes "And then truly works justify—deified works, that is, done in faith—so that a man creates the stars—a deified man, that is."[89] Luther's notes are sketchy, and the reference here is not entirely clear, but he may again be referring to Christ according to his human nature, of whom one can say, "this Man is the Creator of the universe." In this way, Christ's works are in fact the "*opera deificata*" that justify.

Luther's meaning becomes much clearer in his thematic introduction ("Argument") to the commentary. There he begins by distinguishing between every kind of righteousness conceived of as any human activity whatsoever, whether political, ceremonial, or moral in nature. Against all these he posits "the righteousness of faith or Christian righteousness . . . which God imputes to us through Christ."[90] The human sinners who are thus justified by imputation of Christ's righteousness are purely passive, simply receiving what is given to them by God: "for here we work nothing, render nothing to God; we only receive and permit someone else to work in us, namely, God."[91] It is precisely this passive character of the righteousness grasped by faith that makes it a "solid and certain" comfort for the conscience, since it depends utterly on something outside of us. To be thus comforted, the conscience is directed in faith to the word of the gospel, "to take hold of the promise of grace offered in Christ, that is, the righteousness of faith."[92] The content of that comforting promise of grace is none other than the forgiveness of sins: "I embrace only that passive righteousness which is the righteousness of grace, mercy, and the forgive-

89. WA 401.20.29f. "*Et recte opera tunc iustificant scil. deificata, fideifica[ta], Sicut homo creat stellas sed deificatus . . .*"

90. WA 401.40.28–41.16. LW 26.4.

91. WA 401.41.18–20. LW 26.5.

92. WA 401.42.26–28. LW 26.5.

ness of sins."[93] This grace, mercy, and forgiveness is the *favor Dei* bestowed on us through the promise of the gospel, and as such it always remains a promise to be received by faith, never a possession which I can have apart from the promise ("*non habemus, sed accipimus*").[94] Luther can speak of this righteousness being worked "in me,"[95] but he just as often speaks of it as located outside of and completely independent of me.[96] The crucified, risen, and triumphant Christ is the location of this righteousness of faith, because God himself imputes his life and righteousness to us: he declares it ours by saying "for you."[97]

In the light of such a clear summary of how Christ's life and righteousness is imputed to us through the promise of the forgiveness of sins, Luther then proceeds with his detailed exposition of Galatians. It is in the light of this understanding of imputed (forensic) righteousness spelled out so plainly in the "Argument" that we should read Luther's comments on verses such as 2:19–20, from which Mannermaa draws many of his conclusions. Luther marvels at the radical, even shocking language Paul uses here to describe how the Christian has no other life or "being" than what is given to him in Christ through the promise of the gospel. Against the death of sin in us, Luther (following Paul) pits the death of Christ in our place: "Thus in my flesh I find a death that afflicts and kills me; but I also have a contrary death, which is the death of my death and which crucifies and devours my death."[98] This means that my sin is given to Christ in the same way that his righteousness and life are given to me, i.e., by the promise of the gospel. The identification of Christ and the sinner, upon which Mannermaa builds his anthropology as if it were descriptive of some kind of empirical reality in the Christian, is the content of the promise which presents the death and resurrection of Christ and says that it is "for me."[99] What follows from God's saving action in Christ, and from the promise of forgives and life received in faith, is a new life, which

---

93. WA 40I.43.12–15. LW 26.6.

94. WA 40I.43.16.

95. E.g., WA 40I.41.20 and 47.21.

96. E.g., WA 40I.47.16–20 and 48.22–25.

97. WA 40I.50.18–23.

98. WA 40I.273.23–25. LW 26.160.

99. Luther devotes a special section to emphasizing how the "*pro me*" of God's promise in Christ makes the word of the gospel not just information but powerful, effective declaration. WA 40I.295.35—300.22. LW 26.176–79.

Luther describes as "an alien life" ("*vita aliena*").[100] Such new, alien life is "not inborn in me but is granted to me in faith through Christ."[101] And then Luther (again following Paul) goes on to describe the life of faith of the person thus justified; but that description of the life of the justified cannot be equated with the way in which the person is justified, or the righteousness of faith would become an active righteousness again. In short, the "identification" language of Luther's comments on these verse echoes Paul's languages in the biblical text, but Luther understands it as fleshing out the passive, imputed righteousness he sketched briefly in the "Argument."

Luther has much to say in the Galatians commentary about the law and the gospel and their respective effects. The function of the law is to kill and reduce to nothing, says Luther, but it is God's nature, his "proper" work through the gospel, to create out of nothing:

> "If the Law does not justify, what is its purpose?" . . . It produces in man the knowledge of himself as a sinner. . . . Therefore the Law is a minister and a preparation for grace. For God is the God of the humble, the miserable, the afflicted, the oppressed, the desperate, and of those who have been brought down to nothing at all. And it is the nature of God to exalt the humble, to feed the hungry, to enlighten the blind, to comfort the miserable and afflicted, to justify sinners, to give life to the dead, and to save those who are desperate and damned. For He is the almighty Creator, who makes everything out of nothing.[102]

Following soon after this is another passage which makes clear that God the Creator-Savior is at work through his word. That is, Luther focuses on the word of God's promise. What matters to him is not an "ontological" union with Christ, but rather "hearing" Christ in the preaching of grace.

100. WA 40I.287.30. LW 26.170.
101. WA 40I.288.16. LW 26.170.
102. AE 26:314. WA 40I:487.30—488.19.

Si lex non iustificat, ad quid valet? . . . Deinde aperit homini cognitionem sui, quod sit peccator . . . Sic ergo lex ministra et praeparatrix est ad gratiam. Nam Deus est Deus humilium, miserorum, afflictorum, oppressorum, desperatorum et eorum qui prorsus in nihilum redacti sunt; Estque Dei natura exaltare humiles, cibare esurientes, illuminare caecos, miseros et afflictos consolari, peccatores iustificare, mortuos vivificare, desperatos et damnatos salvare etc. Est enim Creator omnipotens ex nihilo faciens omnia.

Now I have been crushed and troubled enough. Now it is time for grace and for listening to grace. . . . It follows, therefore, that the Law with its function does contribute to justification—not because it justifies, but because it impels one to the promise of grace and makes it sweet and desirable.[103]

For faith, according to Luther, everything depends on this "hearing" Christ, that is, the believer is directed exclusively to God's word of promise that is addressed to him. Whatever "ontological" change may be wrought in the human person, it fades into the background when one speaks of the justification of the sinner before God.

What we have seen so far would seem to indicate that Luther certainly used the vocabulary of deification, and in a mostly positive fashion. With such language he refers either to the deification of Christ's own human nature (Christologically), or to the effect of the word of God's promise on the human person (in terms of faith or of the believer's "alien life" of sanctification flowing out of faith). However, toward the end of his life, in his Genesis lectures (with reference to the text of 17:10), Luther's mention of the notion of deification has a completely and unambiguously negative force.

It is just as Satan says: "Then you will be like gods." You will no longer be creatures who will be concerned about carrying out the commands of God; you yourselves will be gods, you will judge God, and you will do other things—things that are proper for God alone. Oh, the wretched divinity with which Satan surrounded us through sin when he had this one design, that we should disregard the commands and promises of God. Therefore it is original sin to become a god. Against this disease we must fight throughout our entire life, and we must say with Paul: "I know nothing except Jesus Christ and Him crucified."[104]

---

103. AE 26:315. WA 40I: 488.31—489.29.

. . . Iam satis contritus et conturbatus sum, satis misere afflixit me tempus legis. Iam tempus est gratiae et audiendi Christi, ex cuius ore procedunt sermones gratiae. . . . Sic per consequens Lex cumsuo officio etiam prodest ad iustificationem, Non quidem iustificans, sed urgens ad promissionem gratiae et faciens eam dulcem ac desiderabilem.

104. AE 3:139. WA 42:647.22–29.

Sicut Satan dicit: 'Eritis tum sicut Dii'. Non eritis amplius creaturae, cum soliciti eritis de mandatis Dei exequendis, ipsi eritis Dii, iudicabitis Deum, et facietis alia, quae solum Deum decent. O miseram divinitatem, quam nobis per peccatum Satan

"Deification" is seen here as the original temptation, which draws human creatures away from God's word of command and promise. The same negative use of "deification" terminology to describe the idea occurs much earlier, and appears already in Luther's "Disputation Against Scholastic Theology" (1517): "Man is by nature unable to want God to be God. Indeed, he himself wants to be God. . . ."[105] Later, in a letter from Luther to Spalatin, written from the Coburg to Augsburg just a few days after the *Confessio* had been presented (30 June 1530):

> Be strong in the Lord, and on my behalf continuously admonish Philip not to become like God, but to fight that innate ambition to be like God, which was planted in us in paradise by the devil. This [ambition] doesn't do us any good. It drove Adam from paradise, and it alone also drives us away, and drives peace away from us. In summary: we are to be men and not God; it will not be otherwise, or eternal anxiety and affliction will be our reward.[106]

It now remains to place Luther's use of terminology related to deification into the broader context of his theological development, an area conspicuously ignored by scholars of the Finnish school

Luther's Theological Development: "Early" vs. "Late" Luther

The most obvious example of the Finnish inattention to history is the almost complete omission in the Luther studies of the Mannermaa school of any discussion about the nature and date of Luther's so-called evangelical breakthrough. A watershed question for understanding Luther's development as a theologian is whether this "breakthrough" occurred before or after (or during) his engagement in the controversy over indulgences.

---

circumdedit, hoc unicum agens, ut praecepta et promissiones Dei negligamus. Fieri igitur Deum est peccatum originale. Contra hunc morbum pugnandum nobis est per omnem vitam, et cum Paulo dicendum: "Nihil scio, nisi Iesum Christum, eumque crucifixum."

105. AE 31:10. WA 1:221–28. *"No(n) potest homo naturaliter velle deum esse de(um). Immo vellet se e(ss)e de(um), (et) deum non esse deum."*

106. AE 49:337. WABr 5.415.40–46.

Tu esto fortis in Domino, & Philippum meo nomine Exhortare semper, ne fiat Deus, Sed pugnet contra illam iññatam & a Diabolo in paradiso implantatam nobis ambitionem diuinitatis, Ea enim non expedit nobis. Eiecit Adam paradiso, Nos quoque ipsa sola exturbat & extra pacem trudit. Wir sollen menschen und nicht Gott sein. Das ist die summa; Es wird doch nicht anders, odder ist ewige unruge und Herzleid unser lohn.

How one answers this question largely determines—or is determined by—one's understanding of Luther's distinctive insight into justification as the *iustitia Dei*. The implications of answering this question one way or the other for the interpretation of Luther's thought are enormous. For example, it is a serious question with enormous consequences whether one should read the first lectures on the Psalms (1513–1515), the Romans lectures (1515–1516), the 95 Theses on Indulgences (1517), the Heidelberg Disputation (April 1518), and the Explanations of the 95 Theses (1518) as expressions of Luther's "reformation insight," or as works which reflect various stages of Luther's development toward (but prior to) that insight. Scholars have produced an impressive body of literature over several decades in the course of this debate,[107] and it cannot be our task in this chapter even to cite all the major arguments on both sides. Nor is such an undertaking necessary, since our purpose is to illustrate why the question of an "early" or "late" date for Luther's evangelical insight is important for evaluating the studies of Mannermaa, Peura, and the rest of the Finnish school. The magnitude of the question and its ramifications for the interpretation of Luther make the Finnish school's wholesale neglect of the topic border on the incomprehensible. A brief discussion will show how the decision about the date and character of Luther's "breakthrough" must actually imply also the decision between a sympathetic reading of Mannermaa and his school and an ultimate rejection of their central arguments.

The question about dating Luther's insight into the gospel is framed partly by Luther himself. In his introduction to the 1545 edition of his Latin works, Luther sets down in brief his memoir of the early years of the Reformation.[108] This description places his new and decisive insight chronologically during the indulgence controversy, and connects it materially with an exegetical discovery of the meaning of *iustitia Dei* in Romans 1:17. The problem this creates for scholars is that such a dating makes not only the *Dictata* "pre-Reformation" in their theology, but also casts the lectures on Romans and those on Hebrews under the same suspicion. There are some other references scattered among Luther's later writings that also provoke this kind of investigation. In a sermon in 1537, Luther remarked that he was unaware of the comfort of the gospel when he be-

---

107. For a representative sampling of the literature, cf. two indispensable collections edited by Bernhard Lohse: *Durchbruch* and *Neuere Untersuchungen*.

108. WA 54:179–87. AE 327–38.

came a doctor (i.e., in 1512).[109] In another place he recounts his diligent study of the Scriptures and the fathers (naming particularly Chrysostom, Jerome, Ambrose, and Augustine), emphasizing his struggle to understand the real meaning of the Scriptures.[110] Veit Dietrich records a remark in which Luther says he began to escape from the "exegetical mysticism" of allegory through his study of Romans.[111] Luther's own testimonies about the development of his theology are an important ingredient in the scholarly debate,[112] but are not by themselves conclusive. A number of responsible scholars have preferred to suppose that Luther's memory in 1545 was in error, rather than accept his own testimony that his understanding of *iustitia Dei* was not yet clear in those important early lectures. The general consensus in the earlier part of the twentieth century was disturbed by studies such as those of Ernst Bizer[113] and Oswald Bayer[114] in which the "turning point" or "breakthrough"[115] in Luther's understanding of the gospel was located later in his development, about 1518 or 1519.[116]

The question of when one should date Luther's evangelical insight is only partially a historical question. The chronology one is prepared to accept depends to a very large extent on a prior theological decision. That is to say, what theologians understand to be "evangelical" determines which

---

109. WA 45:86.18f.

110. WA 50:519.20–28. AE 41:19–20. ("On the Councils and the Church," 1539) However, neither this reference nor the following quip from Luther's table talk necessarily has to refer to preparations for specific lectures on the biblical books in question, but could be meant more generally.

111. WA TR 1:136, no. 335. AE 54:46f. Cf. another remark from the *Tischreden* where Luther looks back and describes even his first commentary on Galatians (1519) as "weak," "*infirmos*," WA TR 2:281.11–13.

112. Cf. the helpful collection of material in Otto Scheel, ed., *Dokumente zu Luthers Entwicklung*.

113. Bizer, *Fides Ex Auditu*.

114. Bayer, *Promissio*.

115. Despite Bernhard Lohse's plea for more precision and clarity about the meaning of such terms (cf. his *Vorwort* to the important collection, *Neuere Untersuchungen*, x–xi), scholars continue to operate with divergent understandings of exactly what "new insight" they are looking for in Luther. It is therefore not surprising that they find "it" at different places. The proposal of Otto Hermann Pesch, that the so-called "turning point" and the "tower experience" be understood as two separate events and separated by as much as four years, has likewise not convinced the majority of scholars or led the way to greater consensus.

116. Cf. also Uuras Saarnivaara, *Luther Discovers the Gospel*.

writings of Luther they will read as "evangelical," and thus also governs how they date the chronology of Luther's development. As a general rule, scholars who wish to date Luther's "discovery" early (before the indulgence controversy—or in some cases even before the *Dictata*), decline to take Luther's 1545 recollections at face value. In other words, if scholars identify what they consider to be expressions of a genuinely evangelical understanding of *iustitia Dei* or some related concept in, say, the lectures on Romans, then they account for this by either postulating that Luther's memory lapsed in old age, or by interpreting the 1545 account as something other than the autobiographical chronology it appears to be. But in order to do this, scholars must begin with their own conception of what constitutes a "genuinely evangelical understanding," and their arguments run the risk of begging the question by imposing their own theological prejudices on Luther's theology. This is a dubious methodology that frequently interferes with the task of establishing what Luther himself regarded as "genuinely evangelical." One decides in advance what the gospel is, and when one finds *that* in Luther, the reformer is deemed to have "discovered" the true gospel. Such an approach makes it almost impossible to listen to Luther's own testimony. What was it that Luther did not (by his own account) understand before the indulgence controversy, but which ultimately transformed his theology after it did become clear to him?

This is a crucial question for evaluating the Finnish school, as well, since Mannermaa and his colleagues assume a basic continuity in Luther's understanding of justification from his earliest writings, and in fact rely heavily on "early" Luther to support their arguments. In the case of Mannermaa, as we have seen, the central theme of *theosis*, deification, or "real-ontic" participation in Christ is assumed to be in place by the end of 1514, which he says expresses "the core of [Luther's] doctrine of justification."[117] In a more recent essay, Mannermaa cites the same early sermon, and then adds: "I am familiar with the objection that this sermon is pre-Reformation and therefore cannot be used as a direct source for Luther's theology. Without being able here to substantiate my claim, I only answer that the theological construct I am noting permeates every aspect of the Reformer's thinking from its beginning all the way to his final commentary on Genesis."[118] Such an unsupported claim, however, is

117. Mannermaa, "Theosis as a Subject of Finnish Luther Research," 43.
118. Mannermaa, "Why Is Luther So Fascinating?"

completely unsatisfactory as a basis for a fundamental shift in our understanding of Luther's theology. What Mannermaa asks us to accept, without substantiation, is not only that *all Luther scholars have been wrong* about when Luther reached his fundamental insight concerning justification, but that *Luther himself was wrong* about this, as well. The result of Mannermaa's premise is that all of Luther's discussions of justification after 1514 are read in the light of the mystical, participatory language of that early Christmas sermon. If the core of that doctrine was in place as early as 1514, then certainly a very radical re-evaluation of Luther's theology (and Lutheran theology) is called for. But the weight of the evidence is really not quite so seismic.

Luther's use of deification language most closely approximated the thought of medieval mysticism very early in his career (when, as he put it, he was initially attracted to the Neoplatonic aspect[119]). Therefore it is important to know whether Luther's idea of justification as early as 1514 was substantially the same as in his later thinking, as Mannermaa asserts. The scholarly debate about precisely this question has reached nothing even close to a consensus which would allow Mannermaa and his school to take for granted that such early expressions of Luther should be recognized as representing "authentic reformation theology."

In fact, a strong case can be made for dating Luther's "evangelical" view of the justification of the sinner before God much later.[120] Doing so does not necessarily challenge the actual data that the Finnish school have assembled; in fact, it should be noted that Luther's early work did appropriate the mystical vocabulary of deification, and this theme deserves the attention that the Finns have devoted to it. It is also true that Luther continued to use some of the vocabulary of deification later, but with a distinctly evangelical emphasis on God's word of promise (as discussed above). What can and must be challenged, however, is the claim that the deification motif in Luther's early theology retains a central place in his more mature thought, and therefore that *theosis* can legitimately be regarded as the primary focus of "authentically evangelical" theology.

---

119. See Paul Rorem, "Martin Luther's Christocentric Critique of Pseudo-Dionysian Spirituality," 292.

120. In the following sketch of Luther's early theological development, I am largely following Bizer. However, one need not agree with Bizer in all details in order to recognize that numerous keys changes in Luther's theology *after* 1517 challenge the major conclusions of the Finnish school.

What, then, was the shape of Luther's early understanding of justification, and what was the path by which his views changed? Justification in the earliest period of Luther's theology that can be documented was understood as the process by which God reduces the sinner to nothing, brings him to a consciousness of his own sinfulness. This early "theology of the cross" is really a theology of contrition and of humility, according to which the sinner is made righteous by being put through the "paradigm" of the cross.[121] Thus man is "justified" (as Mannermaa might say) "*realiter*" but also (in this life) partially, and only in so far as God has worked in him the death which must precede resurrection.

Understanding the orientation of Luther's early theology in this way explains his objections to the promotion of indulgences. The whole purpose of an indulgence is to escape the penalties and sufferings imposed by the Law, which Luther at the time saw as the only way the sinner could hope to be saved. God's work of humiliation and death had to be carried out in the person of the believer, and the believer's whole life was to be one of repentance. Far from trying to escape the humbling, indeed crushing and killing, work of God, the true Christian embraces such penalties, as he embraces contrition: "A Christian who is truly contrite seeks and loves to pay penalties for his sins."[122] The most authentic Christian experience, according to this understanding, is contrite self-condemnation. In such a state the Christian agrees with the crushing verdict of God's righteous judgment and verges on despair.[123]

It is important to keep in mind that the place in the Christian's life where the indulgence controversy made the most difference was in the confessional, that is, in the regular, pastoral practice of the sacrament of penance. It was in that context, which formed the heart of medieval pastoral care, that questions of contrition, absolution, and satisfaction came especially to the fore. Wrestling with the issues surrounding indulgences in the context of pastoral care through the sacrament of penance, Luther gradually came to focus more and more on the centrality of objective absolution, rather than subjective contrition or subsequent satisfaction, as the source of Christian comfort and the object of faith. Previously, Luther had emphasized contrition and *humilitas* as the way of the cross for the

---

121. Cf. Luther's comments on Psalm 2 from the *Dictata*, WA 3:31ff. AE 10:35ff.

122. AE 31:29. WA 1:235.16. (Thesis 40).

123. Leske, "Another Look at Luther's Indulgence Theses."

Christian, in which ultimate uncertainty about the adequacy of one's own contrition (and hence about one's salvation) was an important part of the psychology of faith. By contrast, in the wake of the indulgence controversy, Luther began to direct the attention within the practice of penance to the absolution spoken by the priest. That word is a sure guarantee of forgiveness, not based on the penitent's contrition—about which the confessor, after all, must necessarily remain uncertain[124]—but rooted in the promise of Christ: "If you forgive anyone his sins, they are forgiven" (John 20:23). Precisely in the context of the sacrament of penance, therefore, Luther formulates this distinctively new and evangelical understanding in a little known disputation prepared in 1518,[125] apparently shortly after his "Explanations of the 95 Theses" and perhaps before (though this is less certain) his hearing with Cajetan at Augsburg. Here he describes the main role of the priest as speaking the absolution to the penitent as a confident and unconditional word of forgiveness based on Christ's own word and authority. The priest functions as a servant of that word of promise, and the goal or object of the priest's ministry is that the penitent trust that forgiveness which is promised is given in absolution.[126]

The focus on the centrality of the word in the "*Pro veritate*" theses signals an important new emphasis in Luther's theology as it had developed up to late 1518, a focus which would come to be much more pervasive in Luther's thought far beyond the bounds of the controversy about indulgences. Not only in the confessional should the focus be concentrated on the word of the promise of the forgiveness of sins. Luther came to see God's way of working with human creatures, in creation and in re-creation, as characteristically *per verbum*. The richness of Luther's theology of the word depends on the recognition that the word is never to be understood merely as "information," not even of divinely accurate and revealed information. For Luther God's word is always directed to man; it is the Creator's address to his creatures. Human creatures find themselves inescapably *coram Deo* as they are addressed by this divine word. The divine word is never simply a word "about" the human creatures but always and especially a word directed "to" them, and the creatures thus addressed

124. Cf. WA 1:586.21—587.2. AE 31:178f. ("Explanation" of Thesis 30).

125. WA 1:630ff., under the title "*Pro veritate inquirenda et timoratis conscientiis consolandis hec sub R. P. Martino Luther Augustiano disputabuntur per vices circulares pro nostro more.*"

126. Priests function as "*ministratores verbi in fidem remissionis,*" WA 1:631.33f.

cannot respond with mere intellectual assent or agreement but only with faith understood as trust.

The word which God directs to his human creatures has two distinct and even contradictory functions. Its "alien" work is to condemn, judge, and kill by declaring human beings to be sinners. But its own "proper" function is to create, make alive, and forgive. Law and gospel are not to be understood as conceptual categories by which one may classify the data of Scripture, but rather as two ways in which God himself works through his living word. The word of *promise* came to be decisive for Luther in the whole divine economy of the justification of sinners, and that word operates on human beings from outside.

Mannermaa and others of the Finnish school have failed to appreciate the centrality of the word in Luther's theology, and the all-sufficient creative function the "word the promise" came to play. For Luther, God's word of promise does not simply convey accurate information (in the sense that "God does not lie"), but above all the promise gives what it says. God's promise is not merely a dependable guarantee of some future action (i.e., accurate information about what God will do in the future): the promise is the word of the Creator, the same word that creates *ex nihilo*. As such, God's word of promise (even when what it says runs directly contrary to all the evidence of our senses) is more "real" than any description of reality, since only God's word has the power to bring about and perform what it says.

The evangelical "insight" of Luther was not a new formulation of this or that individual doctrine, but rather (by implication, at least—it took some time for this new way of thinking to work itself out in all aspects of Luther's theology) a whole new paradigm or framework for theological thought that linked declaratory (unconditional) forgiveness, absolution, the promise of Christ, faith as confident *fiducia* with forgiveness as its object, etc., together in an organic whole. This means that the exact details of chronology turn out to be rather less important than has been generally supposed, since the "new paradigm" of evangelical theology did not make itself apparent everywhere at once in Luther's thinking and writing. Even in 1519, in a single set of sermons, his new theology is apparent in the context of the sacrament of penance, while the older "transformative" understanding of the gospel characterizes the sermon on baptism.[127]

---

127. WA 2:714–23 and 727–37. AE 35:9–22 and 29–43.

Unevenly and according to the demands of his immediate situation, sometimes in small incremental stages and sometimes by huge leaps of insight, Luther's new evangelical paradigm was brought to bear across the whole range of his theology, as he rethought old questions and confronted new challenges.[128] When Luther, in 1545, looked back and said that something fundamental had changed in his theology through his struggle with the indulgences controversy, it is best to understand him to refer to this kind of basic re-design of the whole theological system, a new way of connecting items and concepts in an "evangelical" matrix, rather than to an isolated insight into one single text or *locus*.

The question is, then, does an understanding of justification as *theosis* or deification, emphasized by Mannermaa, Peura, and their colleagues, fit into the matrix of Luther's evangelical theology? The brief answer seems to be that it does not, at least not in the way that the *theosis* school have argued. For Luther, justification came to be correlated more and more with an external word of declaratory (not "descriptive") forgiveness, which is never *separate* but always *distinct* from the new life engendered in the believer because he is connected to Christ. The Finns' insistence on an ontological transformation as the essence of justification seeks to make such ontology primary, in a way that views God's verdict of righteousness as descriptive rather than creative. Our survey of Luther's mature use of deification vocabulary and themes has shown that he came to more clearly understand the Christian's new life in Christ as an effect and fruit of God's powerful and creative word of promise.

What mattered to Luther more and more as he grew older was not the prospect of raising the human person beyond his or her humanity to an ontological union with the divine, but rather the restoration of created humanity to its divinely ordered place in the world: "*wir sollen menschen und nicht Gott sein.*" That is to say, Luther became less interested in "deification" and more interested in "humanization," accomplished through the performative word of the Creator. His foundational insight about the sinner's justification before God by sheer grace, for Christ's sake, and through faith alone permitted a new appreciation of the doctrine of creation, and a deeper grasp of what it means to be human creatures of God. The framework for understanding Lutheran anthropology must reckon

128. Examples of such new challenges are Luther's conflict with the antinomianism of Agricola, his experience in the Saxon visitation, or his struggles against the sacramentarians, etc.

with both the doctrine of creation and the doctrine of justification, and that will be our topic in the next chapter.

4

Anthropology in the Lutheran Confessions

INTRODUCTION

UP TO THIS POINT, our attention has been focused on Luther and his theology, especially his theological understanding of anthropology and his use of the vocabulary of deification. This was necessary as the first step in evaluating the credibility of the Mannermaa school's claims that a doctrine of *theosis* is central to genuine Lutheran theology. The next step is to consider the Finnish notions of deification in light of the anthropology of the Lutheran Confessions. In order to pursue that consideration, we will shift our approach from a largely historical examination of claims about Luther's theology to a more systematic analysis of *theosis*.

It will be the central argument of this chapter that the Finnish assertions about theosis are inconsistent with the Lutheran anthropology articulated in the Lutheran Confessions. This argument in turn is based upon at least two presuppositions that should be made explicit at the outset: one about the inner consistency of the documents collected in the Book of Concord of 1580, and a second about what constitutes normative, definitive, authoritative "Lutheran" doctrine.

Regarding the first of these presuppositions, it will be argued in this chapter that the Lutheran Confessions exhibit a unified and coherent theological perspective on what it means to be human, one that is congruent with a unified confessional doctrine of justification and that is only comprehensible with reference to that justification. Of course, it lies outside the scope of the present study to defend the unity or cohesion of the Lutheran confessional documents in any kind of comprehensive way. I mean to assert and defend a narrower and more modest claim, namely that a close study of the anthology of documents known as the

Book of Concord reveals a consistent but richly nuanced understanding of human nature and human identity. Mannermaa, together with his colleagues and students, often argues against such theological cohesion, being especially critical of Melanchthon's influence on the development of the later Reformation. They have in mind especially the Formula of Concord, but sometimes also refer to the Augsburg Confession.[1] I intend to sketch the Lutheran understanding of human existence under the three aspects of creation, sin, and justification; and to show that this theological anthropology is both characteristic of Luther and consistent throughout the Lutheran Confessions.

My second premise for this chapter has to do with the question of what counts as "Lutheran doctrine." It should be clear that this point relates intimately with the preceding one. That is to say, when Mannermaa, Peura and others identify what they consider to be discrepancies between Luther and Melanchthon, it is because they wish to side *with* Luther *against* Melanchthon, or at least against the Formula. The theologians of the Mannermaa school repeatedly contrast what they regard as Luther's core understanding of justification with the theology of later Lutheranism, especially under the (in their judgment, detrimental) influence of Melanchthon. For example, Mannermaa and his colleagues are not prepared to accept FC III as a clarification of distinctions (especially between the "righteousness of faith" and the indwelling of Christ in the believer) which were implicit already in Luther's own theology. Instead, they argue that there are fundamental differences between Luther's theology and what came to be defined as orthodox Lutheranism by the end of the sixteenth century, and they appeal to Luther in opposition to the Formula. Such claims obviously raise the larger question of the relationship between Luther and Lutheranism. What defines "genuine" Lutheran theology? What authority do Luther's writings have for Lutheran theology? Such questions have ramifications far beyond the debate over *theosis* in Luther studies, a point that is recognized by Carl Braaten:

> In case of fundamental disagreement between Luther's theology and the Lutheran Confessions on an article so crucial as justification, which is normative? Is Luther normative for Lutheran churches today? . . . It would seem that, when push comes to shove,

---

1. Mannermaa, "Why Is Luther So Fascinating?," 20; and Peura, "Christ as Favor and Gift," 45f.

many Lutheran dogmaticians would rather have Luther on their side than the Formula of Concord.[2]

Braaten's alternative—either Luther or the Formula—is spurious if pressed absolutely, since the Formula of Concord itself cites some key works of Luther as at least "quasi-confessional," which means that certain of Luther's writings are given more weight than others, as Luther himself suggested.[3] Braaten apparently includes himself in that company of dogmaticians, since he agrees with Peura's assessment that an important element of Luther's understanding of justification was lost through the Formula's "over-reaction to Osiandrianism."[4]

This attempt to accentuate contrasts within Lutheran theology applies most pointedly to the Formula of Concord, but it raises broader and more basic questions of the theological coherence of Lutheranism. Indeed, much of the Finnish argument depends precisely on sharpening this contrast, for their interest is not confined to a historical question about the shape of Luther's theology, but aims necessarily at a fresh answer to the question of what constitutes authentic Lutheran theology. And this quest for what Simo Peura calls "genuine Lutheran tradition"[5] is closely related to their ecumenical concerns, which lead the Finns and their supporters to search for "resources" from which to develop theological common ground, particularly with the Russian Orthodox Church. The theology of the Book of Concord, and especially of the Formula, seems to frustrate these ecumenical aspirations. "My interest in Luther," comments Robert W. Jenson, "is not that of a *Lutherforscher*, but that of a systematic theologian and ecumenist." And with those specific interests in mind, Jenson concludes that:

> the sort of Lutheranism that constantly appeals to that Luther [as filtered through the theology of the Formula] has been an ecumenical disaster. With Luther according to the Finns, on the other

2. Carl E. Braaten, "Response to Simo Peura, 'Christ as Favor and Gift,'" in *Union with Christ: The New Finnish Interpretation of Luther* (Grand Rapids: Eerdmans, 1998), 72.

3. FC SD "Binding Summary" 9 (BSLK 836.36—837.15). Frequent citations of Luther are made in many places in the FC.

4. Carl E. Braaten, "Response to Simo Peura," 73.

5. Peura, "Christ as Favor and Gift," 67. It is interesting to note that Peura's immediate reference seems to identify the Regensburg Book of 1541 with that "genuine Lutheran tradition," in implied opposition to the Formula of Concord.

hand, there can be much systematically and ecumenically fruitful conversation.[6]

Thus Jenson would agree with Carl Braaten's assessment that:

> The Finnish scholars discovered their Luther-insight in the context of their ecumenical dialogue with theologians of the Russian Orthodox Church. I am immensely interested in what they have found of ecumenical relevance in Luther. That leads me to want to place the most favorable construction on what they are teaching us.[7]

One may, of course, make "ecumenically fruitful" use of Luther in various ways, including the approach of Mannermaa, Peura, and their colleagues. But a process of selectively co-opting some of his writings and ignoring others does not lead to genuine understanding of his thought. Taken as a whole, Luther's writings surely provide almost as many ways to offend as to conciliate. Many of his comments about Jews and Muslims— to say nothing of his polemics against the papacy—would seem unlikely to provide much in the way of resources for building mutual understanding today. Perhaps the real reason Mannermaa and his admirers are "fascinated" by Luther but unsatisfied with the Book of Concord is precisely because his writings are diverse enough that they can find there what they are looking for (already and for other reasons). And even such a selective gleaning of Luther for ecumenical purposes depends on a very modern and limited definition of ecumenism; both the doctrinal content and the public character of the collected documents that make up the Book of Concord argue for at least a serious consideration of their claim of catholicity.[8]

If the present study cannot provide a comprehensive defense of the inner unity of the Book of Concord, then much less can it pretend to establish that standard as the authoritative *corpus doctrinae* for Lutheranism for those who still wish to dispute that claim. I am, of course, aware that Lutheran churches differ in their formal confessional subscription (e.g.,

---

6. Jenson, "Response to Tuomo Mannermaa," in *Union with Christ: The New Finnish Interpretation of Luther*, 21.

7. Carl E. Braaten, "Response to Simo Peura," 75.

8. Cf. Preface to the Book of Concord, 23: "We are minded not to manufacture anything new through this work of concord nor to depart in either substance or expression to the smallest degree from the divine truth . . ."

some churches regard the AC as authoritative but do not subscribe to other documents in the Book of Concord). I am also aware that there is continuing discussion and debate, even among those who formally subscribe to the same writings, about the "internal hermeneutics" of the Lutheran Confessions, including such questions as to the priority or weight given to each document, their respective function within the church, etc.[9] But not all such broader questions can be adequately evaluated in this context—nor need they be so evaluated for our present purposes. It must suffice here simply to take note of these other questions, and hope that my narrower argument may be found convincing in favor of a consistent anthropology—understandable only in the context of the Lutheran doctrine of justification—throughout the Lutheran Confessions. As we shall see, that consistent, evangelical, Lutheran anthropology differs fundamentally from the anthropology of *theosis*.

LUTHER'S CATECHISMS AS BRIDGE

Charles Arand remarks that Luther's catechisms served as a bridge by which the evangelical theology of the Reformation was able to move out of the academic setting of the university and into the parishes and homes of ordinary Christians. It is also true to say that the catechisms of Luther serve as the crucial bridge between *Luther's* theology and *Lutheran* theology, i.e., the public doctrine which became normative for those who identify themselves by their commitment to the Lutheran Confessions. The relationship of Luther to Lutheran theology is a matter of great interest and long-standing debate. Without reproducing that debate here, it is necessary to note that the formal (even legal) authority of Luther's corpus of writings may actually have declined even among his most ardent admirers after the adoption of the Book of Concord.[10] By the end of the 16th century, Luther's writings were held in high regard, but the public doctrine of Lutheran churches was defined by the Book of Concord, in which Luther's catechism functioned not as examples of his private writings but as official standards of public teaching.

9. On the hermeneutical function of the Lutheran Confessions, see Charles P. Arand and James W. Voelz, "The Lutheran Confessions as Normative Guides for Reading Scripture," *Concordia Journal*, 21.4 (October 1995), 366–84.

10. Kolb, "'Perilous Events and Troublesome Disturbances,'" and more recently, *Martin Luther as Prophet, Teacher, and Hero: Images of the Reformer, 1520–1620* (Grand Rapids: Baker and Carlisle, UK: Paternoster Press, 1999), 55–74.

If we are to consider the connection between Luther's theology and Lutheran theology, then, an obvious place to begin is with Luther's catechisms.[11] These served both to connect the theology of the Reformation with the common life of the churches and to link Luther's writings with the public (official) "Lutheran" doctrine. The two functions are related of course, since the pervasive influence especially of the Small Catechism is attested (not introduced) by its inclusion in the *corpus doctrinae* of the Book of Concord. Yet for the Lutheran princes and public officials, as well as for pastors and simple people, the crucial questions could not be decided by asking whether the man Luther thought or believed something. Luther's theology had given birth to public doctrine, formulated in confessions that transcended the influential, but ultimately private, writings of even so great a man as Luther. Luther's catechisms took on this character of public confessions through their extensive use in churches and schools and by their inclusion among the other documents in the Book of Concord. The catechisms, then, can and must be viewed both as important writings in Luther's theological corpus and as normative public documents that help us define what "Lutheran" theology is. For this reason the anthropology of the catechisms will provide us with the central framework for understanding Lutheran anthropology.

What are the Catechisms?

Of course, Luther's catechisms do not present us with systematic theology in the usual (modern) sense of the word.[12] And it is also good to remember Tuomo Mannermaa's warning against the temptation to "systematize" Luther too much.[13] Nevertheless, the catechisms (and especially the Small Catechism) serve an important hermeneutical function in Lutheran theology, providing as they do a "map" to guide the believer through the in-

---

11. Another approach would be to begin by arguing for the substantial agreement between Luther and Melanchthon, as for example in the Augsburg Confession, which is persuasive where Melanchthon's authority rivals that of Luther; cf. Kolb's discussion of Selnecker, in *Martin Luther as Prophet, Teacher, and Hero*, 70ff. In the present discussion, and given the Finns' assertion of Luther as authoritative for "Lutheran" theology, the catechisms provide a more natural point of contact between Luther's writings and the *corpus doctrinae* of Lutheran churches.

12. Arand, *That I May Be His Own*, 147.

13. Mannermaa, "*Über die Unmöglichkeit*."

exhaustible details that arise as one lives by faith and reflects on the faith.[14] The Small Catechism, for all its brevity and simplicity—simplicity that is real without being reductionistic—is at the same time perhaps Luther's most systematic work.[15] This quasi-systematic (or better: hermeneutical) character of the catechism was occasioned by its purpose: to provide ordinary preachers and simple people an introduction and orientation to the most important essentials of Christianity. Luther's career as a theologian prompted most of his writings to emerge *ad hoc* as responses to specific situations and challenges. But the specific challenge that gave birth to the catechism was the challenge of foundations; not in learned theological arguments on subtle controversies of the day, but in the normal course of everyday Christian life. "Having preached and written on the parts of the catechism regularly over a period of thirteen years, [Luther] was arguably better prepared to write the catechism than any other writing."[16] With that extensive background and preparation, Luther sets out in the SC to offer a "brief, plain, and simple version" of the basics which every Christian can be expected to know (SC Intro 1).

Knowledge, in the sense of information, was not Luther's only (or even primary) goal in the SC, although he had seen clearly enough the "deplorable, wretched deprivation" that resulted from sheer ignorance. The effect of unchristian ignorance is unchristian life, and he found the people living "like simple cattle or irrational pigs" (SC Intro 3). So Luther urged that people be taught the basics, i.e., that they memorize in a fixed form the Ten Commandments, the Creed, and the Lord's Prayer. These were texts that would be practiced and used in regular, even daily, repetition in the context of each Christian's life in the church. Only after these texts were committed to memory would the goal be to instill a clearer, more thorough understanding of what the texts meant (SC intro 14). For this purpose Luther offers the brief explanations contained in his SC. This process was expected to take considerable time, and the assumption was that the people would gradually come to understand what they already knew and practiced. On the one hand, such an approach to teaching the faith may seem repetitive and artificial; but Luther saw the core of Christian essentials (Decalogue, Creed, and Lord's Prayer) as the

14. Arand, *That I May Be His Own*, 109–15.

15. *Ibid.*, 147f.

16. *Ibid.*, 148.

basic architecture of Christian living, so that the believer never "outgrew" these simple rudiments, or advanced to a point where they were no longer needed. Luther offered himself as an example of this (LC Preface 7f).

The catechism (in the sense of the three core texts Luther received from the tradition, apart from any commentary or explanation on those texts) has a "centering" and stabilizing effect on the theological life of Christians, however educated and subtle they may become. Luther's "catechisms" (i.e., those core texts plus Luther's explanations) work in much the same way; this is particularly true of the SC, the length and style of which facilitate easy memorization and frequent repetition. Form, theological content, and function are interwoven in the catechisms, so that the "knowledge" imparted by the catechism(s) is far more than merely a body of information; it is a practical knowledge that forms the life of faith and informs reflection on the faith. The goal of the catechisms can thus be described, in Arand's phrase, as the "art of living by faith."[17]

The Voice of the Catechisms

All of the foregoing orientation to the nature and use of Luther's catechisms helps us understand more clearly the content and function of Luther's understanding of what it means to be human. As we have noted, this is especially important for our present purpose because the catechisms bridge the distinction between Luther's (essentially private, however influential) theology and (public) Lutheran doctrine. Unlike many of the other sixteenth-century documents in the Book of Concord, the catechisms are largely free of the polemical tone and the narrow focus of theological battle which necessarily characterize, for instance, the Augsburg Confession and the Formula of Concord. Luther's catechisms set out to explain the essentials of basic Christianity by forming in the believer certain distinctively Christian patterns of thinking and living. Within these basic patterns, as part of this "map" to all of Scripture and all of Christian living,[18] the key insights about anthropology are part of "a seamless integration of doctrine and life,"[19] and correspond to various features on the larger landscape of the other Lutheran confessional docu-

17. *Ibid.*, 145ff.

18. Arand & Voelz, "The Lutheran Confessions as Normative Guides for Reading Scripture," 367f.

19. *Ibid.*, 20.

ments. If the catechisms teach the "art of living by faith," then where does anthropology fit into that art?

To begin with, we must note that the catechisms teach the Christian to speak and think of human life in concrete rather than abstract terms. This concrete specificity is most obvious in the explanation of the creed in the SC. Thus there is not a "theory" of human origins developed in the Catechisms, but only the confident confession "that God has made me." There is no discussion of "sin" in general, but rather the stark recognition of my own state as "a lost and condemned human being." The work of the Spirit is not "systematized" in the usual sense of the word in a locus on pneumatology, but involves a series of verbs with "me" as the object: the Spirit calls, enlightens, sanctifies, keeps, forgives, and raises me.

The decisive, central issue in Luther's treatment of the catechism is faith.[20] It is precisely faith which God demands in the Decalogue, especially the first commandment; faith which is given as a gift of the triune God in the Creed; faith which is exercised and practiced in the Lord's Prayer; and faith which grasps the promise of God's sacramental word. The catechism aims not just to educate or inform, but to inculcate a faith-centered way of thinking, speaking, and living in believers who know themselves to be addressed by God's command and promise, and who respond to God's command and promise in concrete ways.

The first-person voice in Luther's catechisms results from this central concern with faith. The first-person voice is natural enough, perhaps, when explaining the creed (the *ego* is explicit in the "*credo* . . . ," "I believe . . ."). But Luther maintains the same first-person perspective in his explanation of other parts of the catechism as well. Thus in the Decalogue, God addresses the Christian as "you" ("*Du*"), and the responding explanations are not generalized descriptions of human religious obligations, but framed in the first person plural. "We" who are addressed by God in the commandments are the ones who are to answer him with fear and love. When explaining the Lord's Prayer, Luther naturally follows the voice of the prayer itself, namely that of believers who pray with other believers. Here again we learn what we are praying for and what we may expect from our heavenly Father. But Luther's explanation of the LP does not so much teach *about* prayer as it teaches Christians to pray.

---

20. Arand, *That I May Be His Own*, 148ff.

Theses comments about the centrality of faith and the first-person "voice" of Luther's catechisms provide a foundational anthropological insight, namely that our knowledge of ourselves and our understanding of what it means to be human are never self-referential or autonomous. Understanding anthropology from a Lutheran perspective means to chart our knowledge of human existence in the service of faith. And to do that we need to develop what Oswald Bayer calls a "catechetical-systematics"[21] that mines the themes sketched in the catechisms and developed throughout the Lutheran Confessions. Lutheran anthropology stands in service of faith, and therefore it seeks to understand human existence as a matter of the word of God; for only that divine word is the object of faith. As Gerhard Ebeling put it, with reference to Luther's understanding of faith, "The word decides about the human being's existence as human."[22] The same is true of the Lutheran anthropology of the catechisms and the other Lutheran Confessions. To be, and to be human, is to be addressed by God's word. For the Word does not merely communicate divinely accurate information, but actually brings about the reality it speaks. This utter reliance on the word of God to "decide" about human existence is simply another way of expressing the Lutheran commitment to *sola fide*, for faith's object is the effective promise of God, the Creator and Redeemer.

In what follows, basic insights from Luther's catechisms will be developed as the framework around which the consistent "Lutheran anthropology" in the Book of Concord is built.

LUTHERAN ANTHROPOLOGY: TWO 'SIMUL'S

The anthropology of the Lutheran Confessions can be described in terms of two paradoxes, each involving a tension between interrelated contradictions. These paradoxes are summed up in two *simul*-relationships. To be genuinely and fully human means to be "*simul creatus et peccator*," and also to be "*simul peccator et iustus*." We need to explore both of these tensions to appreciate the Lutheran understanding of what it means to be human. As we shall see, this understanding contrasts sharply with the anthropology of *theosis* which emerges from the Mannermaa school.

---

21. Bayer, "I Believe That God Has Created Me With All That Exists. An Example of Catechetical-Systematics." *Lutheran Quarterly* VIII n.s., no. 2 (Summer 1994), 133–37.

22. Ebeling, "Problem des Natürlichen," 284.

Simul Creatus et peccator: Creation and Sin in the Lutheran Confessions and the Anthropology of Theosis

HOMO CREATUS

The anthropology of the Lutheran Confessions does not begin with human beings, but with God. The first thing to be said about human existence is in fact a statement about God. Thus the Lutheran doctrine of humanity begins with a confession of God as "Maker of heaven and earth." This terse assertion of the Apostles' and Nicene Creeds is echoed with no elaboration in AC I and SA I. But the confession about God is explicitly developed and connected to anthropology in Luther's catechetical explanations in the SC and LC. The focus of such a confession is not on the creature, but on the Creator.

This truth is as counter-cultural and counter-intuitive today as it was uncontested in the sixteenth century. Yet nothing else of the Lutheran theological understanding of human life can be understood without some careful attention to this prime axiom. Schlink is therefore correct when he finds (*Theology of the Lutheran Confessions*, 37ff) the anthropology of the Confessions emerging from the revelation of God as Creator: the starting point for anthropology is not *homo creatus* but rather *Deus creator*. God reveals himself to be the maker of heaven and earth, and of all things visible and invisible. In the explanation of the First Article of the Creed, Luther teaches the believer to take the short but crucial step to conclude that God is thus *my* maker, the maker and source of everything that makes and keeps me as the creature I am, and thus the source of my being and my identity. The human creature does not, in fact, live as a self-existent and autonomous being, but only as one who is made by Another and is always dependent on Another, i.e., as a creature of the Creator. And as human existence is dependent on God as the Source, so also the human being cannot arrive at proper and accurate self-understanding from a vantage point of autonomy and self-existence.[23]

---

23. This point about not only the "ontological" but also the "epistemological" priority of creation for anthropology is echoed in Luther's "Disputation Concerning Man" (1536): "[human reason] does not know itself a priori, but only a posteriori. Therefore, if philosophy or reason itself is compared with theology, it will appear that we know almost nothing about man. . . . Nor is there any hope that man . . . can himself know what he is until he sees himself in his origin which is God" (AE 34:137f; WA 39I).

What do we mean when we confess that we are creatures? To begin with, God's work of original creation *ex nihilo* is confessed in the Book of Concord, both in the ecumenical creeds themselves, and in the close paraphrases of the creeds that begin both the Augustana (AC I) and the Smalcald Articles (SA I.1). In the light of Luther's catechisms, the "*ex nihilo*" of God's act of creation includes but is not limited to a proposition about the original material of the universe. In terms of the catechisms, the creation *ex nihilo* correlates with the aspect of God's free and gracious and undeserved initiative. Thus the catechism explains the first article of the creed by confessing that God does all his (present and ongoing) creative work "without any merit or worthiness of mine at all." Human creatures stand before their Creator utterly without merit or worthiness, entirely dependent on God's unearned love and goodness, not only because they are sinners but already because they are *creatures*. One might say that the "*ex nihilo*" is the "*sola gratia*" of the doctrine of creation. As Oswald Bayer puts it, "out of nothing' (*ex nihilo*) means: undeservedly, gratuitously."[24]

But original creation as such is never really in the foreground of the discussion. There was no need to focus discussion on this matter, since this doctrine was not disputed in the sixteenth century. The lack of emphasis in the Confessions on the particulars of God's original creation (e.g., the precise length of the six days in Genesis 1) corresponds to the way in which creation is used by the Confessions as a resource for theological insight. Such insight grows out of a theological system in which the Creator's ongoing and constant work of creation, provision, and preservation takes center stage.

The Small Catechism's simple assertion, "I believe that God has made me together with all creatures," is the classic expression of such a Lutheran theological articulation of the doctrine of creation. The voice of faith (which, as we have seen, is the voice of the Catechism) is less interested in the details of original creation, than in the present[25] reality of God's creative work in and for me. This focus on the fact of creation (the "what" in this doctrinal locus) is completely characteristic of the theology

24. Bayer, "I Believe That God Has Made Me . . . ," 157.

25. Bayer comments on the significance of Luther's use of the present tense in the SC, "I Believe That God Has Made Me . . . ," 146. Albrecht Peters also points to the "presence" of the Creator in the sense of nearness and in the sense of time, Peters, *Der Glaube*, 74–76. See also Johannes Schwanke, "Luther on Creation," in *Lutheran Quarterly* XVI n.s., no. 1 (Spring 2002), 2–4.

of the Lutheran Confessions. It is therefore not unimportant that Luther's catechetical question is *"Was ist das?"* ("what is that?"), which does not probe for hidden "meanings" but rather prompts a clear restatement of the material.[26]

This celebration of the "what" of creation, which is exemplified in the SC, stands in sharp contrast to a preoccupation with what may be called creation's technology or apparatus (the "how"). In the face of contemporary challenges, that contrast gives the Lutheran understanding of creation a depth and durability that is perhaps missed in some other contemporary Christian approaches. Modern humans simply do not define themselves as creatures at all, so that assertions and arguments about the "how" of creation seem utterly out of touch with their experience. But when the Lutheran doctrine of creation focuses rather on the "what" of creation, it does so in terms of a host of tangible, immediate realities from everyday life, not in terms of unique and unrepeatable events in the remote past and out of reach of direct human knowledge.

It is worth comparing the Lutheran approach to, or use of, the doctrine of creation with that of classic Calvinism. If a Lutheran theology of creation concentrates on the "what" and contemporary fundamentalism argues for the "how," it might be accurate to describe a Calvinist view as a focus on the "why." "What is the chief and highest aim of man?" asks the Westminster Catechism. When the answer is given, "Man's chief and highest end is to glorify God and fully to enjoy him forever," this is certainly understood to be based on the presupposition that man is a creature. It is precisely this creatureliness that puts the human creature into a particular relationship vis a vis the Creator, and defines human purpose and responsibility. But the point here is simply that the *fact* of creation is implicit rather than explicit, and that man's being as creature recedes into the background as the focus concentrates on the "theological purpose" of human creatures. In this perspective, the vertical, theological dimension of human life is the only aspect of existence that has any real meaning. But what is missing from this "radically theological" view of man and his created *purpose* is the connection of human creatures with each other and with all of creation—the *"samt allen Kreaturen"* of Luther's Small Catechism. Human creatures do not exist solely in the vertical dimension of their relationship with God, *coram Deo,* but live concretely in the world

26. Cf. Arand, *That I May Be His Own,* 102f.

where they find themselves in a complex web of relationships. *Homo creatus* lives before God, in community with other human creatures and as steward of the world. That is to say, we live also *coram hominibus* and *coram mundo*. Indeed, secular disciplines focus exclusively on the *coram mundo* aspect of life—and properly so. This horizontal dimension of human life is appreciated and celebrated as a gift from the Creator in the Lutheran understanding. And this is because, following Luther's lead, the Confessions focus with some care on what creation actually is, rather than deeming only the "how" and the "why" as worthy of theological attention. Similarly, in the Westminster Catechism God's work of "creation" is explicitly limited to his work of making the universe *ex nihilo* in the beginning (Question 15), thus removing it some distance from the life of normal believers. The Lutheran Confessions, following the lead of Luther's catechisms, refuse to draw any real distinction between creation and preservation.[27]

The anthropology of the Lutheran Confessions provides rich resources for confessing faith in God the Creator in the contemporary world. The details of the origins of the world and of human beings seem to have preoccupied Christian defense of the doctrine of creation since the challenge of Darwin's theories about human origins. Anti-Darwinian Christian apologetics have produced energetic attempts either to refute biological evolution altogether or to appropriate it within a theistic frame of reference. By contrast, the Lutheran confessional starting point for the doctrine of creation defends the theologically more significant point that "I am a creature of God." In other words, the argument about creation is not really an argument about Adam and Eve but an argument about who *I* am and my place in the universe. The simple assertion which the Catechism places in the mouth of the confessing believer ("I believe that God has created me . . .") addresses the really urgent question in contemporary minds, more than arguments about the age of the earth or the interpretation of fossils. As Edmund Schlink notes, "the problem of the doctrine of creation is by no means confined to the *how* of the original divine creative process, but also includes the *what* of the creative activity of God today amid the fluctuations of catastrophe and renewal within the present-day world."[28] Behind Schlink's remark is the insight that creation

---

27. Schlink, *Theology of the Lutheran Confessions*, 39.
28. *Ibid.*, 38.

does not become a "problem" for people today primarily because we won-der whether Adam and Eve were real individuals in remote history, but rather because we are uncertain whether we as living individuals stand in any real relationship with a Creator God.

The Creator brings human creatures into being through his word of creation, so that human creatures have real and structured existence. The "nature" of human creatures consists in that reality and structure called into being by the Creator's word: we are what and who he says we are. The reality and structure of human creatures includes physical, bodily life, life which is affirmed, even emphasized, in the Lutheran Confessions. Lutheran theology rejects all kinds of dualism which denigrate the body, as well as all attempts to set up some kind of higher "spiritual" life based on an ascetic monastic ideal. Instead, such things as marriage and "secular" activities are stressed as not only acceptable and appropriate for human creatures, but even the normal and highest expressions of genuine hu-manity, blessed by the Creator's word of command and promise. Exercises of bodily discipline and mortification "should not serve the purpose of earning grace but of keeping the body in a condition that does not pre-vent performing the duties required by one's calling."[29]

With regard to the soul, the Lutheran Confessions affirm the reality of the soul but display an almost complete disregard for any metaphysical questions of the substance or nature or specific attributes of the human soul. The soul may be regarded as the whole human creature *coram Deo*, rather than as a separate component part or component of human nature. What must be said about the soul, in defense against a Platonic ideal of the spiritual as superior to the physical, is that just as the body is not viewed as evil in and of itself, so the soul is not imagined to be good by itself. Far from being separate or separable components of a composite human nature, "body and soul" are properly regarded as a way of describing the whole human creature by means of a hendiadys. Closely related to the soul are the non-physical faculties attributed to human creatures: reason, will, and the senses or mental faculties. All of these taken together are what the Creator makes when he makes "me." "God has given me and still preserves my body and soul: eyes, ears, and all limbs and senses; reason and all metal faculties" (SC Creed 2).

29. AC XXVI.38. "Fasting and bodily preparation" are described in similar terms in SC LS 10.

As long as the concept of human nature is confined to "body and soul" (even when that holistic compound is augmented or elaborated by mention of specific faculties), it may seem that God has created self-subsistent individuals with no fundamental connections to each other. Yet the web of relationships in which human creatures are placed by the creative word of God are also constitutive of human nature in the fullest sense. Human beings are created in the complimentary plurality of male and female in fruitful union (Genesis 1:26–28), and this points to the irreducible God-created design of marriage, family, and household. Plurality, mutuality, and complimentarity among human creatures extend into larger relations of wider communities and government, so that these, too, are properly regarded as dimensions of genuine human existence. "Moreover, he gives all physical and temporal blessings—good government, peace, security. . . . All this is comprehended in the word 'Creator'" (LC Creed 15–16).

Human nature, in the sense of the created structure of human existence, extends beyond the single individual. The Creator mediates our very being through other human beings (e.g., our parents), sustains and provides for us through others (e.g., lawful vocations and government), and then does the same for other human beings through us. Any adequate grasp of human nature must not only regard the human individual in isolation but also include this interdependent aspect of what it means to be human. Indeed, this may be extended still further, to embrace the Creator-designed relations with the non-human world: the catechisms mention property, house, clothing, food, and even seemingly distant elements and forces of nature: "Besides, he makes all creation help provide the benefits and necessities of life—sun, moon, and stars in the heavens; day and night; air, fire, water, the earth and all that it yields and brings forth; birds, fish, animals, grain, and all sorts of produce" (LC Creed 14). Wolfhart Pannenberg remarks that "man's community with God directs him back into the world. In any case that is the thought involved in the biblical idea about man as the image of God. Man's destiny for God manifests itself in his dominion over the world."[30] The irreducible plurality and complimentarity of human existence, and the interconnectedness of human creatures with the rest of creation, need to be emphasized and recovered in opposition to the individualism of modernity. A human creature

30. Pannenberg, *What Is Man?*, 14.

who lacks such relationships (e.g., an orphan, a prisoner, a castaway) is nevertheless a human being, but in the same sense as a human being who has lost arms or legs or eyes is still human.

Creation itself, of course, is far from being a self-evident fact, at least to modern eyes and minds. What humans encounter in their everyday experiences may more often be conceptualized as "nature" (that which simply *is*, especially when we consider it prior to and apart from human action upon it), but not necessarily as "creation" (that is, reality which has its source and origin in God the Creator). In fact, the Lutheran understanding of "creation" embraces both God's activity and that which exists as a result of that activity (i.e., us humans "*samt allen Kreaturen*").

Indeed, the two are intimately connected. Oswald Bayer has drawn attention to the fact that to assert that the natural, empirical world is "creation" also implies the acknowledgment that the Creator addresses his creatures *through* his creatures.[31] God the Creator works mediately within and for his creation. This is even clearer in the LC than in the SC's explanation of the 1st article of the Creed. There Luther explains that God not only gives and preserves the immediate necessities of life—body, soul, all faculties, daily necessities, etc. (SC Cr 2), but he expands the horizon of God's creative giving to embrace the whole natural world—even the whole cosmos. "Besides, he makes all creation help provide the benefits and necessities of life—sun, moon, and stars in the heavens; day and night; air, fire, water, the earth and all it yields and brings forth; birds, fish, animals, grain, and all sorts of produce." (LC Creed 14) Everywhere human creatures look in the universe, they are confronted with the giving goodness of the Creator.

Since the Lutheran understanding of creation embraces the mediation of God's gifts of creation, it is not threatened by any exploration of the means God uses. Thus the catechism's confession, "I believe that God has made me together with all creatures," is not shaken or undermined by a detailed knowledge of genetics and embryology, all of which simply help me understand the created means through which my Creator has done his work. Faith in the Creator does not require ignorance or naiveté about the universe, because the Lutheran understanding of creation is that God acts *for* his creatures *through* his creatures. This fact of God's ongoing, mediated work of creation embraces the whole inanimate world,

---

31. Bayer, "*Schöpfung als »Rede«*".

so that the so-called laws of nature can be seen as tools and vehicles of his ongoing work of creation, preservation and provision. For example, the phenomena of climate, seasons, and weather proceed along (at least partially!) understandable "natural" laws, without detracting at all from faith's recognition of good weather and fertile fields as gifts of God.

And as the Creator gives them such necessities through inanimate creation, he also provides what they need through the means of other humans at work in the world: "Moreover, he gives all physical and temporal blessings—good government, peace, security" (LC Creed 15). Through our fellow human creatures, God makes us who we are, gives us what we need, and protects us from the many dangers and threats in the world. This idea of the mediation of God's work of creation through other creatures is echoed in Luther's explanations of the Decalogue, especially in the LC. There the giving hand of the Creator is seen in God's law, as in Luther's comments on the 1st Commandment: "Although much that is good comes to us from men, we receive it all from God through his command and ordinance. Our parents and all authorities—in short, all people placed in the position of neighbors—have received the command to do us all kinds of good. So we receive blessings not from them, but from God through them" (LC TC 26). The same thought recurs in connection with the 4th Commandment: "through civil rulers, as through our own parents, God gives us food, house and home, protection and security" (150). Similarly, parents and those in authority are reminded that God wants to provide for others through them: "[God] has given and entrusted children to us with the command that we train them according to his will; otherwise God would have no need of father and mother" (173). So many and ubiquitous are God's "hands, channels and means" (26) through which he blesses that it is impossible for us to imagine (at least from our own experience and direct knowledge) the Creator at work *except* in this mediated way through other creatures.

It is not at all accidental that Luther's Catechisms (as Schlink notes) "do not distinguish between creation and preservation, nor do the other Confessions make a clear distinction."[32] Nor is this "failure" to make such a distinction a sign of imprecision or neglect of these doctrines in Lutheran theology. Schlink takes this prime assertion of the creatureliness of human beings (not just of humanity originally but also of each man and woman

---

32. Schlink, *Theology of the Lutheran Confessions*, 39.

individually and in the present) as the starting point for his development of the counter-empirical duality of man as both creature and sinner.

To be a creature is to be placed into direct and indirect relationships with our Creator, and this implies that human creatures are not in any sense self-subsisting. Rather, the true existence and identity of human creatures does not reside in themselves, but properly outside of the self, in God (as the source and author of their being) and in the neighbor, through whom the Creator addresses and serves them, and toward whose good they are directed in their vocation.

The revelation of God as *Deus creator* contains within it the recognition of the human being as *homo creatus*. Beyond that, the insight that God's creating work continues in the present world, carried out mediately through other creatures, allows the further assertion that we may also describe the human creature as *homo creator*, at least in a conditioned and limited sense.[33] For the creature joins in the Creator's work in a host of commonplace yet profoundly important ways, from procreation to daily labor to civil government. This human participation or cooperation in acts of creation allows for a theological understanding of human work that is both profoundly important and yet relieved of the burden of contributing something toward salvation. This insight into the real value and place of human creativity and work receives inadequate development in Lutheran theological descriptions of anthropology, but it is alluded to in several places in the Lutheran Confessions. The LC mentions tasks such as government and preservation of temporal peace, functions of human rulers, as ways in which God the Creator provides for life's necessities. The same idea is implicit in AC XVI, where all kinds of legitimate secular life are reclaimed as proper arenas for genuine Christian life. "Christians

33. Indeed, the "limits" on human creation are essential and valuable. G. K. Chesterton described the peculiar character of human creativity well:

> God is that which can make something out of nothing. Man (it may truly be said) is that which can make something out of anything. In other words, while the joy of God be unlimited creation, the special joy of man is limited creation, the combination of creation with limits. Man's pleasure, therefore, is to possess conditions, but also to be partly possessed by them; to be half-controlled by the flute he plays or by the field he digs. The excitement is to get the utmost out of given conditions; the conditions will stretch, but not indefinitely. A man can write an immortal sonnet on an old envelope, or hack a hero out of a lump of rock. But hacking a sonnet out of a rock would be a laborious business, and making a hero out of an envelope is almost out of the sphere of practical politics. (*What's Wrong with the World* [New York: Sheed and Ward, 1910], 112.)

may without sin exercise political authority; be princes and judges; pass sentences and administer justice according to imperial and other existing laws; punish evildoers with the sword; wage just wars; serve as soldiers; buy and sell; take required oaths; possess property; be married; etc." (AC XVI.2). Human beings can and should make use of these "good creations of God" (Ap XVI.1) as they live in the world. This is the basis of the AC's argument in favor of the marriage of priests: the enforcement of celibacy is "contrary to all divine, natural, and civil law" (AC XXIII 13), and seeks to forbid participation in the structured order of marriage "which God himself instituted and left open for people to enter." Having thus abandoned and prohibited the ordered freedom of God's creation, it is no surprise when those who forbid marriage encounter "terrible offense, adultery, and other immorality" (AC XXIII 3). The Apology's argument in this regard stresses even more than the AC the unalterable character of God's created order, defined and set in motion by his word and command.[34]

When human creatures engage in such "good creations of God" and carry out their proper work and vocation in the world, they do so with the exercise of a certain degree of choice or free will with respect to these "secular" matters. This exercise of limited freedom in the affairs of the world and the labors of daily life means that men and women are at the same time actively involved in precisely the created means by which the Creator works to give and sustain life; they are instruments (whether they know it or not) of God's ongoing work of creation. A theology which could take into account the co-creative activity of human beings would be in a position not only to sketch what might be called a theology of artistic creation, but also to embrace the whole spectrum of all kinds of human work and vocation in a theological perspective.[35]

---

34. Cf. Ap XXIII 7 on the Scriptural doctrine of creation of the sexes; and *ibid.*, 9 on an argument from natural law.

35. Dorothy L. Sayers provides a fascinating reflection on the human creative process as an analogue to the doctrine of the Trinity in *The Mind of the Maker*. She also devotes a chapter of her book *Creed or Chaos?* (Manchester, NH: Sophia Institute Press, 1974) to the matter of the value of vocation. And again Chesterton has got here ahead of us, seeing the connection between creation, art, and common human work:

> The average man cannot cut clay into the shape of a man, but he can cut earth into the shape of a garden; and though he arranges it with red geraniums and blue potatoes in alternate straight lines, he is still an artist; because he has chosen. . . . Property is merely the art of democracy. It means that every man should have something that he can shape in his own image, as he is shaped in the image of

To be a creature is to be addressed by the creative word of God, by which he brings us into existence and sustains our lives by providing the ordered freedom of our existence. Thus there is an intimate connection between creation and law in Lutheran theology. But when "law" is understood exclusively in terms of accusation or condemnation, this connection is lost. Then the law becomes a more or less arbitrary word of judgment imposed rather artificially upon self-existent human beings, rather than the moral structure of the universe which human creatures inhabit. In the categories of the Lutheran Confessions, this connection between creation and law is the "first use" of the law, by which "external discipline may be maintained against the unruly and the disobedient" (FC Ep VI.1). It is also referred to as the civil use of the law, which orders human life in marriage, family, and community.

The law of God thus establishes a specific kind of order in the world, sometimes called "orders of creation," which is the shape of God's giving.[36] In the Catechisms, the first and most central fact about human vocations is not whether we *recognize* God's created orders within them, but the fact that God continues to work in the world through human beings and the structures of human life. Of course, the *existence* of such moral structure or created order in the universe (i.e., the *fact* of God's activity through human "marks") and the possibility of human *knowledge* of it are two separate questions. The Decalogue expresses exactly these limits and this order that characterize what we may call "genuine human life" (i.e., life that is ordered and structured as the Creator designed, and as he still creates, gives, and preserves). But to some extent this order is perceptible without revelation. So in some sense the Decalogue is viewed as a summary of natural law, rather than an introduction to something new and uniquely Christian. This is how Luther explains the 3rd Commandment in the LC, having noted that the literal meaning of the Sabbath does not

---

heaven. But because he is not God, but only a graven image of God, his self-expression must deal with limits; properly limits that are strict and even small. (*What's Wrong with the World*)

36. The concept of "orders of creation" ("*Schöpfungsordnungen*") is problematic when it is developed in the way Werner Elert proceeds, because it so easily becomes a means of justifying and legitimizing many different corrupted human institutions. There is a constant temptation to identify structures (including political structures) which exist at the moment with "orders of creation" in a way that forbids any challenge to those structures. The political quietism of well-meaning Lutherans in the face of Nazism is only one example of how "orders of creation" can be misapplied as a theological category.

apply to Germans. Even so, he continues, "We observe them, first, because our bodies need them. Nature teaches and demands that the common people—menservants and maidservants who have gone about their work or trade all week long—should retire for a day to rest and be refreshed." (LC TC 83)

This is obviously not to say that all human beings will automatically or infallibly arrive at an accurate knowledge of this law. But the obscurity or ambiguity of natural law is a consequence of sin, not an intrinsic limitation of creation. Before sin entered the world, human knowledge of God's law was perfect, "for they were created in the image of God" (FC Ep VI.2). In the world after the fall, the goodness of God the Creator is often hidden beneath the various evils of the world, and remains a matter of faith to be asserted sometimes in the teeth of the evidence, rather than an empirical conclusion.

> Those who trust in God and not in mammon suffer grief and want and are opposed and attacked by the devil. They have neither money, prestige, nor honor, and can hardly stay alive.... Therefore, we must hold fast to these words, even in the face of this apparent contradiction, and be certain that they do not lie nor deceive but will yet prove true. (LC TC 42)

As Melanchthon remarked, "man's nature is divided" (*Loci Communes 1543*); this means that humans neither know the law perfectly, nor can they encounter the law without judgment (as we shall see in the next section).

Nevertheless, human reason, even clouded and corrupted by sin after the fall, can arrive at some knowledge of the law by which God orders and preserves our life in the world. The Apology acknowledges this real but imperfect vestige of natural knowledge of the law, when it concedes: "to some extent human reason naturally understands [the law] since reason has the same judgment divinely written on the mind" (Ap IV.7). In particular the requirement of the second table of the Decalogue[37] can be somewhat understood (Ap IV.34), and human beings can engage in a limited external obedience to this naturally grasped law. Such partial, outward obedience Melanchthon refers to as "the righteousness of reason

---

37. In the 1543 *Loci Communes* Melanchthon sketched an argument that the requirements of the first table were also perceived, albeit dimly, by unaided human reason. *Loci Communes 1543*, translated by J. A. O. Preus (St. Louis: Concordia, 1992), 71.

or at the very least, the righteousness of the law" (Ap IV.21), or "civil righteousness" (34). Melanchthon's rebuttal of his opponents allows him just a brief explanation of the place and purpose of such righteousness: "Now we maintain that God requires the righteousness of reason. . . . God even honors it with temporal rewards. Still, it ought not be praised at Christ's expense" (Ap IV.22–24).

In the passage just cited, Melanchthon is engaged in the dispute about justification, and so does not make explicit the connection between the righteousness of reason and creation, which is clearer in the catechisms. But despite this imperfect perception and ambiguous apprehension of natural law, the fact remains that, considered purely in terms of creation, God's law is simply good, for it establishes the limits and conditions which genuine human life require.[38] Here Melanchthon seems to echo thoughts of Luther, as expounded in the treatise "How Christians Should Regard Moses" (1525).[39] Certainly Melanchthon himself later developed his concept of natural law in more detail, not to give it any role in human salvation but to account for the continuing good influence of order and discipline in the world.[40]

Lutheran dogmatic theology has tended to neglect this function of law in the context of creation, providing order and structure which protect

38. Some Lutheran theologians have been sharply critical of the tradition, generally identified with Melanchthon's influence, which reclaims some place in theology for "natural theology," alongside the revelation in Scripture. This criticism seems especially pertinent in the question of anthropology. Schlink, *Der Mensch*, 6ff and 160–70; Elert, *The Structure of Lutheranism*, 49–58. Elert traces what he sees as the line of development from Melanchthon's allowance for some "natural knowledge of God," through the later dogmaticians' discussion of the "two books" of revelation (*liber naturae* and *liber scripturae*), through the Enlightenment's eventual equation of natural knowledge and revelation, causing "the apologetic theology of the eighteenth and nineteenth centuries to bleed to death . . ." (56) His claim that this path led eventually to a fundamentalistic attempt to reconcile all natural knowledge of the world with the words of Scripture seems to oversimplify this development, and he ignores the fact that Fundamentalism's ideas about Scripture had other roots. See Martin E. Marty and R. Scott Appleby, eds. *Fundamentalism Observed*. The Fundamentalism Project, vol. 1 (Chicago and London: The University of Chicago Press, 1991).

39. AE 35:155ff; WA 16:363–93. Melanchthon was thinking about the law and its place in human life on several levels all at once, natural and revealed. For an intriguing case study of his legal thought on the question of property cf. Paul Robinson, "'The Most Learned Discourses of the Philosophers and Lawyers': Roman Law, Natural Law, and Property in Melanchthon's *Loci Communes*" CJ 28 (January 2002), 41–53.

40. Melanchthon, *Loci Communes 1543*, trans. J. A. O. Preus, 70ff; cf. above, note 36.

and provide for life.[41] And indeed the "first use" of the law is described in a somewhat negative way in FC VI, namely as a restraint against overt evil and maintaining "external discipline and respectability against dissolute, disobedient people" (FC SD VI.1). Especially in the context of the debate about justification, as in the passage from the Apology just cited, this understanding of the law as providing "civil discipline to restrain the unspiritual" might be conceded but not emphasized; whatever might be said about creation and the law in that context must conclude: "Nevertheless, it ought not to be praised at the expense of Christ." This necessary defense can be, and sometimes is, understood in a way that overlooks the constructive and positive contribution of the law as the framework of life-fostering order. So in Francis Pieper's *Christian Dogmatics* the connection between creation and law is almost entirely missed, as when Pieper defines the difference between the law and the gospel to be "*Lex est Deus accusans et damnans; evangelium est Deus absolvens et iustificans*" ("the law is God accusing and damning; the gospel is God forgiving and justifying").[42]

But this sharp contrast of the law and the gospel is not the only way to understand the law, and the mere repetition of the one fact that the law does not justify obscures the good gifts which the Creator gives through the structured relationships defined by the law. But those relationships are means through which God does his creative work, as the Lutheran confessions (especially the catechisms) point out. G. K. Chesterton sums up the goodness of that structure of the law with his characteristic flamboyance: "The more I considered Christianity,[43] the more I found that while it had established a rule and order, the chief aim of that order was to give room for good things to run wild."[44] That is to say, the function of the law in creation is to define limits and boundaries, the purpose of which is as much to liberate as it is to confine and restrict. Such liberating limits and ordered freedom are necessary conditions for the life and well-being

41. In one place Schlink describes how "in the old Protestant theology, rebirth, justification, and sanctification . . . were strictly separated from the article *de homine* by Christology," but that this was altered and undermined by Pietism's emphasis on human experience. (*Der Mensch*, 5–6)

42. Pieper, *Christian Dogmatics*, III, 250.

43. Although Chesterton refers to the "rule and order" of *Christianity*, his context makes it plain that most of what he is talking about here is not the particulars of specifically Christian faith, but what might be termed "sub-Christian orthodoxy," a way of looking at the world that corresponds to God's created reality.

44. G. K. Chesterton, *Orthodoxy* (London: The Bodley Head, 1908), 158.

of human creatures, in much the same way that the boundary of a cell's membrane is essential to the cell's life.

There is no trace of this rich and positive view of human creatureliness in the anthropology of *theosis*. In particular, Mannermaa and Peura fail to recognize the way in which creation places human beings among other creatures, both human and non-human (i.e., the "*samt allen Kreaturen*" of Luther's catechisms). This failure means that they are also incapable of appreciating the myriad ways in which the Creator addresses his creatures through other creatures—thus giving intrinsic and continuing value to common human vocations as co-creative "masks of God." If the value of the human being lies exclusively in union with God which transcends ordinary creaturely existence (thus making me "mehr als ein Mensch"), then what the human is as creature has no real significance at all. But the Lutheran central insight about justification by grace apart from works was also the root of the characteristically Lutheran view of vocation and "natural" human life. The vast implications of the Lutheran doctrine of creation have been inadequately appreciated, but not entirely ignored by such theologians as Gustaf Wingren[45] and Oswald Bayer.[46] These scholars have explored the depth of the theological insight in Luther and the Lutheran Confessions on precisely the question of creation. Gerhard Ebeling has also explored how the Lutheran recovery of a proper appreciation of the created world and created (and creative) human nature is in some sense a corollary of the central Lutheran doctrine of the justification of the sinner before God by faith alone—as he points out, it is only a right understanding of justification "which alone truly lets creation be creation and redemption be redemption."[47]

HOMO PECCATOR

Creation is not the only, or the final, thing that must be said about human existence. Indeed, human existence is broken and distorted, and we live amid so many kinds of evils that the goodness of the Creator is not always obvious or clear. The cause of this distortion and corruption is sin. Not only the personal effects of sickness, pain, suffering, and death are traced to the fact of sin; the fallout of sin stretch out into every kind of human

---

45. Wingren, *Creation and Law* and *Creation and Gospel*. Also "*Das Problem des Natürlichen bei Luther.*"

46. E.g., the essays collected in *Schöpfung als Anrede*.

47. Ebeling, "Problem des Natürlichen."

community and into the whole of creation. Every human creature is also a sinner, embroiled in rebellion against the Creator, so that concrete human life in the world is perverted by sin. Because of sin, human creatures do not encounter the structures and limits of the created order as the life-giving, life-preserving shape of God's giving that he intends. God's word of law, which establishes the necessary bounds of human life, becomes a word of judgment which exposes and denounces sin as soon as human creatures abandon the created order and transgress the limits. The fact of human sin makes it at best incomplete, and at worst simply wrong, to draw conclusions about "human dignity" from the statement that "God has created me." The recognition that human beings are creatures affirms the creative and giving goodness of God the Creator. Yet the mere fact of being creatures does not give us a basis from which to make demands on our Creator. The fact of creation does not lay obligations on the Creator, who is and remains free, but it does make it our proper task (duty) to "thank and praise, serve and obey him."

The anthropology of the Lutheran Confessions includes a profound acknowledgment of sin as the corruption of created humanity. The root of this corruption is at the same time both the lack of true fear and trust (which are demanded by the 1st Commandment) and the presence of "evil lust and inclination" (AC II). The AC calls this condition an "innate disease and original sin,"[48] to denote that it is pervasive and inescapable in the concrete realities of human experience in the world. This perversion of created human life is predicated of all human beings who are "born in the natural way." The inborn desire and inclination toward sin corresponded to the traditional understanding of concupiscence, and the Roman Confutation conditionally approved this article of the AC. But the Lutheran insistence that such concupiscence itself is truly sin and that it condemns corrupt human creatures to the eternal wrath of God seemed to go too far and was rejected by the Confutation.[49]

Not only does original sin place every natural human creature under God's wrath as a sinner, but it also corrupts all dimensions of human exis-

---

48. "*angeborne Seuch und Erbsunde*" / "*hic morbus seu vitium originis.*"

49. "This article's declaration that original sin means that humanity is born without fear and trust in God is to be completely rejected. As every Christian acknowledges, adults fail to fear and trust God, but this is not a fault found in children, who lack the use of reason" (Robert Kolb and James A. Nestingen, eds., *Sources and Contexts of the Book of Concord*, 107).

tence. It leaves no aspect or dimension of human life or human capacities untouched. Sin clouds and obscures human reason, so that we are unable to know and understand ourselves, the world, and God as we are designed to know. Sin disorders human relationships, and perverts and twists the human self back upon itself, with the result that relationships such as husbands and wives, or parents and children, do not fully conform to the created orders through which God would continue to create, provide for, and protect life. The creatures who were made to be directed outward toward God and neighbor are now curiously detached from others and collapsed in upon themselves like grotesque spiritual black holes.[50]

If we return to the vocabulary of the catechisms, we note that the shift from creation to sin is abrupt and irreversible. We have seen how the Creed introduces us first to the goodness of creation, in light of which the Decalogue may be seen as descriptive of the created order. But in the Second Article of the Creed, the "I" whom God created "together with all creatures" is at once seen in a sharply different light, and is exposed as "a lost and condemned human being."[51] Such a lost and condemned human inevitably encounters God's law, the moral structure of the universe summarized in the Decalogue, in a far different way than does the mere *homo creatus* of the First Article. Far from recognizing in God's law the shape of the Creator's giving love, human sinners are judged and condemned by that same law precisely because they rebel against the limits and boundaries which it sets for their existence. First and foremost, the first commandment's exclusive claim on the hearts of humans confronts their primal desire to be "like God" and to "set ourselves up as God" (LC TC 23; cp.

---

50. The American novelist Walker Percy describes this predicament of the self in *Lost in the Cosmos*, 47:

> The Self since the time of Descartes has been stranded, split off from everything else in the Cosmos, a mind which professes to understand bodies and galaxies but is by the very act of understanding marooned in the Cosmos, with which it has not connection. It therefore needs to exercise every option to reassure itself that it is not a ghost but rather a self among other selves.

51. Albrecht Peters, following Wingren, points to what he calls a "*doppelter Ansatz*" in the theology of Luther's explanations of the Creed in the SC and LC (*Der Glaube*, 50). But the somewhat jarring discontinuity between the First Article and the Second is not to be accounted for by any lack of focus or consistency in Luther's theology at this point; rather it is an expression of the tension between the First Article's view of *homo creatus* and the Second Article's concern for *homo peccator*.

Genesis 3:5),[52] that is, to abandon the created limits and orders that define the genuine freedom of human creatures and to become self-defining and "self-lawed" (autonomous).

The source and origin of our existence and our daily life is God, but the author of sin is not God the Creator, but the devil. "When we were created by God the Father, and had received from him all kinds of good things, the devil came and led us into disobedience, sin, death, and all misfortune. As a result, we lay under God's wrath and displeasure, sentenced to eternal damnation, as we had merited it and deserved it" (LC Cr 28). As we noted in the discussion of creation, so also here when describing human sin Luther's interest in the catechism is by no means focused on some primeval event; the reality of sin is immediate and personal. As Luther teaches faith to speak, the fall into sin was *my* fall, and its results and aftermath condemn *me* to death and embroil *me* in sin and blindness (LC Cr 27). It is as impossible to place any distance between myself and sin, death, the devil, and all kinds of evil as it is to distance myself from God's creating and sustaining work.

Just as there seems to be an abrupt discontinuity between the catechisms' perspective in treating the First and Second Articles of the Creed, so the Augsburg Confession makes no reference at all to what human nature *before* the fall into sin may have looked like; there is nothing to which the fallen plight of human sinners may be compared. As we saw, the confession of God as Creator (included in AC I) carries in it the implicit acknowledgement of human beings as creatures, with no elaboration of the implications of that fact. After simply beginning with God as Creator in AC I, the attention turns abruptly to human beings as sinners (AC II). The condition of fallen humanity is not mere ignorance or spiritual neutrality, but rebellion and hostility toward God; the human being has "not only turned away from God but has also become God's enemy" (FC Ep II 3). Even though they may exercise a limited scope of freedom when dealing with other created things, their wills are captive and imprisoned and cannot be directed toward God and his will. Whatever might be said of the original, perfect state of human creatures before sin entered the world, now "in spiritual and divine matters, the mind, heart, and will of the unreborn human being can in no way, on the basis of its own natural

---

52. Cf. Luther's remark: "*Fieri igitur Deum est peccatum originale*" AE 3:139. WA 42:647.

powers, understand, believe, accept, consider, will, begin, accomplish, do, effect, or cooperate. Instead, it is completely dead to the good—completely corrupted" (FC SD II 7). The result is that, "in spiritual and divine matters, which concern the soul's salvation" (FC SD II 20), all the human being's gifts, powers, intelligence, and creativity are not even neutral, but inflict further damage and continue to be at war against God, until the person is converted.

As a result of sin, humans become subject to powers that attack and attempt to undo the Creator's work. In the SC these are identified as "all sins, death, and the power of the devil" (SC Cr 4), but Luther mentions other groupings as well.[53] These powers are at odds with the life-giving order and structure of creation. Sinful human creatures will not be defined by their Creator, but insist on self-definitions which can only conceive of freedom as disregard for boundaries and limits. For that reason human creatures cannot hear God's law simply as descriptive of the life he intends for them, but must collide with the law as prohibition and as accusation. And as the law, as the catechisms explain it, centers in the First Commandment, so human disobedience is, at its root, the violation of that command: ". . . being ignorant of God, despising him, lack of fear and confidence in God, hating the judgment of God, fleeing this judging God, being angry with God, despairing of his grace, and placing confidence in temporal things, etc" (Ap II.8).

Having ceased to know their Creator through their disobedience, human sinners can no longer know themselves properly, either. This is true, obviously, in that no one can recognize his own sins fully (AC XI 1–2). But human sinners not only fail to know themselves as sinners; neither can they know themselves as creatures, because they do not know the Creator by themselves.[54] Sin means that "neither God's goodness nor God's wrath, neither man's creatureliness nor his corruption, can

---

53. E.g., "disobedience, sin, death, and all misfortune" (LC Cr 28); "the wicked world, the devil, death, sin, etc." (LC Cr 31); "the flesh, the world, and the devil" (LC LP 101); and many other similar lists of what Peters summarizes as "*Verderbensmächte*" (*Der Glaube*, 122ff).

54. Ebeling points to Luther's identification of "*cognitio Dei et hominis*" ("knowledge of God and humanity") as the sum and substance of theology ("Cognitio Dei et hominis"). When commenting on Luther's "Disputation Concerning Man," Ebeling also mentions the intriguing connection between knowledge of God and self-knowledge: the association goes back to Greek antiquity, with the Delphic inscription *gnōthi seauton* at the temple entrance (*Luthertudien* II, 448–52).

be recognized from the natural reality of man" (Schlink, 48). Schlink is here affirming the hiddenness of God, both as Creator and as Lawgiver. Neither the Creator's love nor his wrath can be observed or deduced from empirical observation in the fallen world. This is also true of human vocations, which as we already noted, function as "masks" of God; but now the masks conceal the Creator as well as perform his work in the world. It is at this point, of course, that the "natural knowledge" of God and of his law becomes problematic for theologians such as Schlink: how is any such "natural knowledge" possible if sin embroils us all in culpable ignorance of God?

The solution of this problem seems to lie in the *simul*-paradox which Schlink himself urges: human beings are at one and the same time *both* creatures *and* sinners. The anthropology of the Lutheran Confessions is not based on a description of what we can observe about human life. It is deeply counter-intuitive and counter-empirical. It begins as God the Creator addresses his creatures with word of command and promise, and that address serves as the key which unlocks what is otherwise concealed behind contradictions and ambiguous evidence. Thus each half of the paradox, the *creatus* as well as the *peccator*, is obscured and fundamentally unknowable by humans purely in terms of themselves. In addition, the two only come into paradoxical tension when they are juxtaposed by the word; creation and sin only become theologically problematic when we insist on affirming them *simul*. And here the issue is not primarily one of knowledge, in the sense of information, but rather the awareness of oneself before God. Ebeling describes Lutheran anthropology well in terms of existential self-knowledge under the impact of God's word: "Self-knowledge is now radicalized in terms of the understanding of sin, and also concentrated on the force of the law and confronted with the gospel; the result is the coexistence in tension of two ways of knowing God."[55] To "know myself" either as creature or as sinner is to be confronted with God's word and to derive my identity from who God is and what he says to me.

As universal and pervasive as sin's corruption is, this second truth about human life does not negate or simply "un-say" the word of creation. Lutheran anthropology arises out of the paradoxical tension between a radical view of sin and a stubborn insistence on the continuing truth of

---

55. Ebeling, *Lutherstudien* II, 450f.

God's creation. This tension, it must be remembered, only arises as long as creation is asserted as a present and continuing reality, rather than simply a question of origins. The Lutheran Confessions do not teach that human beings *were* created by God, but are now sinners. Instead, as Schlink explains, each human being is *at the same time* both creature and sinner, not at various times or in varying proportions but *simul* and *in toto*.[56]

That tension is maintained, and indeed heightened, when the FC insists on distinguishing between original sin and human nature. In a debate with Viktorin Strigel, the Gnesio-Lutheran Matthias Flacius had defended the idea that, after the fall, original sin is identified with the "essence" (or "formal essence") of human nature. While defending the radicalized understanding of sin that articulates the hopeless predicament of human sinners left to their own devices, the FC sharply rejects Flacius's language because it short-circuited the paradox of *simul creatus et peccator*, and "solved" the tension in favor of an unambiguous view of the human being as simply *peccator*. Resisting this temptation to resolve the paradox, the FC warns that it is necessary, even after the fall, to distinguish carefully between human nature *per se* (which is a creature of God) and "the horrible, dreadful, inherited disease corrupting their entire nature" (FC SD I 5). The difference is neither abstract nor merely academic, since Flacius' position casts the first Article of the Creed (or at least the understanding of it expressed in the catechisms) in doubt. The difference between human nature and original sin "is as great as the difference between the work of God and the work of the devil" (FC Ep I 2). After all, as we have seen, when Lutheran anthropology acknowledges that the human being is a creature of God, this is to be understood more a confession of the Creator's goodness than any claim to special dignity or privilege on the part of the creature. The art of the Formula's response lies in its stubborn unwillingness to relinquish that confession of the Creator's work, while at the same time giving no quarter to the corruption of every aspect of human life through sin.

Andreas Osiander proposed an anthropology in some ways similar to that of Flacius, at least in the sense that he regarded created human nature as inherently unrighteous. The difference between the two views is that for Osiander, human nature lacks righteousness not just because of the fall into sin, but because only God himself is righteous; a creature can

---

56. Schlink, *Theology of the Lutheran Confessions*, 40.

only be said to be righteous to the extent it participates that the essential righteousness of God himself. Thus Osiander eliminates the paradox between creatureliness and sin by ultimately denying the goodness (even the limited and penultimate goodness) of creation itself, while Flacius does so by arguing that original, good human nature had been replaced by sin.

This discussion of Flacius and Osiander and original sin is no detour from our purpose, which is to examine Lutheran anthropology and compare it with the anthropology of *theosis* as it emerges in the work of the Finnish school. It is particularly important for that purpose to trace the way the Formula navigates the challenge presented by Flacius to the correct understanding of what it means to be human, since Tuomo Mannermaa seems to approximate one position or the other, either equating human nature with sin like Flacius (although perhaps without the laborious Aristotelian vocabulary),[57] or insisting like Osiander on the divine nature as the only true righteousness. For Mannermaa, human nature is always identified with sin, corruption, and death, even as God's nature is equated with righteousness, holiness, and life. This becomes plain in the way he describes the incarnation as the clash between the divine life and human sinfulness, in which the divine righteousness swallows up, overwhelms, and conquers the human. This concept diverges from that of the Formula, where the incarnation is taken as evidence that human nature after the fall cannot be simply equated with original sin.

> In the article on redemption Scripture gives powerful testimony that God's Son assumed our nature without sin, that he 'became one of us, in every respect like us' apart from sin . . . If there were no difference between the nature or the essence of the corrupted human being and original sin, it would have to follow that Christ either did not assume our nature because he had not assumed our sin, or because he assumed our nature, he would also have assumed sin. (FC SD I 43–44)

Underlying Mannermaa's understanding of the incarnation is his anthropology, which has at this point clearly parted company with the Lutheran

---

57. A significant portion of the Article I in the SD (50–62) is devoted to clarifying the technical and often ambiguous terminology that was used in the controversy. Tuomo Mannermaa says at times that he does not wish to use philosophical jargon, but his repeated insistence on the "real-ontic" nature of the believer's union with Christ would seem to force some kind of metaphysical claim, as well.

confessional consensus regarding the human being as *simul creatus et peccator.*

Simul peccator et iustus: the Anthropology of the Gospel and Faith

Trapped by their fallen nature and unable either to know God or to fear and trust him, human beings are also unable to know themselves or grasp their identity as creatures and sinners. They are enslaved and imprisoned by the "powers of destruction" ("*Verderbensmächte,*" as Albrecht Peters describes them) which threaten to poison and undo the Creator's work.

Into that predicament of human ignorance, powerlessness, and death, God speaks the new, re-creating word of the gospel. This word, like God's first word of creation, is never simply a source of accurate information, but the voice of God addressing human creatures with his forgiveness. It is the performative *promissio* of God the Creator, which does not simply "define" human nature but actually brings about our new existence and makes us who and what we are. For human beings who are unable to discover or define their own identity, everything hangs on the command and promise of God.

Humans are first of all exposed and condemned by God's word of judgment. As we noted earlier, God's law is his design for genuine human life and the boundaries of ordered freedom. For human beings as originally created, the law carried no accusing or condemning force. Only after sin entered the world did human beings find themselves outside the boundaries of life and freedom, thus encountering the law—and even creation itself—as threat and accusation. Creation is good, but it cannot be experienced as unconditionally good in our present state. The reason for this is human sinfulness. The natural, everyday world has been disrupted and disordered by the rebellion of human creatures. Gustaf Wingren writes how this fact "problematizes" human life in the world:

> The actual problem is thus not in nature, neither plants nor things. The problem is the human being. . . . Therefore nature "sighs" and awaits the healing of the human being (Romans 8:20ff.). The "un-problematic" human being, who serves his neighbor and is thankful that he may live—who thus praises the Creator—this human being means that nature has no more problem. "The problem of the natural" has only one solution, namely the redemption of the

human being. For only the human being is fallen. The things, the animals, and the plants are purer than he.[58]

Sin, points out Wingren, is the one really "unnatural" thing in the world, a twisting and distortion of what God has created. The perversion of the world as it is (as distinct from the world as God created and intended it) is that the "unnatural" has become normal. Sin is the universal condition of human creatures since the fall, the only world of which we (ourselves embroiled in the perversion of what God made) have any direct experience. The perverse universality of the abnormality of sin does not change what nature itself (i.e., creation) *is*, but it completely corrupts the stance of the human being over against the Creator. As a consequence, the place of human creatures within and over against the rest of creation is similarly disordered.

The sinner has no choice but to encounter both creation and Creator as *law* in the "theological" sense, that is, as displays of God's wrath and judgment, and this is due to the rebelliousness of the human will. Once the human creature becomes a sinner, and thus an enemy of the Creator, the universe, once permeated by God's gifts and signs of his goodness, becomes a place in which man's divine foe can lurk behind every bush. Human creatures become alienated, not only from God himself, but also from the whole God-haunted universe in which they find themselves. Thus the first people, after they disobeyed God, could only hear the sound of the Creator walking in the garden as a threat (Genesis 3:8). When the sinner encounters creation not as gift but as a mirror of God's wrath, then the law is unavoidably at work in human life in the world, "through what has been made" (Romans 1:20). This means that two different senses of "law" are more closely related than is often recognized. "Natural law," in the sense of the ordered design of the universe, thus also functions as law in the theological sense of accusation and condemnation.[59] God's good and generous will as Creator does not cease to operate, even through the activities of sinners, whether they cooperate or not. Yet God's law *kills* the sinner, both as it operates through the creation and as the sinner is addressed by God's revealed law.

58. Wingren, " Problem des Natürlichen," 157.

59. Luther uses the terms "theological / proper / true use" of the law, cf. Wingren, "Problem des Natürlichen bei Luther," 160 & 161, n. 20. For Luther's positive assessment of "civil" and "natural" law, cf. William H. Lazareth, "Luther on Civil Righteousness and Natural Law."

Precisely to sinners killed by his law, God speaks the gospel. Humans are cast upon God's word of forgiveness. The human being's existence *coram Deo* must be decided by God's promise in Christ, if it is not to be crushed by collision with the law. In either case, to quote Ebeling again, "the word decides about the human being's existence as human."[60] It is very important for Lutheran anthropology (as for Luther's theology) that the word of the gospel not be replaced by any other ground of confidence or certainty; no other basis for being is possible.

This utter reliance on the word of the promise to create and define human existence (to the exclusion of any so-called realist ontological claims) is vividly presented in the explanations of the sacraments in Luther's catechisms. There the focus returns again and again to the promise of forgiveness which is attached to the visible elements. So the benefits of baptism are explained to be that "it brings forgiveness of sins, redeems from death and the devil, and gives eternal salvation to all who believe it, *as the words and promise of God declare*" (SC Bapt 6). When asked how the water of baptism can do such things, the Christian is taught to reply: "Clearly the water does not do it, but the Word of God, which is with and alongside the water, and faith, which trusts this Word of God in the water" (SC Bapt 10). One is reminded of Luther's comments about the water and word of baptism elsewhere:

> I the Father, I the Son, I the Holy Spirit give this water. It is not simply water, but deified water [*durchgottet wasser*], because it and my name are not far apart. It is not watery water, but divine, heavenly water, in which there is deity itself. So do not look at it as water, but wherever someone is baptized, here is poured out water mixed with God's name. . . . Thus in baptism the water is deified [*durch Gottet*], saturated with God's name.[61]

In the SC, Luther replaces the "deified water" language with the more explicit reference to the forgiveness of sins, something which is only possible because the word of God is present.[62]

With regard to the sacrament of the altar, the "reality" or "ontology" of the sacrament—what it really "is" in its substance or essence—became

---

60. Ebeling, "Problem des Natürlichen."

61. WA 37:264.25–34.

62. On Luther's emphasis on the connection of the water of baptism with God's word of promise, see Trigg, *Baptism*, 61–75.

a point of controversy. And of course, Luther and his followers staunchly defended what the sacrament *is* in debates with those who challenged it, such as Zwingli and the sacramentarians. There was no argument in this matter with the church of Rome, so the AC contains only a brief statement: "Concerning the Lord's Supper it is taught that the true body and blood of Christ are truly present under the form of bread and wine . . ." (AC X 1) Similarly, the Smalcald Articles do not engage in any lengthy defense of what the sacrament "is" but state the Luther understanding with simplicity: "We maintain that the bread and wine in the Supper are the true body and blood of Christ and that they are not only offered to and received by upright Christians but also by evil ones" (SA III 6 1). The Lutheran defense of what the sacrament "is" developed out of the controversies with the sacramentarians who denied that the body and blood of Christ were "truly and essentially present"[63] in the bread and wine of the sacrament, and with the "Crypto-Philippists" who wanted to allow only a "spiritual" reception of Christ's body and blood. In this dispute the question of whether unworthy communicants also receive Christ's body and blood (although to their judgment and harm) became a sort of litmus test to distinguish between those who held to the position of the AC and those who "spiritualized" the sacrament in some way. "This presence [of Christ's body and blood in the sacrament] is to be understood as valid not only for those who believe and are worthy, but also for those who do not believe and are unworthy" (SD VII 27) This is because the "reality" of the sacrament does not depend on human experience (either of the celebrant or of the communicant), but is entirely decided by God's word: "Even though a scoundrel receives or administers the sacrament, it is the true sacrament (that is, Christ's body and blood) just as truly as when one uses it most worthily. For it is not founded on human holiness but on the Word of God" (LC Sacr 16; quoted in SD VII 24). [64]

Given this polemical stress on the "ontology" of the sacrament, it would be reasonable to expect the SC to accent the essence of the Supper

63. The phrase preferred in FC Ep VI 2 & 6.

64. John R. Stephenson explores other aspects of Luther's writings on the Lord's Supper in his essay, *"Ein fröhlicher Wechsel: Der Fürst und der Bettler am Kreuz und am Altar,"* in *Einträchtig Lehren: Festschrift für Bischof Dr. Jobst Schöne D.D.*, edited by Jürgen Diestelmann and Wolfgang Schillhahn (Groß Oesingen: Verlag Lutherischer Buchhandlung Heinrich Harms, 1997), 432–42. Stephenson makes sympathetic use of writings by Simo Peura and Risto Saarinen, and his focus does not reflect the catechisms' near-obsession with the forgiveness of sins in and through the sacrament.

as the main thing for Christians. In other words, if one were to expect an ontological emphasis on the believer's union with Christ anywhere in the SC, then surely the section on the sacrament of the altar would be the place. It would be natural to expect Luther to stress the "real-ontic" union of the believer with Christ, the direct (even mystical) participation in Christ for salvation. But, in fact, this is definitely not the case. If the Mannermaa school were correct about assigning a central place in Luther's (and Lutheran) theology to a "real-ontic" union with Christ, then such a central teaching should find a place in what is arguably Luther's most important text on the basic of Christian faith, especially with reference to the sacrament in which Christians partake of Christ himself in the most real and "essential" way. But the catechisms lay emphatic stress on the forgiveness of sins as the main thing in the sacrament.

The theme of the Christian's union with Christ is certainly not unknown in the Lutheran Confessions. In the article on the righteousness of faith, the FC teaches that the believer is united with Christ, and that the whole Trinity dwells in the believer. The relevant passage reads:

> In the same way we must correctly explain the argument regarding the indwelling of the essential righteousness of God in us. To be sure, God the Father, Son, and Holy Spirit, who is the eternal and essential righteousness, dwells through faith in the elect, who have become righteous through Christ and are reconciled with God. (For all Christians are temples of God the Father, Son, and Holy Spirit, who moves them to act properly.) However, this indwelling of God is not the righteousness of faith, which St. Paul treats and calls *iustitia Dei* (that is, the righteousness of God), for the sake of which we are pronounced righteous before God. Rather, this indwelling is a result of faith which precedes it, and this righteousness [of faith] is nothing else than the forgiveness of sins and the acceptance of poor sinners by grace, only because of Christ's obedience and merit. (FC SD III 54)

This indwelling of God is a new reality which results from faith, and God's "eternal and essential righteousness" does become present in the believer as a power which "moves them to act properly." But the Formula also makes two crucial distinctions about this indwelling of God in the believer and its relation to justification. First, this new reality results from, and thus cannot be simply identified with, justification. The true righteousness of faith is thus not a matter decided by the ontology of the believer, not even the ontology of one in whom God dwells, but "is nothing else than the forgiveness of sins and the acceptance of poor sinners by grace, only because of Christ's obedience and merit." In this way the Formula explicitly rejects Osiander's notion of justification which identified the essential righteousness of God dwelling in the believer with the righteousness of faith.

The second distinction maintained by the Formula is between the personal union of the divine and human natures in Christ and the indwelling of God in the believer. This point comes up in the discussion of the Person of Christ in FC VIII, when the argument presents evidence that a "real exchange" ("*realis communicatio*") (SD VIII.63) has occurred between the divine and human natures in Christ's person. Here, indeed, (to mention the favorite expression of Mannermaa) the FC urges what might be called a "real-ontic" union, in opposition to a merely "verbal exchange," that is, a manner of speaking which would allow Christ's human nature to share the divine glory, power, omnipresence, etc. only metaphorically (FC SD VIII 63). But this assertion necessarily leads to the confession that the glorification[65] of Christ's human nature is unique and cannot be predicated of any other human creature. Thus the FC excludes the possibility that the union of the divine and human natures in Christ can be regarded as paradigmatic of the union that takes place in believers (which is precisely the key idea in the anthropology of the Mannermaa school). "In this

65. One can even, perhaps, speak of the "deification" of Christ's human nature according to Chemnitz. In his *The Two Natures of Christ*, Chemnitz is willing to apply the term to the truth that Christ's human nature shared in his divine power, life, and glory. But he also points out (refereeing to John of Damascus) that:

[T]he ancients in using the term 'deification' did not have in mind a transmutation, commingling, conversion, abolition, or equating of the natures, but they wished by this term to describe first of all the plan of the personal union. For just as with respect to the assumed humanity this union could be called a putting on of flesh (*sarkōsis*) or a putting on of man's nature (*anthrōpēsis*), so with respect to the deity which is united to the humanity the ancients called it a putting on of God (*theōsis*) or a putting on of the Logos (*logōsis*).

But even though this terminology could be rightly understood with reference to the personal union, Chemnitz was reluctant to use it because of its association with "the Eutychian controversies and the ravings of Schwenkfeld." He concludes that, in contemporary usage, "the term 'deification' has already become unsuitable [NB even in connection with the discussion of Christ's two natures!], and I would not want to restore the use of this term, for it would require a long explanation and a warning" (*The Two Natures of Christ*, translated by J. A. O. Preus (St. Louis: Concordia, 1971), 396).

way there would be no difference between Christ according to his human nature and other holy people; this would deprive Christ of his majesty, which he has received above all creatures as a human being, according to his human nature" (FC SD VIII 69). Against such a view, the FC stresses the real and unique glorification of the humanity of Christ. To him alone is given "all authority in heaven and on earth" (Matthew 28:18); in him alone "the fullness of the deity dwells bodily" (Colossians 2:9; FC SD VIII 70). But the FC clearly distinguishes in this way between the glorified (or even "deified") human nature of Christ and the human nature of all other people, even of believers in whom Christ dwells.[66]

Furthermore, the FC places special emphasis on the salvific role of Christ's human nature, and points out that the promises by which believers are united to Christ according to his human nature. So in SD VIII 79: "[Christ] instituted his Holy Supper that he might be present with us, dwell in us, work and be mighty in us according to that nature, too, according to which he has flesh and blood." The same section of the FC makes an explicit point of agreeing with Luther on this point, citing Luther's "Great Confession" (1528)[67] and his "Treatise on the Last Words of David" (1543),[68] in both of which Luther likewise stresses the real humanity of Christ and its importance for the salvation and comfort of human sinners. The conclusion drawn by the FC's discussion of the person of Christ is that our union with Christ involves especially union with his human nature.[69] Even when the FC talks of a "twofold eating of Christ's flesh" and identifies the first as the spiritual eating of faith, this is nevertheless directly connected with Christ's human nature, not just his deity.[70]

66. This is affirmed in SD VIII 70: "... it is true that God, together with the fullness of deity which he always has with him, dwells in believers ..."

67. WA 26:232, 24–333, 9; AE 37:218–19. Particularly striking in this passage is Luther's insistence that faith can never settle for "mere God" apart from the human nature of Christ; that would leave us with "nothing more than a mere isolated God ["*ein bloßer abgesonderter Gott*"] and a divine person without the humanity." To such a "mere God" Luther says: "No God like that for me!"

68. WA 54:49, 33–50, 11; AE 15:293–94.

69. This same theme is taken up by Chemnitz, who devotes a chapter to "Comfort Derived by the Ancients from Christ's Human Nature," in which several of the patristic citations deal with the Lord's Supper (*The Two Natures of Christ*, 467–74).

70. "This spiritual eating, however, is nothing other than faith ... [in Christ] as true God and a true human being along with all his benefits ... [which] he won for us with his flesh, which he gave into death for us, and with his blood, which he poured out for us" (SD VII 62).

In the light of this emphasis on Christ's humanity in the FC (and also in Luther's writings as cited there), it is very significant that Mannermaa and Peura virtually ignore the human nature of Christ in their version of the union of the believer with Christ. Instead Mannermaa sees the believer's union with Christ by faith as a parallel of the incarnation, so that the union of the two natures in the person of Christ becomes paradigmatic for the *theosis* of the Christian. For Mannermaa, Christ himself is the Christian's divine nature, and the Christian takes the need and burden of the neighbor as "human nature."[71] In such a conception it becomes largely a matter of indifference that Christ himself is united with the believer according to his *human* nature, since it is his divinity which is decisive for salvation. Simo Peura likes to cite the phrase (from Luther's comments on Psalm 5) "*homo enim homo est, donec fiat deus*,"[72] in support of his contention that union with Christ makes the human being something "more than human," that is, a new ontological reality which surpasses the created human nature. But the passages cited above reveal that the FC (making an explicit point of agreement with Luther on this question) are much more interested in the *homo factus est* of the Creed than in Peura's *homo fiat deus*. Without distortion, one may conclude that the soteriology—and anthropology—of the Lutheran Confessions depends on Christ having a human nature rather than on me having a divine nature.

All that being said with regard to the Lutheran understanding of the believer's union with Christ, it must be seen as all the more significant that the SC does not connect the sacrament of the altar with the believer's union with Christ at all. Rather, the SC's explanation of the sacrament repeatedly emphasizes the word which promises and gives forgiveness of sins. The first question ("What is the Sacrament of the Altar?") asks for a definition, to which the briefest possible answer is given, without the elaboration, polemic, or antitheses that occupy much space in other treatments of the sacrament in the Book of Concord: "It is the true body and blood of our Lord Jesus Christ under the bread and wine, instituted by Christ himself for us Christians to eat and drink" (SC Sacr 2). This is attested with a plain recitation of the biblical passages that contain the words of institution in the Gospels and 1 Corinthians (SC Sacr 4). When our attention is turned to the benefit of the sacrament, the focus fixes

---

71. Mannermaa, "Theosis as a Subject of Finnish Luther Research," 48.

72. AWA 2:305.18–19.

squarely not on the substance or essence of the sacrament, but on the words that speak God's promise there: "The words 'given for you' and 'shed for you for the forgiveness of sins' show us that forgiveness of sin, life, and salvation are given to us in the sacrament through these words" (SC Sacr 6). Of course, Luther would acknowledge and confess that the essence and substance of the sacrament, i.e., the body and blood of Christ, are good and powerful and beneficial in and of themselves, but he stresses the words of promise by which these are delivered to us. "Christ's body cannot be an unfruitful, useless thing that does nothing and helps no one. Yet, however great the treasure may be in itself, it must be set within the Word and offered to us through the Word, otherwise we could never know of it or seek it" (LC Sacr 29–30). This is also why Luther repeatedly highlights the "for you" in the LC (e.g., LC Sacr 21, 34, 64). Certainly Luther wants Christians to be aware of much crucial information about the sacrament: it is the body and blood of Christ, it is for the forgiveness of sins, etc. But when he prints "*FUR EUCH*" in all capital letters, Luther is accentuating the fact that these words are not mere information (even divinely true and accurate information), but a divine promise addressed to the Christians.

It is impossible to overestimate the importance of Luther's decisive emphasis on the words of the promise at precisely this point. "These words," the Christian learns to speak in the catechism, "are the essential thing [*Häuptstück*] in the sacrament" (SC Sacr 8). And, in fact, not only in the sacrament: here we have to do with "the most important topic of Christian teaching which, rightly understood, illumines and magnifies the honor of Christ and brings the abundant consolation that devout consciences need" (Ap IV 2). That is why Luther repeats the "for you" ("*fur Euch*") no fewer than six times, and "forgiveness of sin(s)" seven times, in the brief explanation of the sacrament in the SC. God's promise of forgiveness of sins is the source and center of the Christian's entire life, "because where there is forgiveness of sin, there is also life and salvation." The SC focuses on the promise of forgiveness (forensic justification) as the *Häuptstück* of the sacrament, rather than any "ontological" reference, either in the elements themselves or in the human recipient.

The SC's radical focus on the words in the sacrament, and especially the words as promise rather than as mere information, bring us to the bedrock of the anthropology of the Lutheran Confessions. The words of the promise of the forgiveness of sin not only define but also create the new reality of human creatures, rescued from their self-inflicted alienation from their Creator and the resultant corruption and corrosion of their lives. The promise of forgiveness of sin is thus the heart of the Lutheran understanding of what it means to be human; no other definition of "reality" is to be sought than this word addressed by the Creator to his fallen creatures. The reality of the promise trumps all other evidence and every other claim by which human beings seek to understand themselves. The Lutheran Confessions do not offer a precise definition of human nature, nor do they specify some kind of change to that nature in Christians after conversion. They do not answer all the philosophical or scientific questions that arise about human existence. They provide a theological framework for knowing ourselves that revolves around these two related, paradoxical assertions: that we are creatures and yet sinners, and that we are sinners yet justified, all at the same time.

Conclusion: Anthropology and the Object of Faith

T HE FINNISH *THEOSIS* SCHOOL of Tuomo Mannermaa and his colleagues want to emphasize the *reality* of faith and of the sinner's justification, in opposition to a mistaken construal of faith and justification
as something less than really true, a kind of fiction. The object of faith, in
their view, must be something solid and essential, an "ontological reality"
in which the believer likewise participates in a "real-ontic" (Mannermaa's
favorite designation) union. That object of faith is Christ himself, and the
righteousness by which the sinner is justified is identified with Christ's
own essential, "ontological" righteousness. This means that justification
is attributed to who Christ *is*. And having placed the focus squarely on
Christ's essential being, his "ontological" nature as the source of justification for the sinner, the Mannermaa school then likewise concentrate
entirely on the divine nature as the real source of Christian righteousness. The whole point of talking about justification as *theosis*, after all, is
to draw attention in an emphatic way to the participation of the believer
in the reality of *God*. The human nature of Christ recedes quickly into the
background, and is not involved in any "real" (i.e., ontological) way in the
righteousness that counts in the sinner's justification.

What is important in such an understanding of justification is who
Christ *is*, his essence or ontological nature, and that makes his deity alone
decisive. Strangely absent from this picture is any specific interest in what
Christ *does*, or to be still more precise, what he has done. The suffering,
death, and resurrection of Jesus as actual events in history apparently
have little bearing on the notion of the deification of the believer through
union with God, at least as this is explored by the Finnish theologians
interested in *theosis*. The reality of faith sought by the Mannermaa school
is not the concrete reality of history (". . . crucified under Pontius Pilate
. . .") but only the ontological reality of God's own being. The attributes
of God such as love, righteousness, etc., (and Mannermaa sees no division between God's attributes and his essence) are communicated to the

believer because Christ himself is really present. But in such a theological system there is oddly little for God to *do*. There is more in Mannermaa about Christ as the active subject of the good works of the Christian than about Christ crucified.[1]

This is a major departure from the biblical view of salvation history, in which God has involved himself actively to bring about the salvation of his people. God rolls up his sleeves, he bares his arm, he comes down and fights his enemies, he struggles and gathers and argues and pays. The God of the Bible, and of Lutheran theology, is an active, busy God. The God who took on human flesh in the person of Jesus healed, taught, fed, ate, wept, slept, rebuked, prayed, suffered, bled, died, rose, sent, ascended. All of this is obscured when the justification of the sinner is seen as something that "happens" (if that is the right word) on the level of ontology, of being itself. Or perhaps more exactly, the work of Christ becomes largely irrelevant in view of *theosis*. After reading the works of the Mannermaa school, one is left to wonder whether the historic suffering and death of the Christ are important (let alone necessary) in such a theology. They seek the "reality" of justification elsewhere, not in the events and deeds of Jesus, but in the realm of being itself—and the "real-ontic" transformation of the believer who "is" in union with Christ.

If the reality sought by the Mannermaa school is a reality "beyond" history, it must also be recognized as a reality "beyond" the word. The ontological realities in which the believer is said to participate are ultimately quite separate from the external word by which they are mediated. Again, the ground of reality to which the theologians of the Mannermaa school turn is the "presence of Christ." It is an odd twist in contemporary Luther studies that pits this "presence of Christ" against the forensic word of the gospel, as if the two were competing alternatives.

What has been suggested in response to the anthropology of *theosis*, with its search for "reality" beyond history and beyond the word, is an approach to anthropology in which God's word decides about human identity and human existence. This is an anthropology in which human creatures are addressed by the Creator, and everything hangs on how the Creator answers his own question: "Who do I say that you are?" Such a way of asking and answering anthropological questions has the potential, at least, to open theology to making more public (as opposed to special-

---

1. Cf. the section titled "Christ as Subject of Good Works" in Mannermaa, *Der im Glauben gegenwärtige Christus*, 56–59.

ized "in-house") contributions to reflection about our humanity. In an age when anthropological questions are being raised from many directions and in many disciplines with new urgency, theology needs fresh clarity in its own distinctive way of saying what it means to be human.

If we begin with the premise that the word decides about our "reality" as humans, this calls for further reflection in at least three directions.

First, the word of creation defines and gives us life in the world, and places us as human creatures in special roles and relationships. Our discussion of God's word of creation has helped us appreciate the fact that "creation" is not a single, primordial event, but the continuing, constant reality in which we live. An integral part of that reality is the concept of human vocation, the tasks and functions for which human creatures are placed in the world. A renewed anthropology in which the word determines and gives us our reality will reclaim a deeper value of the various gifts of creation, including human work in the world, not as some kind of resource for soteriology, but as a gift of creation.

Second, the word of the gospel bespeaks a new reality to human creatures alienated from their Creator by their own rebellion and fall. Human sin mars and perverts God's good creation; it dehumanizes those made in God's image. That image, that true and rightly ordered humanity, is restored and recreated in Christ. Sent by the Father in the power of the Spirit, Jesus assumed human nature and also bore human sin. The *pro nobis* of the gospel word makes his righteousness and life ours, and our sin and death his. Justification through the "alien righteousness" of Christ not only promises and gives forgiveness of sin and hope for resurrection in the new heaven ad new earth, it also frees human creatures to live now in creation as creatures. The salvation promised and given by the gospel is not an escape from creation, but in the best sense a return to it. The gospel lets creation be creation.

Finally, the word in us introduces believers into intimate communion with God. Christ himself dwells in believers, along with the Father and the Holy Spirit, and this begins and shapes a new reality of life grounded in God's own life. This is the communion described by 2 Peter 1:4, in which the "participation in the divine nature" is still directly linked to the Christian's continued dependence on the word, the "very great and precious promises." Life in communion with God is not a state of reality "beyond" or "behind" the word. The divine word works in believers to conform them to Christ, to help them escape the evil desires of a corrupt world, and to grow in love. This process of transformation is incipient and partial, and never forms the ground of the believers' hope or faith. Rather, it is the indication that the word is doing its work in believers to bring about that perfect convergence and agreement of what God now declares us to be in Christ and what we shall be when he appears. From first to last, then, human creatures live from the word.

Bibliography

Aghiorgoussis, Maximos, Bishop. "Orthodox Soteriology." *Salvation in Christ: A Lutheran-Orthodox Dialogue*, edited by John Meyendorff and Robert Tobias, 35–57. Minneapolis: Augsburg, 1992.

Allen, Diogenes. *Philosophy for Understanding Theology.* Atlanta: John Knox Press, 1985.

Arand, Charles P. "Personal Autonomy Versus Creaturely Contingency: The First Article and the Right to Die." *Concordia Journal* 20 (October 1994): 385–401.

———. *That I May Be His Own: An Overview of Luther's Catechisms.* St. Louis: Concordia, 2000.

Asendorf, Ulrich. "*Die Einbettung der Theosis in die Theologie Martin Luthers.*" In *Luther und Theosis*, edited by Joachim Heubach, 85–102. Erlangen: Martin-Luther-Verlag, 1990.

———. "*Die Ökumenische Bedeutung von Luthers Genesis-Vorlesung (1535–1545).*" In *Caritas Dei: Beiträge zum Verständnis Luthers und der gegenwärtigen Ökumene*, edited by Oswald Bayer, Robert W. Jenson, and Simo Knuuttila, 18–40. Helsinki: Luther-Agricola-Gesellschaft, 1997.

———. "*Die Trinitätslehre als integrales Problem der Theologie Martin Luthers.*" In *Luther und die trinitarische Tradition: Ökumenische und philosophische Perspektiven*, edited by Joachim Heubach, 113–30. Erlangen: Martin-Luther-Verlag, 1994.

Athanasius. *On the Incarnation.* Translated by anonymous. Crestwood, NY: St. Vladimir's Orthodox Theological Seminary, 1944.

Aves, John. "Persons in Relation: John Macmurray." In *Persons, Divine and Human: King's College Essays in Theological Anthropology*, edited by Christoph Schwöbel and Colin E. Gunton, 120–37. Edinburgh: T. & T. Clark, 1991.

Bayer, Oswald. "*Geistgabe und Bildungsarbeit: Zum Weltbegriff der Theologie.*" *Lutherische Theologie und Kirche* 23, no. 1 (January 1999): 1–17.

———. "*Luthers Verständnis des Seins Jesu Christi im Glauben.*" In *Luther und Ontologie. Das Sein Christi im Glauben als strukturierendes Prinzip der Theologie Luthers*, edited by Anja Ghiselli, Kari Kopperi, and Rainer Vinke, 94–113. Helsinki & Erlangen: Luther-Agricola-Gesellschaft & Martin-Luther-Verlag, 1993.

———. *Promissio: Geschichte der reformatorischen Wende in Luthers Theologie.* Göttingen: Vandenhoeck & Ruprecht, 1971.

———. "*Die reformatorische Wende in Luthers Theologie.*" In *Der Durchbruch der reformatorischen Erkenntnis bei Luther: Neuere Untersuchungen*, edited by Bernhard Lohse, 98–133. Stuttgart: Franz Steiner, 1988.

———. "*Schöpfung als »Rede an die Kreatur durch die Kreatur«. Die Frage nach dem Schüssel zum Buch der Natur und Geschichte.*" In *Schöpfung als Anrede*, 2nd edition. Tübingen: J. C. B. Mohr (Paul Siebeck), 1990, 9–32.

Bibliography

————. "*Das Wunder der Gottesgemeinschaft. Eine Besinnung auf das Motiv der 'Unio' bei Luther und im Luthertum.*" In *Unio. Gott und Mensch in der nachreformatorischen Theologie,* edited by Matti Repo and Rainer Vinke, 322–32. Helsinki: Luther-Agricola-Gesellschaft, 1996.

Die Bekenntnisschriften der Evangelisch-Lutherischen Kirche. 11. Göttingen: Vandenhoeck & Ruprecht, 1992.

Bielfeldt, Dennis. "Deification as a Motif in Luther's *Dictata Super Psalterium.*" *The Sixteenth Century Journal* 28, no. 2 (1997), 401–20.

————. "Luther, Metaphor, and Theological Language." *Modern Theology* 6, no. 2 (1990): 121–35.

————. "The Ontology of Deification." In *Caritatis Dei: Beiträge zum Verständnis Luthers und der gegenwärtigen Ökumene,* edited by Oswald Bayer, Robert W. Jenson, and Simo Knuuttila, 90–113. Helsinki: Luther-Agricola-Gesellschaft, 1997.

Bienert, Wolfgang. "*Christologische und trinitätstheologische Aporien der östlichen Kirche aus der Sicht Martin Luthers—Korreferat zu Jouko Martikainen.*" In *Luther und die trinitarische Tradition: Ökumenische und philosophische Perspektiven,* edited by Joachim Heubach, 95–112. Erlangen: Martin-Luther-Verlag, 1994.

————. "The Patristic Background of Luther's Theology." *Lutheran Quarterly* 9, no. 3 (Autumn 1995): 263–79.

Birmelé, André. "*Das Thema 'Trinität' in den internationalen ökumenischen Dialogen— Korreferat zu Michael Root.*" In *Luther und die trinitarische Tradition: Ökumenische und philosophische Perspektiven,* edited by Joachim Heubach, 161–74. Erlangen: Martin-Luther-Verlag, 1994.

Bizer, Ernst. *Fides Ex Auditu: Eine Untersuchung über die Entdeckung der Gerechtigkeit Gottes durch Martin Luther.* Neukirchen: Verlag der Buchhandlung des Erziehungsvereins, 1958.

Braaten, Carl E. "The Finnish Breakthrough in Luther Research." *Pro Ecclesia* V, no. 2 (1996): 141–43.

————, and Robert W. Jensen, editors. *Christian Dogmatics.* Philadelphia: Fortress, 1984.

————, and Robert W. Jensen, editors. *Union with Christ: The New Finnish Interpretation of Luther.* Grand Rapids: Eerdmans, 1997.

Brecht, Martin. "*Iustitia Christi. Die Entdeckung Martin Luthers.*" In *Der Durchbruch der reformatorischen Erkenntnis bei Luther: Neuere Untersuchungen,* edited by Bernhard Lohse, 167–211. Stuttgart: Franz Steiner, 1988.

————. "*Neue Ansätze der Lutherforschung in Finnland.*" *Luther* 61 (1990): 36–40.

Breck, John. "Divine Initiative: Salvation in Orthodox Theology." In *Salvation in Christ: A Lutheran-Orthodox Dialogue,* edited by John Meyendorff and Robert Tobias, 105–20. Minneapolis: Augsburg, 1992.

Burns, J. Patout. *Theological Anthropology.* Sources of Early Christian Thought. Philadelphia: Fortress Press, 1981.

Catechism of the Catholic Church. New York: ImageDoubleday, 1994.

Chemnitz, Martin. *Justification: The Chief Article of Christian Doctrine as Expounded in Loci Theologici.* Translated by J. A. O. Preus. St. Louis: Concordia, 1985.

Chemnitz, Martin, and Johann Gerhard. *The Doctrine of Man in Classical Lutheran Theology.* Translated by Mario Colacci, et al. Edited by Herman A. Preus and Edmund Smits. Minneapolis: Augsburg, 1962.

Christian Perspectives on Being Human: A Multidisciplinary Approach to Integration. Edited by J. P. Moreland and David M. Ciocchi. Grand Rapids: Baker, 1993.

Bibliography

Collins, Carr. "*Theosis*: Deification of Man." *Diakonia* 15, no. 3 (1980): 229–35.

"Common Statement: Christ 'in Us' and Christ 'for Us' in Lutheran and Orthodox Theology." In *Salvation in Christ: A Lutheran-Orthodox Dialogue,* edited by John Meyendorff and Robert Tobias, 17–33. Minneapolis: Augsburg, 1992.

Der Franckforter. *Theologia Deutsch. Kritische Textausgabe.* Edited by Wolfgang von Hinten. München: Artemis Verlag, 1982.

Dingel, Irene. "*An patres et concilia possint errare: Georg Majors Umgang mit den Vätern.*" In *Auctoritas Patrum II: New Contributions on the Reception of the Church Fathers in the 15th and 16th Centuries,* edited by Leif Grane, Alfred Schindler, and Markus Wriedt, 1–11. Mainz: Verlag Philipp von Zabern, 1998.

Dyson, Esther. *Release 2.0: A Design for Living in The Digital Age.* Online: http://www.release2-0.com/main.html. [6 November 1997].

Ebeling, Gerhard. "*Cognitio Dei et hominis.*" In *Lutherstudien,* vol. I, 221–72. Tübingen: J. C. B. Mohr (Paul Siebeck), 1971.

———. "*Das Leben—Fragment und Vollendung: Luthers Auffassung vom Menschen im Verhältnis zu Scholastik und Renaissance.*" In *Lutherstudien,* vol. 3, 311–36. Tübingen: J. C. B. Mohr (Paul Siebeck), 1985.

———. *Die philosophische Definition des Menschen: Kommentar zu Thesen 1–19.* Vol. II2 of *Lutherstudien.* Tübingen: J. C. B. Mohr (Paul Siebeck), 1982.

———. "*Das Problem des Natürlichen bei Luther.*" In *Lutherstudien,* vol. I, 273–85. Tübingen: J. C. B. Mohr (Paul Siebeck), 1971.

———. "*Das Sein des Menschen als Gottes Handeln an ihm.*" In *Anthropologie und Christologie,* edited by Joachim Heubach, 23–68. Erlangen: Martin-Luther-Verlag, 1990.

Elert, Werner. *Das Kampf um das Christentum: Geschichte der Beziehungen zwischen dem evangelischen Christentum in Deutschland und dem allgemeinen Denken seit Schleiermacher und Hegel.* München: Oskar Beck, 1921.

———. *The Structure of Lutheranism.* Translated by Walter Hansen. St. Louis: Concordia, 1962.

Erikson, Leif. "*Lutherforschung in Finnland.*" In *Luther in Finnland—der Einfluß der Theologie Martin Luthers in Finnland und finnische Beiträge zur Lutherforschung,* edited by Mikka Ruokanen, 30–41. Helsinki: Luther-Agricola-Gesellschaft, 1984.

———. "*Unio in der Theologie Fredrik Gabriel Hedbergs.*" In *Unio. Gott und Mensch in der nachreformatorischen Theologie,* edited by Matti Repo and Rainer Vinke, 310–21. Helsinki: Luther-Agricola-Gesellschaft, 1996.

Flogaus, Reinhard. *Theosis bei Palamas und Luther: Ein Beitrag zum ökumenischen Gespräch.* Göttingen: Vendenhoeck & Ruprecht, 1996.

Fraenkel, Peter. *Testimonia Patrum: The Function of the Patristic Argument in the Theology of Philip Melanchthon.* Geneva: E. Droz, 1961.

Friedman, Maurice. *The Hidden Human Image.* New York: Delacorte Press, 1974.

Ganoczy, Alexandre. "New Tasks in Christian Anthropology." In *Humanism and Christianity,* edited by Claude Geffré, 73–85. New York: Herder and Herder, 1973.

Grane, Leif. "Some Remarks on the Church Fathers in the First Years of the Reformation (1516–1520)." In *Auctoritas Patrum: Contributions on the Reception of the Church Fathers in the 15th and 16th Centuries,* edited by Leif Grane, Alfred Schindler, and Markus Wriedt, 21–32. Mainz: Philipp von Zabern, 1993.

Grenz, Stanley J. *Theology for the Community of God.* Nashville: Broadman & Holman, 1994.

Bibliography

Gritsch, Eric W. "Response to Tuomo Mannermaa: 'Glaube, Bildung und Gemeinschaft bei Luther/Faith, Culture and Community.'" Presented at the Ninth International Congress for Luther Research. In *Glaube und Bildung/Faith and Culture*, 69–74. Heidelberg, 17–23 August, 1997.

Grönvik, Lorenz. "*Der Beitrag des finnischen Luthertums zum heutigen ökumenischen Gespräch.*" In *Luther in Finnland—der Einfluß der Theologie Martin Luthers in Finnland und finnische Beiträge zur Lutherforschung*, edited by Mikka Ruokanen, 42–59. Helsinki: Luther-Agricola-Gesellschaft, 1984.

Gunton, Colin. *The Triune Creator: A Historical and Systematic Study.* Grand Rapids: Eerdmans, 1998.

Gunton, Colin E. "Trinity, Ontology and Anthropology: Towards a Renewal of the Doctrine of the *imago Dei.*" In *Persons, Divine and Human: King's College Essays in Theological Anthropology*, edited by Christoph Schwöbel and Colin E. Gunton, 47–61. Edinburgh: T. & T. Clark, 1991.

Haendler, Gert. "Mannermaa, Tuomo, *et al.*, editors. *Thesaurus Lutheri. Auf der Suche nach neuen Paradigmen der Luther-Forschung.*" *Theologische Literaturzeitung* 113, no. 8 (1988): 602–4.

Haikola, Lauri. "*Melanchthons und Luthers Lehre von der Rechtfertigung.*" In *Luther in Finnland—der Einfluß der Theologie Martin Luthers in Finnland und finnische Beiträge zur Lutherforschung*, edited by Mikka Ruokanen, 71–90. Helsinki: Luther-Agricola-Gesellschaft, 1984.

Hakamies, Ahti. "*Das 'Natürliche' und das 'Christliche' in der Ethik.*" In *Luther in Finnland—der Einfluß der Theologie Martin Luthers in Finnland und finnische Beiträge zur Lutherforschung*, edited by Mikka Ruokanen, 187–98. Helsinki: Luther-Agricola-Gesellschaft, 1984.

Hägglund, Bengt. *History of Theology.* Translated by Gene J. Lund. St. Louis: Concordia, 1968.

———. "*Luther und die Mystik.*" In *The Church, Mysticism, Sanctification and the Natural in Luther's Thought*, edited by Ivar Asheim, 84–94. Philadelphia: Fortress, 1967.

———. "'*Was ist der Mensch?' Psalm 8,5: Eine Grundfrage der altlutherischen Bibeldeutung.*" In *Anthropologie und Christologie*, edited by Joachim Heubach, 69–80. Erlangen: Martin-Luther-Verlag, 1990.

Heschel, Abraham J. *Who Is Man?* Palo Alto: Stanford University Press, 1965.

Hinlicky, Paul. "Theological Anthropology: Toward Integrating *theosis* and Justification by Faith." *Journal of Ecumenical Studies* 34, no. 1 (Winter 1997): 38–73.

Hoffman, Bengt R. *Luther and the Mystics.* Minneapolis: Augsburg, 1976.

Horne, Brian L. "Person as Confession: Augustine of Hippo." In *Persons, Divine and Human: King's College Essays in Theological Anthropology*, edited by Christoph Schwöbel and Colin E. Gunton, 65–73. Edinburgh: T. & T. Clark, 1991.

Hödl, Ludwig. "*Die Gottebenbildlichkeit des Menschen und der sakramentale Charakter des Christen.*" In *Der Mensch als Bild Gottes*, edited by Leo Scheffczyk, 499–525. Darmstadt: Wissenschaftliche Buchgesellschaft, 1969.

Hughes, Philip Edgcumbe. *The True Image: The Origin and Destiny of Man in Christ.* Grand Rapids: Eerdmans, 1989.

Huovinen, Eero. "*An der Unsterblichkeit teilhaftig—das ökumenische Grundproblem in der Todestheologie Luthers.*" In *Luther in Finnland—der Einfluß der Theologie Martin Luthers in Finnland und finnische Beiträge zur Lutherforschung*, edited by Mikka Ruokanen, 130–44. Helsinki: Luther-Agricola-Gesellschaft, 1984.

Bibliography

———. "*Der infusio-Gedanke als Problem der Lutherforschung.*" In *Caritas Dei: Beiträge zum Verständnis Luthers und der gegenwärtigen Ökumene*, edited by Oswald Bayer, Robert W. Jenson, and Simo Knuuttila, 192–204. Helsinki: Luther-Agricola-Gesellschaft, 1997.

———. "*Opus Operatum. Ist Luthers Verständnis von der Effektivität des Sakraments richtig verstanden?*" In *Luther und Theosis*, edited by Joachim Heubach, 187–214. Erlangen: Martin-Luther-Verlag, 1990.

Hytönen, Maarit. "*Unio in der Reformation nach der evangelisch-katholischen Theologie Friedrich Heilers.*" In *Unio. Gott und Mensch in der Nachreformatorischen Theologie*, edited by Matti Repo and Rainer Vinke, 392–414. Helsinki: Luther-Agricola-Gesellschaft, 1996.

Iserloh, Erwin. "*Luther und die Mystik.*" In *The Church, Mysticism, Sanctification and the Natural in Luther's Thought*, edited by Ivar Asheim, 60–83. Philadelphia: Fortress, 1967.

Jaki, Stanley L. *Angels, Apes, & Men*. Peru, IL: Sherwood Sugden & Co., 1983.

Jenson, Robert W. "Theosis." *Dialog* 32 (Spring 1993): 108–12.

———. "*Die trinitarische Grundlegung der Theologie—östliche und westliche Trinitätslehre als ökumenisches Problem.*" In *Luther und die Trinitarische Tradition: Ökumenische und Philosophische Perspektiven*, edited by Joachim Heubach, 9–23. Erlangen: Martin-Luther-Verlag, 1994.

———. *Triune Identity*. Philadelphia: Fortress, 1982.

Joest, Wilfried. "*Das Heiligungsproblem nach Luthers Schrift 'Wider die himmlischen Propheten'.*" In *The Church, Mysticism, Sanctification and the Natural in Luther's Thought*, edited by Ivar Asheim, 189–93. Philadelphia: Fortress, 1967.

———. *Ontologie der Person bei Luther*. Göttingen: Vandenhoeck & Ruprecht, 1967.

Jónsson, Gunnlaugur A. *The Image of God: Genesis 1:26–28 in a Century of Old Testament Research*. Coniectanea Biblica Old Testament Series, vol. 26. Stockholm: Almqvist & Wiksell International, 1988.

Junghans, Helmar. "The Center of the Theology of Martin Luther." In *And Every Tongue Confess: Essays in Honor of Norman Nagel*, edited by Gerald S. Krispin and Jon D. Vieker, 179–94. Dearborn, Michigan: Nagel Festschrift Committee, 1990.

Juntunen, Sammeli. *Der Begriff des Nichts bei Luther in den Jahren 1510 bis 1523*. Helsinki: Luther-Agricola-Gesellschaft, 1996.

———. "Luther and Metaphysics: What is the Structure of Being According to Luther?" In *Union with Christ: The New Finnish Interpretation of Luther*, edited by Carl E. Braaten and Robert W. Jenson, 129–60. Grand Rapids: Wm. B. Eerdmans, 1998.

Kamppuri, Hannu T. "*Theosis in der Theologie Des Gregorios Palamas.*" In *Luther und Theosis*, edited by Joachim Heubach, 49–60. Erlangen: Martin-Luther-Verlag, 1990.

Kelly, J. N. D. *Early Christian Doctrines*. Revised. San Francisco: Harper, 1978.

Kirjavainen, Heikki. "*Luther und Aristoteles: Die Frage der zweifachen Gerechtigkeit im Lichte der transitiven vs. intransitiven Willenstheorie.*" In *Luther in Finnland—der Einfluß der Theologie Martin Luthers in Finnland und Finnische Beiträge Zur Lutherforschung*, edited by Mikka Ruokanen, 111–29. Helsinki: Luther-Agricola-Gesellschaft, 1984.

———. "*Die Spezifizierung der Glaubensgegenstände bei Luther im Licht der spätmittelalterlichen Semantik.*" In *Thesaurus Lutheri: Auf der Suche Nach Neuen Paradigmen der Luther-Forschung*, edited by Tuomo Mannermaa, Anja Ghiselli, and Simo Peura, 237–58. Helsinki: Finnische Theologische Literaturgesellschaft, 1987.

Bibliography

Kjelgaard-Pedersen, Steffen. "*Der finnische Beitrag zur heutigen Lutherforschung.*" In *Nordiskt Forum I. Referate des ersten forums für das Studium von Luther und lutherischen Theologie in Helsinki 21.-24.11.1991*, edited by Tuomo Mannermaa, et al., 7–23. Helsinki, 1993.

Knuuttila, Simo. "*Uniometaphysik und lutherische Orthodoxie im Turku des 17. Jahrhunderts.*" In *Unio. Gott und Mensch in der nachreformatorischen Theologie*, edited by Matti Repo and Rainer Vinke, 296–309. Helsinki: Luther-Agricola-Gesellschaft, 1996.

Kolb, Robert. "The Fathers in the Service of Lutheran Teaching: Andreas Musculus' Use of Patristic Sources." In *Auctoritas Patrum II: New Contributions on the Reception of the Church Fathers in the 15th and 16th Centuries*, edited by Leif Grane, Alfred Schindler, and Markus Wriedt, 105–23. Mainz: Verlag Philipp von Zabern, 1998.

———. "God Kills to Make Alive: Romans 6 and Luther's Understanding of Justification (1535)." *Lutheran Quarterly* XII (1998): 33–56.

———. "*Gott tötet, um lebendig zu machen: das Taufmotiv von Römer 6 in Luthers Verständnis der Rechtfertigung in Galaterkommentar von 1535.*" *Lutherische Theologie und Kirche* 20, no. 4 (November 1996): 153–75.

———. "'Perilous Events and Troublesome Disturbances': The Role of Controversy in the Tradition of Luther to Lutheran Orthodoxy." In *Pietas et Societas: New Trends in Reformation Social History*, edited by Kyle Sessions and Phillip N. Bebb, 181–201. Kirksville, MO: Sixteenth Century Journal Publishers, 1985.

———. "'That I May Be His Own': The Anthropology of Luther's Explanation of the Creed." *Concordia Journal* 21 (January 1995): 28–41.

Kopperi, Kari. "*Luthers theologische Zielsetzung in den philosophischen Thesen der Heidelberger Disputation.*" In *Nordiskt Forum I. Referate des ersten forums für das Studium von Luther und lutherischen Theologie in Helsinki 21.-24.11.1991*, edited by Tuomo Mannermaa, et al., 67–87. 1993.

Kraft, Charles H. *Anthropology for Christian Witness.* Maryknoll, NY: Orbis, 1996.

Kretschmar, Georg. "*Kreuz und Auferstehung in der Sicht von Athanasius und Luther.*" In *Der auferstandene Christus und das Heil der Welt. Das Kirchberger Gespräch über die Bedeutung der Auferstehung für das Heil der Welt zwischen Vertretern der evangelischen Kirche in Deutschland und der russischen orthodoxen Kirche*, edited by Kirchliche Aussenamt der evangelischen Kirche in Deutschland, 40–82. Witten: Luther-Verlag, 1972.

———. "*Die Rezeption der orthodoxen Vergöttlichungslehre in der protestantischen Theologie.*" In *Luther und Theosis*, edited by Joachim Heubach, 61–84. Erlangen: Martin-Luther-Verlag, 1990.

———. "*Der Weg der kirchlichen Theologie zum Bekenntnis des dreieinigen Gottes— Korreferat zu Robert W. Jenson.*" In *Luther und die trinitarische Tradition: ökumenische und philosophische Perspektiven*, edited by Joachim Heubach, 25–41. Erlangen: Martin-Luther-Verlag, 1994.

Lane, Anthony N. S. "Justification in 16th-Century Patristic Anthologies." In *Auctoritas Patrum: Contributions on the Reception of the Church Fathers in the 15th and 16th Centuries*, edited by Leif Grane, Alfred Schindler, and Markus Wriedt, 69–96. Mainz: Philipp von Zabern, 1993.

Lawrenz, Carl J. "On Justification, Osiander's Doctrine of the Indwelling Christ." In *No Other Gospel: Essays in Commemoration of the 400th Anniversary of the Formula of*

Bibliography

Concord 1580–1980, edited by Arnold J. Koelpin, 149–73. Milwaukee: Northwestern, 1980.

Lazareth, William H. "Luther on Civil Righteousness and Natural Law." In *The Church, Mysticism, Sanctification and the Natural in Luther's Thought*, edited by Ivar Asheim, 180–8. Philadelphia: Fortress, 1967.

Leske, Elmore. "Another Look at Luther's Indulgence Theses in the Context of a Study of Luther's Progress Towards His Radical Understanding of Repentance." In *And Every Tongue Confess: Essays in Honor of Norman Nagel on the Occasion of His Sixty-Fifth Birthday*, edited by Gerald S. Krispin and Jon D. Vieker, 61–85. Dearborn, MI: The Nagel Festschrift Committee, 1990.

Link, Christian. *Schöpfung*. Handbuch Systematischer Theologie, vol. 7. Gütersloh: Gütersloher Verlagshaus Mohn, 1991.

Lohse, Bernhard, editor. *Der Durchbruch der reformatorischen Erkenntnis bei Luther*. Darmstadt: Wissenschaftliche Buchgesellschaft, 1968.

———. *Der Durchbruch der reformatorischen Erkenntnis bei Luther. Neuere Untersuchungen*. Stuttgart: Franz Steiner, 1988.

———. "Luther and the Common Christian Heritage." *Lutheran Theological Seminary Bulletin* 75, no. 1 (Winter 1995): 13–24.

———. "Luther und Athanasius." In *Auctoritas Patrum: Contributions on the Reception of the Church Fathers in the 15th and 16th Centuries*, edited by Leif Grane, Alfred Schindler, and Markus Wriedt, 97–116. Mainz: Philipp von Zabern, 1993.

———. *Luthers Theologie in ihrer historischen Entwicklung und in ihrem systematischen Zusammenhang*. Göttingen: Vandenhoeck & Ruprecht, 1995.

———. *Martin Luther: An Introduction to His Life and Work*. Translated by Robert C. Schultz. Philadelphia: Fortress, 1986.

Lossky, Vladimir. *The Mystical Theology of the Eastern Church*. Crestwood, NY: St. Vladimir's Seminary Press, 1976.

———. *Orthodox Theology: An Introduction*. Translated by Ian Kesarcodi-Watson and Ihita Kesarcodi-Watson. Crestwood, NY: St. Vladimir's Seminary Press, 1978.

Luther, Martin. "Disputation *de Homine*." In *WA*, vol. 39I, 175–80, 1536.

———. "Sermo de Duplici Iustitia." In *WA*, vol. 2, 145–52, 1519.

———. "Sermo in Natali Christi." In *WA*, vol. 1, 20–29, 1514.

MacKay, Donald. *Human Science and Human Dignity: London Lectures in Contemporary Christianity*. London: Hodder & Stoughton, 1979.

Macquarrie, John. *In Search of Humanity: A Theological and Philosophical Approach*. New York: Crossroad, 1983.

Madson, Margaret Haried. "*Froehliche Wechsel* and Church: The Implications of Justification as Eschatological Exchange for the Doctrine of the Church." Ph.D. dissertation, St. Paul, MN, Luther Seminary, 1997.

Mahlmann, Theodor. "Die Stellung der unio cum Christo in der lutherischen Theologie des 17. Jahrhunderts." In *Unio. Gott und Mensch in der Nachreformatorischen Theologie*, edited by Matti Repo and Rainer Vinke, 72–199. Helsinki: Luther-Agricola-Gesellschaft, 1996.

Malter, Rudolf. "*Luther und die Geschichte der Metaphysik*." In *Thesaurus Lutheri: Auf der Suche Nach Neuen Paradigmen der Luther-Forschung*, edited by Tuomo Mannermaa, Anja Ghiselli, and Simo Peura, 37–52. Helsinki: Finnische Theologische Literaturgesellschaft, 1987.

Bibliography

"Man." In *The New International Dictionary of New Testament Theology*, edited by Colin Brown, 562–72. Grand Rapids: Zondervan, 1976.

Mannermaa, Tuomo. "The Doctrine of Justification and Christology. Chapter A, Section One of *The Christ Present in Faith*." *Concordia Theological Quarterly* 64, no. 3 (July 2000): 206–39.

———. "*Einig in Sachen der Rechtfertigung? Eine lutherische und eine katholische Stellungnahme zu Jörg Baur*." *Theologische Rundschau* 55 (1990): 325–35.

———. "*Glaube, Bildung und Gemeinschaft bei Luther*." Presented at the Ninth International Congress for Luther Research. In *Glaube und Bildung/Faith and Culture*, 49–68. Heidelberg, 17–23 August, 1997.

———. "*Grundlagenforschung der Theologie Martin Luthers und die Ökumene*." In *Thesaurus Lutheri: Auf der Suche Nach Neuen Paradigmen der Luther-Forschung*, edited by Tuomo Mannermaa, Anja Ghiselli, and Simo Peura, 17–35. Helsinki: Finnische Theologische Literaturgesellschaft, 1987.

———. "*Hat Luther eine trinitarische Ontologie?*" In *Luther und Ontologie. Das Sein Christi im Glauben als strukturierendes Prinzip der Theologie Luthers*, edited by Anja Ghiselli, Kari Kopperi, and Rainer Vinke, 9–27. Helsinki & Erlangen: Luther-Agricola-Gesellschaft & Martin-Luther-Verlag, 1993.

———. *Der im Glauben gegenwärtige Christus. Rechtfertigung und Vergottung. Zum ökumenischen Dialog*. Hanover: Lutherisches Verlagshaus, 1989.

———. "Justification and *theosis* in Lutheran-Orthodox Perspective." In *Union with Christ: The New Finnish Interpretation of Luther*, edited by Carl E. Braaten and Robert W. Jenson, 25–41. Grand Rapids: Wm. B. Eerdmans, 1998.

———. "Response to Vilmos Vajta." In *Luther's Ecumenical Significance: And Interconfessional Consultation*, edited by Peter Manns and Harding Meyer, 150–53. Philadelphia: Fortress Press, 1984.

———. "*Theosis als Thema der finnischen Lutherforschung*." In *Luther und Theosis*, edited by Joachim Heubach, 11–26. Veröffentlichungen der Luther-Akademie Ratzeburg, vol. 16. Erlangen: Martin-Luther-Verlag, 1990.

———. "Theosis as a Subject of Finnish Luther Research," translated by Norman M. Watt. *Pro Ecclesia* IV, no. 1 (1991): 37–48.

———. "*Über die Unmöglichkeit, gegen Texte Luthers zu systematisieren. Antwort an Gunther Wenz*." In *Unio. Gott und Mensch in der Nachreformatorischen Theologie*, edited by Matti Repo and Rainer Vinke, 381–91. Helsinki: Luther-Agricola-Gesellschaft, 1996.

———. "*Das Verhältnis von Glaube und Liebe in der Theologie Luthers*." In *Luther in Finnland—der Einfluß der Theologie Martin Luthers in Finnland und finnische Beiträge zur Lutherforschung*, edited by Mikka Ruokanen, 99–110. Schriften der Luther-Agricola-Gesellschaft. Helsinki: Luther-Agricola-Gesellschaft, 1984.

———. "Why is Luther So Fascinating? Modern Finnish Luther Research." In *Union with Christ: The New Finnish Interpretation of Luther*, edited by Carl E. Braaten and Robert W. Jenson, 1–20. Grand Rapids: Wm. B. Eerdmans, 1998.

Manns, Peter. "*Fides absoluta—fides incarnata. Zur Rechtfertigungslehre Luthers im großen Galater-Kommentar*." In *Reformata Reformanda. Festgabe für Hubert Jedin*, edited by Erwin Iserloh and Konrad Repgen, 265–312. Münster: Aschendorff, 1965.

———. "*Zum Gespräch zwischen M. Luther und der katholischen Theologie. Begegnung zwischen patristisch-monastischer und reformatorischer Theologie an der Scholastik vorbei*." In *Thesaurus Lutheri: Auf der Suche Nach Neuen Paradigmen der Luther-*

Forschung, edited by Tuomo Mannermaa, Anja Ghiselli, and Simo Peura, 63–154. Helsinki: Finnische Theologische Literaturgesellschaft, 1987.

Mantzaridis, Georgios I. *The Deification of Man. St. Gregory Palamas and the Orthodox Tradition.* Translated by Liadain Sherrard. Crestwood, New York: St. Vladimir's Seminary Press, 1984.

Marin, Louis. "The Disappearance of Man in the Humane Sciences—A Linguistic Model and Signifying Subject," in *Humanism and Christianity.* New York: Herder and Herder, 1973) 29–41.

Marquart, Kurt E. "Luther and Theosis." *Concordia Theological Quarterly* 64, no. 3 (July 2000): 182–205.

Martikainen, Eeva. "*Der Doctrina-Begriff in Luthers Theologie.*" In *Thesaurus Lutheri: Auf der Suche Nach Neuen Paradigmen der Luther-Forschung*, edited by Tuomo Mannermaa, Anja Ghiselli, and Simo Peura, 205–20. Helsinki: Finnische Theologische Literaturgesellschaft, 1987.

———. "*Die finnische Lutherforschung seit 1934.*" *Theologische Rundschau* 53 (1988): 371–87.

———. "*Kommunion der Liebe oder Relation der Personen? Die Trinität als Gegenstand ökumenischer Auslegung.*" In *Caritas Dei: Beiträge Zum Verständnis Luthers und der Gegenwärtigen Ökumene*, edited by Oswald Bayer, Robert W. Jenson, and Simo Knuuttila. Festschrift für Tuomo Mannermaa zum 60. Geburtstag, 287–314. Helsinki: Luther-Agricola-Gesellschaft, 1997.

———. "*Die Lehre und die Anwesenheit Gottes in der Theologie Luthers.*" In *Luther und Theosis*, edited by Joachim Heubach, 215–32. Veröffentlichungen der Luther-Akademie Ratzeburg, vol. 16. Erlangen: Martin-Luther-Verlag, 1990.

———. "*Die Unio im Brennpunkt der theologischen Forschung.*" In *Unio. Gott und Mensch in der Nachreformatorischen Theologie*, edited by Matti Repo and Rainer Vinke, 10–32. Helsinki: Luther-Agricola-Gesellschaft, 1996.

Martikainen, Jouko. "*Bild und Sein Gottes in der Theologie Luthers.*" In *Luther und Ontologie. Das Sein Christi im Glauben als strukturierendes Prinzip der Theologie Luthers*, edited by Anja Ghiselli, Kari Kopperi, and Rainer Vinke, 155–66. Helsinki & Erlangen: Luther-Agricola-Gesellschaft & Martin-Luther-Verlag, 1993.

———. "*Christologische und trinitätstheologische Aporien der östlichen Kirche aus der Sicht Martin Luthers.*" In *Luther und die Trinitarische Tradition: Ökumenische und Philosophische Perspektiven*, edited by Joachim Heubach, 71–94. Erlangen: Martin-Luther-Verlag, 1994.

Mau, Rudolf. "*Die Kirchenväter in Luthers früher Exegese des Galaterbriefes.*" In *Auctoritas Patrum: Contributions on the Reception of the Church Fathers in the 15th and 16th Centuries*, edited by Leif Grane, Alfred Schindler, and Markus Wriedt, 117–28. Mainz: Philipp von Zabern, 1993.

McDaniel, Michael C. D. "Salvation as Justification and *theosis*." In *Salvation in Christ: A Lutheran-Orthodox Dialogue*, edited by John Meyendorff and Robert Tobias, 67–83. Minneapolis: Augsburg, 1992.

McFarlane, Graham. "Strange News from Another Star: An Anthropological Insight from Edward Irving." In *Persons, Divine and Human: King's College Essays in Theological Anthropology*, edited by Christoph Schwöbel and Colin E. Gunton, 98–119. Edinburgh: T. & T. Clark, 1991.

McGrath, Alister E. *Luther's Theology of the Cross.* Grand Rapids: Baker, 1990.

Bibliography

McLeod, Frederick G., SJ. *The Image of God in the Antiochene Tradition.* Washington, D.C.: The Catholic University of America Press, 1999.

Meilaender, Gilbert. *Faith and Faithfulness: Basic Themes in Christian Ethics.* Notre Dame, IN: University of Notre Dame Press, 1991.

Metropolitan of Nafpaktos Hierotheos. *St. Gregory Palamas as a Hagiorite.* Translated by Esther Williams. Levadia, Greece: Birth of the Theotokos Monastery, 1997.

Meyendorff, John. "Humanity: 'Old' and 'New'—Anthropological Considerations." In *Salvation in Christ: A Lutheran-Orthodox Dialogue,* edited by John Meyendorff and Robert Tobias, 59–65. Minneapolis: Augsburg, 1992.

———. *A Study of Gregory Palamas.* Translated by George Lawrence. London: The Faith Press, 1964.

Meyer, Johannes. *Historischer Kommentar zu Luthers Kleinen Katechismus.* Gütersloh: C. Bertelsmann, 1929.

Midgley, Mary. *Beast and Man: The Roots of Human Nature.* Ithaca, NY: Cornell University Press, 1978.

Moltmann, Jürgen. "Man and the Son of Man." In *No Man is Alien,* edited by J. Robert Nelson, 203–24. Leiden: E. J. Brill, 1971.

Morris, Desmond. *The Naked Ape.* New York: Dell, 1967.

Murtorinne, Eino. "*Luthers Bedeutung für die neuere Theologie in Finnland.*" In *Luther in Finnland—der Einfluß der Theologie Martin Luthers in Finnland und Finnische Beiträge Zur Lutherforschung,* edited by Mikka Ruokanen, 24–29. Helsinki: Luther-Agricola-Gesellschaft, 1984.

Nellas, Panayiotis. *Deification in Christ: The Nature of the Human Person.* Crestwood, NY: St. Vladimir's Seminary Press, 1987.

Nilsson, Kjell Ove. *Simul: Das Miteinander von Göttlichem und Menschlichem.* Göttingen: Vandenhoeck & Ruprecht, 1966.

Oberman, Heiko. "*Simul Gemitus et Raptus*: Luther and Mysticism." In *The Dawn of the Reformation: Essays in Late Medieval and Early Reformation Thought,* 126–54. Grand Rapids: Wm B. Eerdmans, 1992.

Oberman, Heiko A. "*Simul Gemitus et Raptus: Luther und die Mystik.*" In *The Church, Mysticism, Sanctification and the Natural in Luther's Thought,* edited by Ivar Asheim, 20–59. Philadelphia: Fortress, 1967.

Olsson, Herbert. *Schöpfung, Vernunft und Gesetz in Luthers Theologie.* Studia Doctrinae Christianae Upsaliensia, vol. 10. Uppsala: Acta Universitatis Upsaliensis, 1971.

Osiander, Andreas. "*Disputatio de iustificatione.*" In *Andreas Osiander d. .Ä Gesamtausgabe,* edited by Gerhard Müller and Gottfried Seebaß, vol. 9, 426–46. Gütersloh: Gütersloher Verlagshaus, 1550.

———. "*Eine Disputation von der Rechtfertigung.*" In *Andreas Osiander d. .Ä Gesamtausgabe,* edited by Gerhard Müller and Gottfried Seebaß, vol. 9, 427–47. Gütersloh: Gütersloher Verlagshaus, 1551.

———. "*An Filius Dei fuerit incarnandus, si peccatum non introvisset in mundum, item: de imago Dei, quid sit.*" In *Andreas Osiander d. .Ä Gesamtausgabe,* edited by Gerhard Müller and Gottfried Seebaß, vol. 9, 456–91. Gütersloh: Gütersloher Verlagshaus, 1550.

Ozment, Steven E. *Homo Spiritualis: A Comparative Study of the Anthropology of Johannes Tauler, Jean Gerson and Martin Luther (1509-1516) in the Context of Their Theological Thought.* Studies in Medieval and Reformation Thought, vol. VI. Leiden: E. J. Brill, 1969.

Bibliography

Palamas, Gregory. *The Triads*. Translated by Nicholas Gendle. Edited by John Meyendorff. The Classic of Western Christian Spirituality. Mahwah, NJ: Paulist Press, 1983.

Pannenberg, Wolfhart. *Anthropology in Theological Perspective*. Translated by Matthew J. O'Connell. Philadelphia: Westminster, 1985.

———. "The Christological Foundation of Christian Anthropology." In *Humanism and Christianity*, edited by Claude Geffré, 86–100. New York: Herder and Herder, 1973.

———. *Jesus—God and Man*. Translated by Lewis L. Wilkins and Duane A. Priebe. Philadelphia: Westminster, 1968.

———. *Systematic Theology*. Translated by Geoffrey W. Bromiley. 3 vols. Grand Rapids: Eerdmans, 1991–1997.

———. *Toward a Theology of Nature: Essays on Science and Faith*. Edited by Ted Peters. Louisville, Kentucky: Westminster/John Knox Press, 1993.

———. *What Is Man?* Translated by Duane A. Priebe. Philadelphia: Fortress, 1970.

Papapetrou, Konstantinos E. *Über die anthropologischen Grenzen der Kirche: Ein philosophisch-theologischer Entwurf zum Thema simul iustus et peccator aus orthodox-katholischer Sicht*. Arbeiten Zur Geschichte und Theologie Des Luthertums, vol. XXVI. Hamburg: Lutherisches Verlagshaus, 1972.

Pieper, Franz. *Christliche Dogmatik*, vol. 1. St. Louis: CPH, 1924.

Pelikan, Jaroslav. *The Emergence of the Catholic Tradition (100–600)*. The Christian Tradition: A History of the Development of Doctrine, vol. 1. Chicago: University of Chicago Press, 1971.

———. *The Spirit of Eastern Christendom (600–1700)*. The Christian Tradition: A History of the Development of Doctrine, vol. 2. Chicago: University of Chicago Press, 1974.

Percy, Walker. *Lost in the Cosmos: The Last Self-Help Book*. New York: Washington Square Press, 1983.

Peters, Albrecht. *Der Glaube*. Vol. 2 of *Kommentar zu Luthers Katechismen*. Göttingen: Vandenhoeck & Ruprecht, 1991.

———. *Der Mensch*. Handbuch Systematischer Theologie, vol. 8. Gütersloh: Gütersloher Verlagshaus Mohn, 1979.

Peura, Simo. "Christ as Favor and Gift: The Challenge of Luther's Understanding of Justification." In *Union with Christ: The New Finnish Interpretation of Luther*, edited by Carl E. Braaten and Robert W. Jenson, 42–69. Grand Rapids: Wm. B. Eerdmans, 1998.

———. "Christus als Gunst und Gabe. Luthers Verständnis der Rechtfertigung als Herausforderung an den ökumenischen Dialog mit der römisch-katholischen Kirche." In *Caritas Dei: Beiträge Zum Verständnis Luthers und der Gegenwärtigen Ökumene.*, edited by Oswald Bayer, Robert W. Jenson, and Simo Knuuttila, 340–63. Helsinki: Luther-Agricola-Gesellschaft, 1997.

———. "Christus Praesentissimus: The Issue of Luther's Thought in the Lutheran-Orthodox Dialogue." Review essay. *Pro Ecclesia* II, no. 3 (1993): 364–71.

———. "Gott und Mensch in der Unio. Die Unterschiede im Rechtfertigungsverständnis bei Osiander und Luther." In *Unio. Gott und Mensch in der Nachreformatorischen Theologie*, edited by Matti Repo and Rainer Vinke, 33–61. Helsinki: Luther-Agricola-Gesellschaft, 1996.

———. *Mehr als ein Mensch? Die Vergöttlichung als Thema der Theologie Martin Luthers von 1513 bis 1519*. Mainz: Philipp von Zabern, 1994.

Bibliography

————. "*Das Sich-Geben Gottes—Korreferat zu Ulrich Asendorf.*" In *Luther und die Trinitarische Tradition: Ökumenische und Philosophische Perspektiven*, edited by Joachim Heubach, 131–46. Erlangen: Martin-Luther-Verlag, 1994.

————. "*Die Teilhabe an Christus bei Luther.*" In *Luther und Theosis*, edited by Joachim Heubach, 121–61. Erlangen: Martin-Luther-Verlag, 1990.

————. "*Der Vergöttlichungsgedanke in Luthers Theologie 1518–1519.*" In *Thesaurus Lutheri: Auf der Suche Nach Neuen Paradigmen der Luther-Forschung*, edited by Tuomo Mannermaa, Anja Ghiselli, and Simo Peura, 171–84. Helsinki: Finnische Theologische Literaturgesellschaft, 1987.

————. "What God Gives Man Receives: Luther on Salvation." In *Union with Christ: The New Finnish Interpretation of Luther*, edited by Carl E. Braaten and Robert W. Jenson, 76–95. Grand Rapids: Wm. B. Eerdmans, 1998.

————. "Wort, Sakrament und Sein Gottes." In *Luther und Ontologie. Das Sein Christi Im Glauben Als Strukturierendes Prinzip der Theologie Luthers*, edited by Anja Ghiselli, Kari Kopperi, and Rainer Vinke, 35–69. Helsinki & Erlangen: Luther-Agricola-Gesellschaft & Martin-Luther-Verlag, 1993.

Pico della Mirandola, Giovanni. "On the Dignity of Man," translated by Charles Glenn Wallis. In *"On the Dignity of Man" and Other Works*, 1–34. Indianapolis: The Bobbs-Merrill Company, 1965.

Pihkala, Juha. "Die Anwesenheit Christi und die Taufe in der Auslegungsgeschichte der Lutherischen Tauflehre." In *Thesaurus Lutheri: Auf der Suche Nach Neuen Paradigmen der Luther-Forschung*, edited by Tuomo Mannermaa, Anja Ghiselli, and Simo Peura, 291–308. Helsinki: Finnische Theologische Literaturgesellschaft, 1987.

Pinomaa, Lennart. "*Die Dialektik des Glaubens in der Theologie Luthers.*" In *Luther in Finnland—der Einfluß der Theologie Martin Luthers in Finnland und Finnische Beiträge Zur Lutherforschung*, edited by Mikka Ruokanen, 91–98. Helsinki: Luther-Agricola-Gesellschaft, 1984.

Pirinen, Kauko. "*Luther und die Ökumene.*" In *Luther in Finnland—der Einfluß der Theologie Martin Luthers in Finnland und Finnische Beiträge Zur Lutherforschung*, edited by Mikka Ruokanen, 158–86. Helsinki: Luther-Agricola-Gesellschaft, 1984.

Plathow, Michael. "*Mannermaa, Tuomo. Der im Glauben gegenwärtigen Christus.*" Review. *Theologische Literaturzeitung* 115 (1990): 766–68.

Posset, Franz. "'Deification' in the German Spirituality of the Late Middle Ages and in Luther: And Ecumenical Historical Perspective." *Archiv Für Reformationsgeschichte* 84 (1993): 103–26.

Prenter, Regin. "*Der Gott, der Liebe ist. Das Verhältnis der Gotteslehre zur Christologie.*" In *Theologie und Gottesdienst: Gesammelte Aufsätze. Theology and Liturgy: Collected Essays*, 275–91. Arhus: Forlaget Aros; Göttingen: Vandenhoeck & Ruprecht, 1977.

————. "Worship and Creation." In *Theologie und Gottesdienst: Gesammelte Aufsätze. Theology and Liturgy: Collected Essays*, 152–65. Arhus; Göttingen: Forlaget Aros; Vandenhoeck & Ruprecht, 1977.

Raabe, Paul R. "Why Prophetic Oracles Against the Nations?" In *Fortunate the Eyes That See: Essays in Honor of David Noel Freedman in Celebration of His Seventieth Birthday*, edited by Astrid B. Beck, et al., 236–57. Grand Rapids: Eerdmans, 1995.

Radler, Aleksander. "*Theologische Ontologie und reale Partizipation an Gott in der frühen Theologie Luthers.*" In *Luther und Ontologie. Das Sein Christi Im Glauben Als Strukturierendes Prinzip der Theologie Luthers*, edited by Anja Ghiselli, Kari Kopperi, and Rainer Vinke, 28–34. Helsinki & Erlangen: Luther-Agricola-Gesellschaft & Martin-Luther-Verlag, 1993.

Ratzinger, Joseph Cardinal, and Christoph Schönborn. *Introduction to the Catechism of the Catholic Church.* San Francisco: Ignatius, 1994.

Raunio, Antti. "*Die goldene Regel als Gesetz der göttlichen Natur. Das natürliche Gesetz und das göttliche Gesetz in Luthers Theologie 1522-1523.*" In *Luther und Theosis,* edited by Joachim Heubach, 163–86. Erlangen: Martin-Luther-Verlag, 1990.

———. "Natural Law and Faith: The Forgotten Foundations of Ethics in Luther's Theology." In *Union with Christ: The New Finnish Interpretation of Luther,* edited by Carl E. Braaten and Robert W. Jenson, 96–124. Grand Rapids: Wm. B. Eerdmans, 1998.

———. "*Die 'Goldene Regel' als theologisches Prinzip beim jungen Luther.*" In *Thesaurus Lutheri: Auf der Suche Nach Neuen Paradigmen der Luther-Forschung,* edited by Tuomo Mannermaa, Anja Ghiselli, and Simo Peura, 309–27. Helsinki: Finnische Theologische Literaturgesellschaft, 1987.

Repo, Matti. "*Die christologische Begründung der Unio in der Theologie Johann Arndts.*" In *Unio. Gott und Mensch in der Nachreformatorischen Theologie,* edited by Matti Repo and Rainer Vinke, 249–74. Helsinki: Luther-Agricola-Gesellschaft, 1996.

Ruether, Rosemary Radford. *Gaia & God: An Ecofeminist Theology of Earth Healing.* San Francisco: Harper, 1992.

Rist, John. "Plotinus and Christian Philosophy." In *The Cambridge Companion to Plotinus,* edited by Lloyd P. Gerson, 386–413. Cambridge, UK: Cambridge University Press, 1996.

Ritter, Adolf Martin. "*Dionysius Areopagita im 15. und 16. Jahrhundert.*" In *Auctoritas Patrum: Contributions on the Reception of the Church Fathers in the 15th and 16th Centuries,* edited by Leif Grane, Alfred Schindler, and Markus Wriedt, 143–58. Mainz: Philipp von Zabern, 1993.

Robinson, Paul W. "Luther's Explanation of *Daily Bread* in Light of Medieval Preaching." *Lutheran Quarterly* XIII (1999): 435–47.

Root, Michael. "*Die ökumenische Bedeutung der jüngeren Entwicklungen in der lutherischen Diskussion um die Trinität—eine bescheidene Analyse, die zur Bescheidenheit aufruft.*" In *Luther und die Trinitarische Tradition: Ökumenische und Philosophische Perspektiven,* edited by Joachim Heubach, 147–60. Erlangen: Martin-Luther-Verlag, 1994.

Ruokanen, Mikka. "Luther und Ekstase." In *Luther in Finnland—der Einfluß der Theologie Martin Luthers in Finnland und Finnische Beiträge Zur Lutherforschung,* edited by Mikka Ruokanen, 199–218. Helsinki: Luther-Agricola-Gesellschaft, 1984.

Saarinen, Risto. "*Gottes Sein—Gottes Wirken. Die Grunddifferenz von Substanzdenken und Wirkungsdenken in der evangelischen Lutherdeutung.*" In *Luther und Theosis,* edited by Joachim Heubach, 103–19. Erlangen: Martin-Luther-Verlag, 1990.

———. *Gottes Wirken auf uns: Die transzendentale Deutung des Gegenwarts-Christi-Motivs in der Lutherforschung.* Stuttgart: Franz Steiner, 1989.

———. "*Ipsa dilectio Deus est. Zur Wirkungsgeschichte von 1. Sent. Dist. 17 des Petrus Lombardus bei Martin Luther.*" In *Thesaurus Lutheri: Auf der Suche Nach Neuen Paradigmen der Luther-Forschung,* edited by Tuomo Mannermaa, Anja Ghiselli, and Simo Peura, 185–204. Helsinki: Finnische Theologische Literaturgesellschaft, 1987.

———. "The Presence of God in Luther's Theology." *Lutheran Quarterly* 8, no. 1 (Spring 1994): 3–13.

Bibliography

————. "Salvation in the Lutheran-Orthodox Dialogue." In *Union with Christ: The New Finnish Interpretation of Luther,* edited by Carl E. Braaten and Robert W. Jenson, 167–81. Grand Rapids: Wm. B. Eerdmans, 1998.

————. *"Die Teilhabe an Gott bei Luther und in der finnischen Lutherforschung."* In *Luther und Ontologie. Das Sein Christi Im Glauben Als Strukturierendes Prinzip der Theologie Luthers,* edited by Anja Ghiselli, Kari Kopperi, and Rainer Vinke, 167–82. Helsinki & Erlangen: Luther-Agricola-Gesellschaft & Martin-Luther-Verlag, 1993.

Saarnivaara, Uuras. *Luther Discovers the Gospel: New Light upon Luther's Way from Medieval Catholicism to Evangelical Faith.* St. Louis: Concordia, 1951.

Sayers, Dorothy L. *The Mind of the Maker.* New York: Harper & Row, 1941.

Scheel, Otto, editor. *Dokumente zu Luthers Entwicklung (Bis 1519).* 2d ed. Tübingen: J. C. B. Mohr (Paul Siebeck), 1929.

Scheffczyk, Leo. *"Die Frage nach der Gottesebenbildlichkeit in der modernen Theologie. Eine Einführung."* In *Der Mensch Als Bild Gottes,* edited by Leo Scheffczyk, IX–LIV. Wege der Forschung, vol. CXXIV. Darmstadt: Wissenschaftliche Buchgesellschaft, 1969.

Schlink, Edmund. *Der Mensch in der Verkündigung der Kirche. Eine Dogmatische Untersuchung.* München: Chr. Kaiser, 1936.

————. *Theology of the Lutheran Confessions.* Translated by Paul F. Koehneke and Herbert J. A. Bouman. Philadelphia: Fortress Press, 1961.

Schulze, Manfred. "Martin Luther and the Church Fathers." In *The Reception of the Church Fathers in the West: From the Carolingians to the Maurists,* edited by Irena Backus, vol. 2, 573–626. Leiden: E. J. Brill, 1997.

Schumacher, Ernst Friedrich. *A Guide for the Perplexed.* New York: Harper & Row, 1977.

Schwöbel, Christoph. "Human Being as Relational Being: Twelve Theses for a Christian Anthropology." In *Persons, Divine and Human: King's College Essays in Theological Anthropology,* edited by Christoph Schwöbel and Colin E. Gunton, 141–70. Edinburgh: T. & T. Clark, 1991.

Seebaß, Gottfried. "The Importance of Luther's Writings in the Formation of Protestant Confessions of Faith in the Sixteenth Century." In *Luther's Ecumenical Significance: An Interconfessional Consultation,* edited by Peter Manns and Harding Meyer, 71–80. Philadelphia: Fortress Press, 1984.

————. *Das Reformatorische Werk des Andreas Osiander.* Nürnberg: Verein für Bayerische Kirchengeschichte, 1967.

Seils, Martin. "Luthers Konzepte zu einem 'Buchlein de Iustificatione' (1530)." In *Caritas Dei: Beiträge Zum Verständnis Luthers und der Gegenwärtigen Ökumene.,* edited by Oswald Bayer, Robert W. Jenson, and Simo Knuuttila. Festschrift für Tuomo Mannermaa zum 60. Geburtstag, 385–404. Helsinki: Luther-Agricola-Gesellschaft, 1997.

Slenczka, Notger. *"Über Aristoteles hinaus?—Korreferat zu Tuomo Mannermaa."* In *Luther und die trinitarische Tradition: ökumenische und philosophische Perspektiven,* edited by Joachim Heubach, 61–70. Veröffentlichungen der Luther-Akademie Ratzeburg, vol. 23. Erlangen: Martin-Luther-Verlag, 1994.

Slenczka, Reinhard. *"Die Gemeinheit mit Gott als Grund und Gegenstand der Theologie. Vergöttlichung als ontologisches Problem."* In *Luther und Theosis,* edited by Joachim Heubach, 27–48. Erlangen: Martin-Luther-Verlag, 1990.

Söderlund, Rune. *"Der Unio-Gedanke der Konkordienformel."* In *Unio. Gott und Mensch in der nachreformatorischen Theologie,* edited by Matti Repo and Rainer Vinke, 62–71. Helsinki: Luther-Agricola-Gesellschaft, 1996.

Sparn, Walter. "*Begründung und Verwirklichung: zur anthropologischen Thematik der lutherischen Bekenntnisse.*" In *Bekenntnis und Einheit der Kirche: Studien Zum Konkordienbuch*, edited by Martin Brecht and Reinhard Schwarz, 129–53. Stuttgart: Calwer, 1980.

Spence, Alan. "Christ's Humanity and Ours: John Owen." In *Persons, Divine and Human: King's College Essays in Theological Anthropology*, edited by Christoph Schwöbel and Colin E. Gunton, 74–97. Edinburgh: T. & T. Clark, 1991.

Stevenson, Leslie. *Seven Theories of Human Nature*. 2d ed. New York/Oxford: Oxford University Press, 1987.

Stevenson, Leslie and David L. Haberman, *Ten Theories of Human Nature*. 3rd edition. New York/Oxford: Oxford University Press, 1998.

Stupperich, Martin. *Osiander in Preußen 1549–1552*. Berlin: Walter de Gruyter, 1973.

———. "*Zur Vorgeschichte des Rechtfertigungsartikels in der Konkordienformel.*" In *Bekenntnis und Einheit der Kirche: Studien Zum Konkordienbuch*, edited by Martin Brecht and Reinhard Schwarz, 175–94. Stuttgart: Calwer, 1980.

Tauler, Johannes. *Predigten*. Vollständige Ausgabe. Edited by Georg Hofmann. Freiburg: Herder, 1961.

———. *Sermons*. Translated by Maria Shrady. The Classic of Western Christian Spirituality. New York: Paulist Press, 1985.

Teilhard de Chardin, Pierre. *Man's Place in Nature: The Human Zoological Group*. Translated by René Hague. New York: Harper & Row, 1966.

Theologia Deutsch. Edited by Hermann Mandel. Quellenschriften Zur Geschichte Des Protestantismus. Leipzig: A. Deichert, 1908.

Thielicke, Helmut. *Being Human. Becoming Human: An Essay in Christian Anthropology*. Translated by Geoffrey W. Bromiley. Garden City, NY: Doubleday, 1984.

Thunberg, Lars. *Microcosm and Mediator: The Theological Anthropology of Maximus the Confessor*. Lund: C. W. K. Gleerup, 1965.

Towers, Bernard. "The Scientific Revolution and the Unity of Man." In *No Man is Alien*, edited by J. Robert Nelson, 162–82. Leiden: E. J. Brill, 1971.

Trigg, Jonathan D. *Baptism in the Theology of Martin Luther*. Leiden and New York: E. J. Brill, 1994.

Trillhaas, Wolfgang. "*In welchem Sinne sprechen wir beim Menschen von 'Natur'?*" *Zeitschrift für Theologie und Kirche* 52 (1955): 272–96.

———. "*Natur und Christentum.*" In *Religion in Geschichte und Gegenwart*. 3.

Työrinoja, Reijo. "*Nova Vocabula et Nova Lingua*. Luthers Conception of Doctrinal Formulas." In *Thesaurus Lutheri: Auf der Suche nach neuen Paradigmen der Luther-Forschung*, edited by Tuomo Mannermaa, Anja Ghiselli, and Simo Peura, 221–36. Helsinki: Finnische Theologische Literaturgesellschaft, 1987.

Vaahtoranta, Martti. "*Unio und Rechtfertigung bei Johann Gerhard.*" In *Unio. Gott und Mensch in der nachreformatorischen Theologie*, edited by Matti Repo and Rainer Vinke, 200–248. Helsinki: Luther-Agricola-Gesellschaft, 1996.

van Leeuwen, Mary Stewart. *The Person in Psychology: A Contemporary Christian Appraisal*. Grand Rapids: Eerdmans, 1985.

Vinke, Rainer. "*Der Unio-Gedanke in der Theologie des Pietismus.*" In *Unio. Gott und Mensch in der nachreformatorischen Theologie*, edited by Matti Repo and Rainer Vinke, 275–95. Helsinki: Luther-Agricola-Gesellschaft, 1996.

Bibliography

Vogelsang, Erich. *"Luther und die Mystik."* In *Luther-Jahrbuch*, edited by Th. Knolle, 32–54. Jahrbuch der Luther-Gesellschaft, vol. XIX. Weimar: Verlag Herman Böhlaus Nachf., 1937.

Volz, Carl A. "Human Participation in the Divine-Human Dialogue." *Salvation in Christ: A Lutheran-Orthodox Dialogue*, edited by John Meyendorff and Robert Tobias, 85–103. Minneapolis: Augsburg, 1992.

Vorländer, Dorothea. *Deus Incarnatus: Die Zweinaturenchristologie Luthers bis 1521.* Witten: Luther-Verlag, 1974.

Wentzlaff-Eggebert, Friedrich-Wilhelm. *Deutsche Mystik zwischen Mittelalter und Neuzeit: Einheit und Wandel ihrer Erscheinungsformen.* 3d ed. Berlin: Walter de Gruyter, 1969.

Wenz, Gunther. *"Mannermaa, Tuomo: Der im Glauben gegenwärtigen Christus . . . Saarinen, Risto: Gottes Wirken auf Uns . . ."* Review. *Theologische Revue* 86, no. 6 (1990): 469–73.

———. Review. *Theologische Revue* 86, no. 6 (1990): 469–73.

———. *"Unio. Zur Differenzierung einer Leitkategorie finnischer Lutherforschung im Anschluß an CA I–VI."* In *Unio. Gott und Mensch in der Nachreformatorischen Theologie*, edited by Matti Repo and Rainer Vinke, 333–80. Helsinki: Luther-Agricola-Gesellschaft, 1996.

Wilken, Robert L. "The Image of God in Classical Lutheran Theology." In *Salvation in Christ: A Lutheran-Orthodox Dialogue*, edited by John Meyendorff and Robert Tobias, 121–32. Minneapolis: Augsburg, 1992.

Williams, Anna Ngaire. "Deification in Thomas Aquinas and Gregory Palamas." PhD dissertation, Yale University, 1995.

———. *The Ground of Union: Deification in Thomas Aquinas and Gregory Palamas.* New York/Oxford: Oxford University Press, 1999.

Wingenbach, Gregory C. "Theanthropos in History and Cosmos." *Pro Ecclesia* VI, no. 3: 309–18.

Wingren, Gustaf. *Creation and Gospel: The New Situation in European Theology.* Toronto Studies in Theology. New York and Toronto: The Edwin Mellen Press, 1979.

———. *Creation and Law.* Translated by Ross Mackenzie. Edinburgh: Oliver & Boyd, 1961.

———. *The Flight from Creation.* Minneapolis: Augsburg, 1971.

———. *Luther on Vocation.* Translated by Carl C. Rasmussen. Evansville, IN: Ballast Press, 1999.

———. *"Das Problem des Natürlichen bei Luther."* In *The Church, Mysticism, Sanctification and the Natural in Luther's Thought*, edited by Ivar Asheim, 156–68. Philadelphia: Fortress, 1967.

———. *Schöpfung und Gesetz.* Göttingen: Vandenhoeck & Ruprecht, 1960.

Wolff, Hans Walter. *Anthropologie des Alten Testaments.* München: Chr. Kaiser, 1973.

———. *Anthropology of the Old Testament.* Translated by Margaret Kohl. Philadelphia: Fortress, 1974.

Zimmermann, Gunter. "Die Thesen Osianders zur Disputation 'de Iustificatione.'" *Kerygma und Dogma* 33 (1987): 224–44.

Zizioulas, John D. "On Being a Person: Towards an Ontology of Personhood." In *Persons, Divine and Human: King's College Essays in Theological Anthropology*, edited by Christoph Schwöbel and Colin E. Gunton, 33–46. Edinburgh: T. & T. Clark, 1991.

zur Mühlen, Karl-Heinz. "*Die auctoritas Patrum in Martin Luthers Schrift 'Von Den Konziliis und Kirchen'.*" In *Auctoritas Patrum II: New Contributions on the Reception of the Church Fathers in the 15th and 16th Centuries*, edited by Leif Grane, Alfred Schindler, and Markus Wriedt, 141–52. Mainz: Verlag Philipp von Zabern, 1998.

———. "*Korreferat zu Tuomo Mannermaa: Glaube, Bildung und Gemeinschaft bei Luther.*" Presented at the Ninth International Congress for Luther Research. In *Glaube und Bildung/Faith and Culture*, 75–82. Heidelberg, 17–23 August, 1997.

———. "*Mystik des Wortes: Über die Bedeutung mystischen Denkens für Luthers Lehre von der Rechtfertigung des Sünders.*" *Zeitwende* 52 (1981): 206–25.

Made in the USA
Columbia, SC
28 September 2020

21697173R00117